Magic in the Middle Ages
Second Edition

MAGIC IN THE
MIDDLE AGES

Second Edition

RICHARD KIECKHEFER

*Professor of
Religion and History
Northwestern University*

CAMBRIDGE
UNIVERSITY PRESS

CAMBRIDGE
UNIVERSITY PRESS

University Printing House, Cambridge CB2 8BS, United Kingdom

Cambridge University Press is part of the University of Cambridge.

It furthers the University's mission by disseminating knowledge in the pursuit of education, learning and research at the highest international levels of excellence.

www.cambridge.org
Information on this title: www.cambridge.org/9781107431829

© Cambridge University Press 1989, 2000, 2014

First published 1989
Reprinted 1990, 1991, 1992, 1993, 1995 1997
Canto edition 2000
10th printing 2010
Canto Classics edition 2014
Reprinted 2016

Printed in the United States of America by Sheridan Books, Inc.

A catalogue record for this publication is available from the British Library

ISBN 978-1-107-43182-9 Paperback

CONTENTS

v

ILLUSTRATIONS

FOREWORD TO THE
CANTO EDITION

The history of magic is in some respects closely linked to that of witch-craft, but the issues in the history of magic are not so well established. In historical scholarship over the last three decades, certain problems have emerged as basic to the study of witchcraft: why did the witch trials in Western Europe occur just when they did, from the fifteenth to the seventeenth centuries? Why did many of the religious and intellectual leaders of the age encourage this prosecution? What does it mean that women were disproportionately accused of witchcraft, and that when witch-hunting reached its severest intensity women were overwhelm-ingly its victims? Why was witch-hunting less virulent in countries with tightly centralized judicial apparatus, such as Spain and Italy?[1] But when we turn to the history of magic we find that the questions and issues are much less sharply defined.

One might even be tempted to ask whether magic in fact has a history, if by history one means the story of distinct beginnings, developments, and endings that can be explained with reference to other factors in the society and culture of an era. Magic, some might argue, is simply a perennial dimension of culture: people were practising forms of magic in earliest recorded times, and well into modern days some people have continued to experiment with these same forms. It might be taken as only slight hyperbole to suggest that magic has no more history than the rising and setting of the moon.

[1] Brian P. Levack, *The Witch-Hunt in Early Modern Europe* (London: Longman, 1987), gives a systematic survey of postmedieval witch trials that discusses all these issues and others. My own latest study in this area is "Avenging the blood of children: anxiety over child victims and the origins of the European witch trials," in Alberto Ferreiro, ed., *The Devil, Heresy and Witchcraft in the Middle Ages: Essays in Honor of Jeffrey B. Russell* (Leiden: Brill, 1998), 91–109.

Yet one of the challenges to which historians have risen in the twentieth century is discovering the history of phenomena that extend without dramatic change over long periods, and magic too does have a history. Its forms are not absolutely unchanging, its relationship to other areas of culture such as experimental science has shifted over time, and response to its use has ranged from indifference to panic. The history of magic is one of the ninth-century Christian missionaries who negotiated the relationship between their faith and indigenous European cultures, of the twelfth-century scholars who absorbed the occult and other sciences newly available from the Muslim world, and of fifteenth-century humanists who claimed to resurrect the purer Hermetic and Cabalistic traditions of antiquity.

But in all of this, what are the most basic issues?

One question long debated among anthropologists and historians is how to define magic, and how to situate it vis-à-vis religion and science. When this book was first published in 1989, I argued for a set of definitions derived from medieval culture in preference to modern definitions imposed on that culture. Medieval culture recognized different ways to go about healing an illness, finding a lost object, identifying a lost object, identifying a thief, arousing a woman's love, or cursing a neighbor's children or cattle. And what distinguished one method from another was fundamentally the source of power employed: demonic magic, virtually everyone in medieval Europe agreed, could work because it invoked demons; officially approved religion could be effective for material as well as spiritual ends by appealing to God and other beneficent spirits; natural magic, for those who recognized that category, worked because it exploited "occult virtues" or hidden powers within nature; and ordinary science made use of manifest powers in the natural order. To be sure, not everyone recognized all these distinctions, and even those who did might be unsure in practice whether the use of a herb along with recitation of a particular charm was natural or demonic magic. But even when people disagreed about the sources of power actually being used, they generally agreed that the source of power was what mattered most deeply.

This way of approaching the question of definition cannot be taken for granted. Some of the classic anthropological definitions assume that religion and magic stand in a relationship of binary opposition: religion petitions while magic coerces, or religion is public and official while magic is private and unofficial. I argued in this book that these binary oppositions are not helpful in studying medieval culture. It is also problematic, I have furthermore suggested, to speak of the "magic of the medieval Church," whether one means by that to be critical of or sympathetic with the practices in question. Blessings and exorcisms, use of "sacramentals" such as holy water and images, veneration of relics, traveling to pilgrimage shrines in the expectation of miracles – all these forms of religion may seem to a modern eye indistinguishable from magic. But when medieval clerics used the term "magic" (and they were the chief users of that term), or when the laity used other, parallel terms such as "sorcery," they were referring to practices that they believed could work, and if we are to comprehend their culture it is important for us to know precisely how they supposed these practices worked. If we confuse what they called blessings with what they called magic, we are not listening attentively to what they had to say about their conception of the world. We cannot begin with the assumption that magic is irrational; we must ask ourselves why it was that for people whose rationality was otherwise unimpeachable it seemed to fit into a rational view of the universe, and the first step toward answering this question is listening carefully to their formulations, their definitions.[2]

Another question that needs careful examination is the basic one: what sorts of people were using magic in medieval society? Some kinds of magic were quite widely used, and it may be futile to try associating them with particular classes of user – to ask, for example, who was most likely to use herbal remedies for illness, even though in medieval literature it is often women who are represented as specialists in such arts. Yet some forms of magic do seem to have been devised for the use of particular specialists, and this is perhaps nowhere more clearly the case than with the explicitly demonic magic sometimes called necromancy (or "nigromancy"). In the original edition of this book I suggested that the main users of necromancy were members of a clerical underworld. In this book I cite (and more recently I have published) a fifteenth-century manuscript from Munich which with startling clarity and nuance tells us about the beliefs of these clerical necromancers.[3] Their dabbling in the occult helped to heighten anxiety about magic, and at least indirectly it helped to make people nervous about witchcraft. It was men who were more likely to arouse anxiety by actually standing in magic circles and conjuring demons; it was women who were far more likely to be burned in the ensuing bonfires.

[2] On these issues see my article, "The specific rationality of medieval magic," *American Historical Review*, 99 (1994), 813–36. For a particularly instructive study of how magic makes sense to practitioners in the modern West, see T. M. Luhrmann, *Persuasions of the Witch's Craft: Ritual Magic in Contemporary England* (Cambridge, Mass.: Harvard University Press, 1989).

[3] Richard Kieckhefer, *Forbidden Rites: A Necromancer's Manual of the Fifteenth Century* (Stroud: Sutton, 1997; University Park: Penn State University Press, 1998).

Magic is connected in multiple ways with mainstream religious practice: prayers are recited over magical herbs, gospel verses are written on bread and then scraped into potions, charms can be virtually identical in form sometimes to blessings and sometimes to exorcisms, and the exorcisms used to dispel demons can with the necessary adjustments be made to summon them as well. Recent scholarship has centered on the extreme case of a link between magic and approved religion: the apparent parallel between the witch and the saint. As much a theme in the history of magic as in that of witchcraft, this parallel calls to our attention the role of stereotyping, positive or negative, in attitudes toward wonder-workers.[4] The stereotypical roles of witch and saint tell us at least as much about society's needs and expectations as about any actual individuals distinguished for either sainthood or magic.

That the occult sciences in Western Europe were largely derived from Arabic sources in the twelfth and following centuries is well established and widely known. What we still need to explore are the links between magic within medieval Christendom and the magic of Jews. In the late fifteenth century, humanists such as Giovanni Pico della Mirandola and Johannes Reuchlin learned and incorporated in their own writings the Cabalistic magic of the Jewish tradition, but already for several generations there had been forms of Christian magic so closely parallel to Jewish precedent that influence seems clear. The *Sworn Book* ascribed to a Honorius son of Euclid gives magical formulas to be used for various ends but particularly for a vision of God; the highlighting of this goal, along with other features of the work, points to connections with Merkabah mysticism and other Jewish traditions. And a magical practice known as the *ars notoria* uses a hybrid of magical and devotional techniques to gain knowledge of the liberal arts, evidently building on long-standing Jewish magic for enhancing one's learning.[5] But we will better

---

[4] See Peter Dinzelbacher, *Heilige oder Hexen? Schicksale auffälliger Frauen in Mittelalter und Frühneuzeit* (Zurich: Artemis, 1995), and Gábor Klaniczay, "*Miraculum* und *maleficium*: Einige Überlegungen zu den weiblichen Heiligen des Mittelalters in Mitteleuropa," *wissenschaftskolleg Jarhbuch*, 1990/1, 220–48. I have raised qualifications in my article, "The holy and the unholy: sainthood, witchcraft, and magic in late medieval Europe," *Journal of Medieval and Renaissance Studies*, 24 (1994), 355–85, published also in Scott L. Waugh and Peter D. Diehl, eds., *Christendom and Its Discontents: Exclusion, Persecution, and Rebellion, 1000–1500* (Cambridge: Cambridge University Press, 1996), 310–37.

[5] For Jewish magic, see now especially Michael D. Swartz, *Scholastic Magic: Ritual and Revelation in Early Jewish Mysticism* (Princeton, N. J.: Princeton University Press, 1996). I have discussed Christian borrowings in "The Devil's contemplatives: the *Liber iuratus*, the *Liber visionum*, and Christian appropriation of Jewish occultism," in Claire Fanger, ed., *Conjuring Spirits: Texts and Traditions of Medieval Ritual Magic* (Stroud: Sutton; University Park: Penn State University Press, 1998), 250–65.

grasp the full extent of Christians' magic on Jews' and vice-versa only when the magic of both cultures has been examined more extensively.

Cross-cultural study of magic is particularly important when the cultures in question were in historical contact with each other. But even when they were not, comparison can be valuable, sometimes because of close parallels that emerge, and perhaps even more instructively when the study of another culture shatters our expectations and forces us to raise new questions. Gananath Obeyesekere, for example, has shown how religious authorities in Buddhist, Hindu, and Muslim shrines of Sri lanka work sorcery for their clients by invoking the powers of deities and saints. Obeyesekere challenges traditional distinctions between religion and magic. Perhaps more importantly, he has found that the clients are not criminal personalities but rather law-abiding middle-class citizens who have been pushed against a wall by their enemies and see no recourse other than sorcery.[6] Obeyesekere's findings do not oblige us to assume the same was the case in medieval Europe, but they do call into question any simple link between magic, even in its maleficent forms, and criminality.

These, then, are some of the issues that have been and still must be pursued in the history of magic: we need to know more about how magic was defined and perceived in medieval culture, what sorts of people used magic, and how magic in Christendom was linked with that of other cultures (Arabic and especially Jewish), and we need to see how the study of magic in other cultures can help us frame questions about magic in the West. This book does not answer all these questions, but it attempts to provide a framework that may help in exploring them

---

[6] Gananath Obeyesekere's "Sorcery, premeditated murder, and the canalization of agression in Sri Lanka," *Ethnography*, 14 (1975), 1–23.

PREFACE

Some years ago I wrote a book about notions of witchcraft in late medieval Europe. My own greatest reservation about that book, after I had written it, was that it seemed artificial to discuss witchcraft in isolation from the broader context of magic in general. I thus accepted the invitation to write this present book partly as an opportunity to do what I did not do earlier: examine the full range of medieval magical beliefs and practices. In the process of research and writing I have come to realize more fully the complexity of this topic, and the need to see each of its parts in the light of the whole.

I have written for an undergraduate audience, although I hope others as well may find the book useful. In attempting to do a rounded survey I have had to synthesize a wealth of secondary literature in some areas, while for other topics there is such a dearth of usable material that I have turned mainly to manuscripts. The result is in some ways a new interpretation. I have tried, first of all, to rethink the fundamental distinction between demonic magic and natural magic. Secondly, I have tried to locate the cultural setting of the magicians (as members of various social groups) and of magic (as a cultural phenomenon related to religion and science). Especially in my presentation of necromancy I have had to tread on uncharted ground.

Nonetheless, I have of course stood on the shoulders of Lynn Thorndike and other giants. While I have provided only a minumum of notes, I trust that the notes and bibliography taken together will sufficiently indicate my indebtedness to these scholars.

My personal debts of gratitude are many. My colleague Robert Lerner and my wife and colleague Barbara Newman read the book as it progressed, provided numerous valuable suggestions about matters of detail, and helped in repeated conversation to clarify the focus of my presentation; their aid has been invaluable. I am grateful also to Robert Bartlett, Charles Burnett, Amelia J. Carr, John Leland, Virginia Leland, and Steven Williams for reading one or another version of the typescript, making helpful comments, and correcting errors. David d'Avray, Timothy McFarland, W.F. Ryan, and students in my classes were useful sounding-boards for my ideas and sources of further insight and information. Dr. Rosemary Morris and the staff of Cambridge University Press provided expert assistance. Christine E. E. Jones of the Museum of London gave me important references, and Margaret Kieckhefer helped by providing valuable bibliography.

Librarians at several institutions aided my efforts patiently. Without listing them all, I must at least thank those at Northwestern University and the University of Chicago, the Warburg Institute, the Bodleian Library, and the libraries of Trinity College and St. John's College, Cambridge. My debt to both the British Library and the British Museum goes well beyond what the notes and the list of illustrations might suggest.

I am indebted also to the National Endowment for the Humanities, whose support for an unrelated project allowed me the opportunity to gather materials and carry out revision of this book.

Finally I must thank T. William Heyck, without whom this book could have been written but might not have been.

Richard Kieckhefer

Note. Translations in Chapter 2 are from the sources cited. Elsewhere translations are my own except where noted. Biblical quotations are from the Revised Standard Version, but are consistent with the Vulgate text.

I

INTRODUCTION: MAGIC AS A CROSSROADS

·

This book will approach magic as a kind of crossroads where different pathways in medieval culture converge. First of all it is a point of intersection between religion and science. Demonic magic invokes evil spirits and rests upon a network of religious beliefs and practices, while natural magic exploits "occult" powers within nature and is essentially a branch of medieval science. Yet demonic and natural magic are not always as distinct in fact as they seem in principle. Even when magic is clearly nondemonic it sometimes mingles elements of religion and science: a magical cure, for example, may embody both herbal lore from folk medicine and phrases of prayer from Christian ritual. Secondly, magic is an area where popular culture meets with learned culture. Popular notions of magic got taken up and interpreted by "intellectuals" – a term here used for those with philosophical or theological education – and their ideas about magic, demons, and kindred topics were in turn spread throughout the land by preachers. One of the most important tasks in cultural history is working out these lines of transmission. Thirdly, magic represents a particularly interesting crossroads between fiction and reality. The fictional literature of medieval Europe sometimes reflected the realities of medieval life, sometimes distorted them, sometimes provided escapist release from them, and sometimes held up ideals for reality to imitate. When this literature featured sorcerers, fairies, and other workers of magic, it may not have been meant or taken as totally realistic. Even so, the magic of medieval literature did resemble the magical practices of medieval life in ways that are difficult but interesting to disentangle.

In short, magic is a crossing-point where religion converges with science, popular beliefs intersect with those of the educated classes, and the conventions of fiction meet with the realities of daily life. If we stand at this crossroads we may proceed outward in any of various directions, to explore the theology, the social realities, the literature, or the politics of medieval Europe. We may pursue other paths as well, such as medieval art or music, since art sometimes depicted magical themes and music was seen as having magical powers. Because magic was condemned by both Church and state, its history leads into the thickets of legal development. Indeed, magic is worth studying largely because it serves as a starting-point for excursions into so many areas of medieval culture. Exploration of this sort can reveal the complexity and interrelatedness of different strands in that culture.

Humor and seriousness also converge in the magic of medieval Europe. Many of the recipes for magic that we will encounter in this book may strike a modern reader as amusing or frivolous, and may indeed have been written in a playful spirit, but it is seldom easy to know for sure whether a medieval audience would have been amused or shocked by such material. Some of the magic that medieval people actually employed may now seem merely inane, but the judges who sentenced magicians to death did not take it lightly.

In a further and rather different sense magic represents a crossroads. The ideas about magic that flourished in medieval Europe came from various sources. Magical beliefs and practices from the classical culture of the Mediterranean regions mingled with beliefs and practices of Germanic and Celtic peoples from northern Europe. Later on, medieval Christians borrowed notions about magic from the Jews in their midst or from Muslims abroad. It is sometimes hard to distinguish precisely where a specific belief first arose, but to understand the overall patterns of medieval magic we must be aware of these borrowings from diverse cultures. The study of magic thus becomes an avenue toward understanding how different cultures relate to one another.

TWO CASE STUDIES

What all of this means can perhaps best be clarified by looking at two fifteenth-century manuscripts in which magic plays an important role: a book of household management from Wolfsthurn Castle in the Tyrol, and a manual of demonic magic now kept in the Bavarian State Library in Munich.

The Wolfsthurn handbook shows the place magic might hold in everyday life.[1] Its compiler was an anonymous woman or man involved

---

[1] Oswald von Zingerle, "Segen und Heilmittel aus einer Wolfsthurner Handschrift des xv. Jahrhunderts", *Zeitschrift für Volkskunde*, 1 (1891), 172–7, 315–24.

in running a large estate. Perhaps he or she lived at Wolfsthurn, or came from nearby. At any rate, the book is in the vernacular language, German, rather than in Latin, and the compiler was probably a layperson rather than a priest or monk. The work reflects all the practical concerns of a household. People on the estate were constantly prey to illness. The fields needed cultivation and protection from the elements. Rats had to be driven from the cellar. Much of the knowledge required for these tasks could be kept in one's head, but a literate householder might usefully write down some of the details to ensure that they remained fresh, and the book was a convenient place to record such information. It contains instructions for almost every aspect of running a household. It tells how to prepare leather, make soap or ink, wash clothes, and catch fish. Intermingled with such advice are medical prescriptions for human and animal disease. Claiming the authority of Aristotle and other learned men of antiquity, the compiler tells how to diagnose and treat fevers, ailments of the eyes, and other medical problems. Further added to this potpourri are prayers, blessings, and conjurations.

Medieval people who assembled this and other such manuals would never have thought of themselves as magicians, but the book at hand contains elements of what we can call magic. It recommends taking the leaves of a particular plant as a remedy for "fever of all sorts"; this in itself would count as science, or as folk medicine, rather than magic. Before using these leaves, one is supposed to write certain Latin words on them to invoke the power of the Holy Trinity, and then one is to say the Lord's Prayer and other prayers over them; this in itself would count as religion. There is no scientific or religious reason, however, for repeating this procedure before sunrise on three consecutive mornings. By adding this requirement the author enhances the power of science and religion with that of magic. Religion and magic support each other again in the treatment suggested in this book for a speck in the eye. The prescription begins with a story from the legends of the saints, and then gives an adjuration addressed to the speck itself:

[Legend:] Saint Nicasius, the holy martyr of God, had a speck in his eye, and besought that God would relieve him of it, and the Lord cured him. He prayed [again] to the Lord, that whoever bore his name upon his person would be cured of all specks, and the Lord heard him.
[Adjuration:] Thus I adjure you, O speck, by the living God and the holy God, to disappear from the eyes of the servant of God N., whether you are black, red, or white. May Christ make you go away. Amen. In the name of the Father, and of the Son, and of the Holy Spirit. Amen.

The legend itself is religious, and the formula has some of the trappings of a prayer, but magic enters in with the notion that the disease itself has a

kind of personality and can respond to a command. Similar to this is a cure for toothache that starts with a legend of Saint Peter. The saint is suffering from a worm in his tooth. Christ sees him sitting on a rock and holding his hand to his cheek, and cures him by adjuring the worm to depart, "in the name of the Father and of the Son and of the Holy Spirit." This healing act of Christ becomes an archetype, whose power can be invoked to heal one's own dental afflictions. In the Wolfsthurn book, however, the concrete healing procedure is not explicit. Rather, the legend is followed by a few snippets of religious vocabulary ("Ayos, ayos, ayos tetragramaton"), and then by the unrelated counsel that a person suffering this affliction should write a mixture of Latin and nonsense ("rex, pax, nax in Cristo filio suo") on his cheek.[2]

At times the liturgical formulas in this handbook are put to patently magical uses. For a woman with menstrual problems the book recommends writing out the words from the mass, "By Him, and with Him, and in Him," then laying the slip of paper on the afflicted woman's head. Even more clearly magical is a remedy for epilepsy: first one puts a deerskin strap around the patient's neck while he is suffering a seizure, then one "binds" the sickness to the strap "in the name of the Father and of the Son and of the Holy Spirit," and finally one buries the strap along with a dead man. The sickness is thus transferred from the patient to the strap, then relegated safely to the realm of the dead so it can cause no further harm in the world of the living.

The Wolfsthurn book recommends not only Christian prayers but also apparently meaningless combinations of words or letters for their medical value. At one point it says to copy out the letters "P. N. B. C. P. X. A. O. P. I. L.", followed by the Latin for "in the name of the Father and of the Son and of the Holy Spirit." For demonic possession the book recommends that a priest should speak into the afflicted person's ear the following jumble of Latin, garbled Greek, and gibberish:

> Amara Tonta Tyra post hos firabis ficaliri Elypolis starras poly polyque lique linarras buccabor uel barton vel Titram celi massis Metumbor o priczoni Jordan Ciriacus Valentinus.

As an alternative remedy for possession the book suggests taking three sprigs of juniper, dousing them three times with wine in honor of the

[2] *Hagios* (given here in corrupt form) is Greek for "holy"; Christian liturgy often uses it (or the Latin *sanctus*) in threefold repetition. The Tetragrammaton is the sacred Hebrew name for God, which would have been written in Hebrew without vowels: "YHWH". *Rex* means "king," *pax* means "peace," *in Cristo filio suo* means "in Christ his son," and *nax* does not mean anything.

Trinity, boiling them, and placing them on the possessed person's head without his knowledge.

Prescriptions containing verbal formulas usually come from Christian liturgy, but other prescriptions contain no spoken words at all and have nothing religious in them. To ward off all forms of sorcery, for example, one should carry the plant artemisia on one's person. Or to ensure keen eyesight by night as well as by day one should anoint one's eyes with bat's blood, which presumably imparts that animal's remarkable ability to "see" even in the dark. The appeal to ancient authority might indeed seem plausible in such cases: classical writers like Pliny often referred to cures similar if not identical to what we have here. Tracing exactly where the compiler found any particular recipe, however, would be a hopeless task, leading down labyrinthine byways.

Indeed, little if anything in this compilation is altogether original; much of its material echoes ancient formulas or at least those of other medieval compilations. The cure for toothache beginning with the legend of Saint Peter, for example, is a commonplace. Essentially the same formula occurs in many different manuscripts, from Anglo-Saxon England and elsewhere in medieval Europe.

Not surprisingly, material of this sort could raise eyebrows. Marginal comments added to the Wolfsthurn manual in slightly later handwriting indicate that the manuscript came before disapproving eyes. One passage that gave offense was the above-mentioned cure for menstrual problems. A later reader wrote beside this prescription, "This is utterly false, superstitious, and practically heretical." Indeed, certain pages were excised from the compilation, perhaps by this same reader. Because of this censorship some of the author's formulas are badly mutilated, such as the instructions for making oneself invisible, while others have been lost altogether. At another point, however, the book evoked skepticism rather than disapproval: a reader commented beside a particularly dubious passage, "This would be good – if it were true"!

In short, the Wolfsthurn handbook raises a series of questions regarding the history of magic: how does it relate to religion? How does it relate to science and to folk medicine? What role does the tradition of classical antiquity play in medieval magic? How and why did Christian liturgical formulas get used in magic? To what extent was magic an activity of the laypeople? To what degree did it involve the clergy, such as the priest whose aid is invoked for exorcism? How would a philosopher or theologian such as Thomas Aquinas have reacted to the magic in this book? All these questions will recur in later chapters. The point for now is merely to see how the magic of the Wolfsthurn handbook could serve as a starting-point for exploration in various directions, or as a crossroads in medieval culture.

The second manuscript raises a somewhat different set of questions.[3] Unlike the Wolfsthurn book, the Munich handbook involves straightforwardly demonic magic, or what came to be known as necromancy. Also unlike the Wolfsthurn book, the Munich manual is in Latin (though some vernacular material is appended to it), and the author and owner probably belonged to the clergy. On practically every page this handbook gives instructions for conjuring demons with magic circles and other devices, commanding the spirits once they have appeared, or compelling them to return after they have been dismissed. The purposes served by this magic are many. It can allegedly be used to drive a person mad, to arouse passionate love, to gain favor at court, to create the illusion of a mighty castle, to obtain a horse that can carry the magician anywhere he wants to go, or to reveal future and secret things. The magic of this handbook involves elaborate paraphernalia. Apart from the magic circles, the magician needs wax images of the people he wishes to afflict, or rings, swords, and other objects. In some cases the handbook requires that he sacrifice a hoopoe to the evil spirits,[4] or burn certain herbs so that the smoke can serve as a magical fumigation. Like the Wolfsthurn book, the Munich handbook draws from the riches of Christian liturgy, but it does so much more fully. Rather than merely borrowing short fragments and familiar prayers, the Munich handbook takes over lengthy passages from the Church's ritual, and in other cases uses new formulas clearly modeled on Christian precedent.

Other elements in the work resemble Jewish or Muslim magic. Some formulas involve magical incantation of names for God, as in Jewish magical practice, while the recitation of magical names for Christ is in effect a Christian version of the same thing. Indeed, a great deal of Jewish and Muslim magic seems to have revolved about the basic notion that by magical formulas one can compel the demons to come and do one's bidding. An important Arabic magical text, well known in the later medieval West under the title *Picatrix*, also contains formulas similar to

---

[3] The manuscript in question is Clm 849 (Bayerische Staatsbibliothek, Munich), fols. 3ʳ–108ᵛ. For brief discussion see Lynn Thorndike, "Imagination and magic: force of imagination on the human body and of magic on the human mind", in *Mélanges Eugène Tisserant*, 7 (Vatican City: Biblioteca Vaticana, 1964), 356–8; for a full account see Richard Kieckhefer, *Forbidden Rites: A Necromancer's Manual of the Fifteenth Century* (Stroud: Sutton, 1997; University Park: Penn State University Press, 1998).

[4] The hoopoe is an extraordinary crested bird that figures prominently in magic and in folklore generally. Ulysse Aldrovandi, in his *Ornithologia*, vol. 2 (Bologna: Nicolaus Tebaldinus, 1634), 709, exclaims that he will not record the superstitions that have arisen regarding this bird, but then he does so anyway.

some in the Munich handbook. Furthermore, certain passages in the Munich manuscript presuppose at least a crude knowledge of that astrology which later medieval Western culture had taken over from Arabic sources.

The magic in this Munich handbook is often quite complex. One section, for example, tells how to obtain the love of a woman. While reciting incantations, the magician takes the blood of a dove and uses it to draw a naked woman on the skin of a female dog. He writes the names of demons on various parts of this image, and as he does so he commands the demons to afflict those parts of the actual woman's body, so that she will be inflamed with love of him. He fumigates the image with the smoke of myrrh and saffron, all the time conjuring the demons to afflict her so that day and night she will think of nothing but him. He hangs the image around his neck, goes out to a secret place either alone or with three trustworthy companions, and with his sword traces a circle on the ground, with the names of demons all around its edge. Then he stands inside the circle and conjures the demons. They come (the handbook promises) in the form of six servants, ready to do his will. He tells them to go and fetch the woman for him without doing her any harm, and they do so. On arriving she is a bit perplexed but willing to do as the magician wishes. As long as she is there, one of the demons takes on her form and carries on for her back at home so that her strange departure will not be noticed.

The compiler of this manual had further mischief up his sleeve. He tells, for example, how to arouse hatred between two friends by using a complex ritual in which two stones are buried beneath the friends' thresholds, then unearthed and cast into a fire, then fumigated with sulphur, left three days in water, and smashed together. As the magician fumigates them he conjures forth "all hateful demons, malignant, invidious, and contentious," by the power of God. He demands that these demons arouse between the friends as much hatred as exists among the demons, or as much as existed between Cain and Abel. While striking the stones against each other he says, "I do not strike these stones together, but I strike X. and Y., whose names are carved here." Finally, he buries the stones separately. The handbook warns that the details of this ceremony must be kept secret because of its ineffable power. In case the magician should wish later to undo his damage, he should dig up the stones, heat them, crush them, and cast the fragments into a river.

Another section of the book tells how to become invisible. The magician goes to a field outside of town and traces a circle on the ground. He fumigates the circle, and sprinkles it and himself with holy water while reciting Psalm 51:7. He kneels down and conjures various spirits, compelling them in the name of God to come and do his bidding. The spirits suddenly appear within the circle and ask what he wants. He requests a "cap of invisibility." One of them goes and procures such a headpiece, and gives it to him in exchange for his white robe. The ritual is not without its hazards: if the magician does not return to the same place three days later, retrieve his robe, and burn it, he will die within seven days.

The author of this book is not squeamish about conjuring "demons" or "evil spirits." Sometimes he invokes them by name, as Satan, Lucifer, Berich, and so forth. Even when the ceremonies do not explicitly identify the spirits who come as demonic, the intent is usually clear, and certainly no inquisitor would have thought about the question for more than a moment.

The materials in the Munich handbook, like those in the Wolfsthurn manuscript, are not entirely original. Parallels can be found in other manuscripts, from other parts of Europe, as well as in Arabic and Jewish traditions. Medieval European examples are rare, since whenever possible the inquisitors and other authorities consigned such stuff to the flames. Enough manuscripts escaped this fate, however, to give an idea of the genre.

This handbook, like the first one, raises a series of important questions: How does this magic relate to religion? (Very differently from that of the Wolfsthurn manual!) Precisely how does this material resemble that found in Jewish and Muslim magic, and how does it differ? What historical links can be established between this magic and Jewish or Muslim precedent? What sort of person was likely to own such a book? Did the owners really practice these rituals, or was it all an elaborate game or fantasy? If the owners did actually carry out such magic, how did they resemble the magicians depicted in medieval sermons, or the sorcerers in medieval romances? Once again, these are questions that will arise later in this book, and for now the point is simply to show how magic can lead to such wide-ranging inquiry.

DEFINITIONS OF MAGIC

The most fundamental question for present purposes is how to define magic. If a person rubs bat's blood into his eyes, is that magic, or is it a kind of primitive medical science? How can we define the border between magic and science? Even if we want to say that there are instances that lie near or on the border, it seems that we must be able to define the border itself. So too, we must be able to indicate how magic relates in principle to religion, even if we want to acknowledge many cases where they resemble each other closely. Still further complications arise. Some people, for instance, would want to say that conjuring a demon merely to foretell the future is not magic, since magic involves practical manipulation of things in the world – making people ill, gaining favor at court, and so forth – rather than simply learning about predetermined states of affairs.

What would medieval Europeans have said about these questions? Most of them, perhaps, would have given them little thought. There were people who tried to use knowledge such as that in the Wolfsthurn or Munich handbooks, others who worried about its being used against them, and still others who made it their business to keep it from being used, but few of these people would have asked themselves whether the term "magic" applied to these practices. They might have said that the Wolfsthurn book contained "charms", "blessings," "adjurations," or simply "cures," without calling them specifically "magical." They might have called the Munich handbook a book of "necromancy" or "sorcery" rather than of "magic." Only the theologically and philosophically sophisticated elite bothered greatly about questions of definition. When the intellectuals attended to such matters, however, they were reflecting on contemporary practices, and often they were articulating explicitly what other people merely took for granted. By looking at theological and philosophical notions about magic we can at least take an important step toward understanding how medieval people thought about the subject.

Broadly speaking, intellectuals in medieval Europe recognized two forms of magic: natural and demonic. Natural magic was not distinct from science, but rather a branch of science. It was the science that dealt with "occult virtues" (or hidden powers) within nature. Demonic magic was not distinct from religion, but rather a perversion of religion. It was religion that turned away from God and toward demons for their help in human affairs.

One might quickly conclude that the magic of the Wolfsthurn handbook exemplifies natural magic, and that of the Munich manuscript represents demonic magic. From the viewpoint of the practitioners, this conclusion might be essentially correct. But from the vantage point of medieval theologians, philosophers, preachers, and inquisitors matters were not so simple. Many of these observers would have suspected demonic magic even in the Wolfsthurn book. The unintelligible words that it prescribed might contain names for demons. The use of a deerskin strap to remove a case of epilepsy might be seen as a signal or sacrifice to the demons. If artemisia had power to ward off sorcery, the knowledge of that occult power might have been imparted by demons. Whether knowingly or unknowingly, the person who used the Wolfsthurn handbook might be engaged in demonic magic. The people who went out to gather apparently innocent herbs, or the midwife who seemed blameless and helpful might turn out to be in league with demons (Fig. 1). Indeed,

for many writers in medieval Europe all magic was by definition demonic; not everyone agreed that there was such a thing as natural magic.
For such writers the material in the Wolfsthurn handbook could be called
magical only because it seemed likely to rely on the aid of demons. But the
term "magic" has a history, and understanding what it meant at a given
time requires some knowledge of that history.

In classical antiquity, the word "magic" applied first of all to the arts of
the magi, those Zoroastrian priests of Persia who were known to the
Greeks at least by the fifth century B.C. Some of them seem to have
migrated to the Mediterranean world. What, precisely, did these magi
do? Greeks and Romans generally had imprecise notions of their activities:
they practiced astrology, they claimed to cure people by using elaborate
but bogus ceremonies, and in general they pursued knowledge of the
occult. Whatever they did, however, was by definition "the arts of the
magi," or "the magical arts," or simply "magic." From the outset, the
term thus had an imprecise meaning. Because the magi were foreigners
with exotic skills that aroused apprehension, the term "magic" was a
deeply emotional one, rich with dark connotations. Magic was something
sinister, something threatening. When native Greeks and Romans engaged in practices similar to those of the magi, they too were feared for
their involvement in magic. The term was extended to cover the sinister
activities of occultists whether foreign or domestic.

Early Christian writers who used the term played on these undertones.
If the Greek and Roman pagans could foretell the future, or heal diseases,
that was because they had help from their gods. But the gods of the pagans
were no real gods; from a Christian viewpoint they were in fact demons.
Thus the thaumaturgy of Graeco-Roman paganism was unmasked as
demonic magic. Even if the pagans did not realize they were using the aid
of evil spirits, indeed even if they were merely using curative herbs and
amulets made from precious stones, a Christian writer such as Augustine
of Hippo (A.D. 354–430) was quick to see demonic involvement. The
demons took these objects as signs or tokens calling them to do their work.
It was demons who had founded the magical arts and taught them to
human practitioners, and it was demons who actually carried out the will
of the magicians. Divination (or fortune-telling) also was possible only
with the aid of demons. These are dominant themes in Augustine's classic
book *On the City of God*, and Augustine's authority in medieval culture
was so great that on this issue as on many others his outlook prevailed.

Up through the twelfth century, if you asked a theologian what magic
was you were likely to hear that demons began it and were always
involved in it. You would also be likely to get a catalogue of different

Fig. 1. Group of woman magicians with demons, from Lydgate, *Pilgrimage of the Life of Man*

forms of magic, and most of the varieties would be species of divination.[5] Isidore of Seville (ca. 560–636), borrowing from classical authors such as Varro (ca. 116–ca. 27 B.C.), listed geomancy, hydromancy, aeromancy, and pyromancy (divination by earth, water, air, and fire) under the heading "magic," and then went on under the same heading to discuss divinatory observation of the flight and cries of birds, the entrails of sacrificial animals, and the positions of stars and planets (i.e. astrology). Only after cataloging these and other species of divination did he include enchantment (magical use of words), ligatures (medical use of magical objects bound to the patient), and various other phenomena in his discussion of magic. "All such things," he said, "involve the art of demons, which arises from the pestiferous society of men and bad angels."[6] For centuries, writers repeated and adapted these categories in their discussion of magic. At least into the twelfth century these categories remained standard, and writers repeated and adapted them in their discussion of magic, although no one in the high Middle Ages was still

---

[5] Lynn Thorndike, "Some medieval conceptions of magic", *The Monist*, 25 (1915), 107–39.

[6] Isidore de Séville, *Etymologies*, ed. Peter K. Marshall *et al.* vol. 2, viii.9., (Paris: Les Belles Lettres, 1986).

foretelling the future by inspecting the entrails of sacrificial animals. Not everyone followed Isidore to the letter: in the mid-thirteenth century, the theologian Alexander of Hales (ca. 1185–1245) used "divination" as a generic term under which he distinguished various species of occult art, including sorcery and illusion. In one way or another, however, medieval writers tended to see magic and divination as closely related.[7]

Two major changes began to occur around the thirteenth century. First there were writers who began to see natural magic as an alternative to the demonic form. Secondly, the term came to be used for operative functions such as healing as much as for divination. William of Auvergne (ca. 1180–1249), an influential theologian and then bishop at Paris, recognized the distinction between demonic and natural magic and devoted considerable attention to the latter sort. Albert the Great (ca. 1200–80) also acknowledged the possibility of natural magic in his scientific writings, though in his theological work he was cautious about distinguishing it from the demonic kind.

Many people, to be sure, persisted in thinking of all magic as demonic and in seeing divination as a central purpose of magic. Even those who referred explicitly to occult powers (*virtutes occultae*) in nature did not always use the term "magic" in reference to them. Thomas Aquinas (ca. 1225–74) believed in occult phenomena caused by the influence of stars and planets, but tended to follow Augustine in reserving "magic" for processes involving demons. Roger Bacon (ca. 1214–ca. 1292) also believed in mysterious and awesome powers within nature, but typically used the word "magic" for various kinds of fraud and deception. During the fourteenth and fifteenth centuries, however, the notion of natural magic took firm hold in European culture, even if it still was not universally recognized or uniformly described.

When writers spoke of natural magic as dealing with the occult powers in nature, what precisely did they mean? How did occult powers differ from ordinary, manifest powers? In some cases it seems that the distinction was a subjective one: a power in nature that is little known and arouses awe is occult, unlike those well-known powers that people take for granted. *Picatrix*, for example, remarks at one point that it is dealing with matters which are "hidden from the senses, so that most people do not grasp how they happen or from what causes they arise."[8] The term had a technical sense, however, that referred not to the subjective response of the beholder but to the objective status of the power in question. Most properties of

---

[7] This was not always true of ecclesiastical legislation, which often mentioned them separately without giving precise definitions.

[8] *Picatrix: The Latin Version of the* Ghāyat Al-Ḥakīm, ed. David Pingree (London: Warburg Institute, 1986), 5.

herbs, stones, or animals can be explained in terms of their physical structure. A herb that is "cold" or "moist" can treat an illness caused by excess of "heat" or "dryness." (These are standard Aristotelian categories; a plant might be classed as "hot" or "cold" by nature, regardless of its actual temperature at a given moment.) Other properties, however, cannot be explained in these terms. The power of a plant to cure certain ailments, or the power of a gem to ward off certain kinds of misfortune, may derive not from the internal structure of the object but from an external source: emanations coming from the stars and planets. These latter powers were technically known as occult, and natural magic was the science of such powers. The properties in question were strictly within the realm of nature, but the natural world that could account for them was a broad one: instead of examining the inner structure of a plant to determine its effects, one had to posit influences that flowed from the distant reaches of the cosmos.

By extension, a power might qualify as occult if it was grounded in some symbolic feature of the powerful object, rather than its internal structure alone. Plants with liver-shaped leaves might thus promote the health of the liver, or the keen sight of the vulture might cure eye ailments if it was wrapped in the skin of a wolf and hung around the patient's neck. What we have in these instances is "sympathetic magic," as James G. Frazer called it: magic that works by a "secret sympathy" or symbolic likeness between the cause and the effect.[9] A medical scroll from around 1100 advises that the herb dracontium, so called because its leaves resemble dragons, can counteract snakebite and internal worms.[10] The reverse principle, also important for magic, is that of "antipathy." The wolf is antipathetic toward the sheep, and its antipathy is such that even a drumhead made of wolf's hide will drown out the sound made from a drumhead of sheepskin. For most writers of antiquity and the Middle Ages, sympathy and antipathy were principles of ordinary science, not magic, but writers in the later Middle Ages who worked out the concept of natural magic often included in it phenomena of this sort.

In other cases the effect of the magical object rests on "animistic" principles: the notion that things throughout nature have spirits or personalities dwelling within them. One plant seen as having powerful magical effect was mandrake, the root of which vaguely resembles a human being planted upside-down in the ground. Because this root was thought to have a sort of personality, those who uprooted it to make use of its power feared that it would take vengeance on them. To avoid this fate

---

[9] J. G. Frazer, *The Golden Bough*, 3rd edn. (London: Macmillan, 1913), 54.
[10] Lucille B. Pinto, "Medical science and superstition: a report on a unique medical scroll of the eleventh–twelfth century", *Manuscripta*, 17 (1973), 12–21.

Fig. 2. Extraction of mandrake, from a twelfth-century herbal

they would extract it from the ground by tying a rope around it and
affixing the other end to a hungry dog, then throwing meat to the dog.
The animal would pull the mandrake from the ground and would thus
suffer its vengeance (Fig. 2). Symbolic thought of this sort lay behind
many of the phenomena we will be dealing with in this book.

Even when such symbolic principles underlie magic, however, the
intellectuals seeking to explain the occult powers in question were likely
to posit stellar or planetary influence rather than principles of sympathy,
antipathy, or simple animism.

In this book, then, the term "magic" will be used for those phenomena
which intellectuals would have recognized as either demonic or natural
magic. That which makes an action magical is the type of power it
invokes: if it relies on divine action or the manifest powers of nature it is
not magical, while if it uses demonic aid or occult powers in nature it is
magical.

There is an alternative way of defining magic, which focuses on the
intended force of an action, rather than the type of power invoked. This
way of conceiving magic has its main roots in sixteenth-century religious
debate and gained currency in anthropological writings of the late nine-

teenth and early twentieth centuries.[11] According to this approach, the central feature of religion is that it *supplicates* God or the gods, and the main characteristic of magic is that it *coerces* spiritual beings or forces. Religion treats the gods as free agents, whose good will must be won through submission and ongoing veneration. Magic tries to manipulate the spirits – or impersonal spiritual forces seen as flowing throughout nature – mechanically, in much the same way one might use electricity by turning it on or off. From this perspective the border between religion and magic becomes difficult to discern. A person who tries to coerce God by using rituals mechanically can be seen as practicing magic; indeed, sixteenth-century Protestants charged that this was precisely what Roman Catholics were doing. In recent years even anthropologists have tended to put little stock by this pat distinction, but in the general reading public it remains so deeply entrenched that many people see it as the natural meaning of the terms.

Unfortunately, this way of distinguishing magic from religion is unhelpful in dealing with the medieval material. First of all, the sources tell us little about precisely how medieval people conceived the force of their actions. Did the user of the Wolfsthurn handbook intend to coerce God by incorporating liturgical formulas into curative rituals, or did these rituals reflect a deep (if unsophisticated) faith and piety? The handbook itself gives no clue; nor do other, similar sources. Secondly, ordinary people in medieval Europe probably did not distinguish sharply between coercion and supplication. When they used charms such as those in the Wolfsthurn book they surely expected their efforts to have influence; sometimes this influence might be coercive, and sometimes supplicatory, but there was ample room for uncertainty about which form it would take. Prayer could be likewise ambiguous: Christ had promised to do anything that his followers requested in his name (John 14:14), and a Christian with faith would surely expect this promise to be unfailing, but the attitudes of those who invoked Christ's name could run the gamut from magical incantation at one extreme to mystical piety at the other, and simple Christians were unlikely to analyze precisely where along this spectrum their own intentions lay. Indeed, people in premodern Europe probably viewed their medicine in similarly ambivalent ways: even if a cure was tried and "proven," the force of its influence in a given case would be hard to calculate in advance. In the case of demonic magic, there is still a third reason why it is unhelpful to focus on the intended force: there were magicians who thought they could coerce demons, but only because they had previously supplicated God and obtained divine power

[11] William A. Lessa and Evon Z. Vogt, eds., *Reader in Comparative Religion: An Anthropological Approach*, 4th edn. (New York: Harper & Row, 1979), 332–62.

over the demons. If we start by assuming a fundamental distinction
between coercion and supplication, we will make little sense of these
complexities.

Some of the cases we will examine do indeed suggest that people using
magic were trying to compel demons, or the powers of nature, or God.
The intent to coerce was thus one characteristic of these particular magical
acts. But intentions are so ambiguous, complex, and variable that it is
unhelpful to take the intended force as the crucial and defining characteristic of magic in general.

The definitions given above for natural and demonic magic will be our
starting-points, then, for exploring the role of magic in medieval culture.
We must bear in mind, however, that these definitions came from a
particular class within medieval society, those with theological and philosophical education. In using their definitions we must be careful not to let
their viewpoint overshadow entirely that of their unlettered contemporaries. The problem is a familiar one. All of our sources for medieval
culture come from that small segment of the population that knew how to
write, and there is no shortcut from their mental world to that of the
illiterate populace. The best we can do is read the documents sensitively,
with the right questions in mind. In what ways did the literate elite share
or absorb the mentality of the common people? Do some writings reflect
the views of ordinary people better than others? Can we accurately
reconstruct popular notions from learned attacks on them? Do the definitions of magic used by the intellectuals reflect or distort popular ways of
viewing things? The intellectuals have the advantage of having formu-
lated explicit theories and definitions for us to read and adopt. The rest of
society also had its ways of thinking about the world, but its views are
harder to reconstruct. Popular and learned mentalities were sometimes
alike and sometimes different, and to see the relationship between them
we must read the evidence carefully, case by case.

What we will discover, particularly in comparing popular with
learned notions, is that the history of magic is above all a crossing-point
where the exploitation of natural forces and the invocation of demonic
powers intersect. One could summarize the history of medieval magic in
capsule form by saying that at the popular level the tendency was to
conceive magic as natural, while among the intellectuals there were three
competing lines of thought: an assumption, developed in the early centuries of Christianity, that all magic involved at least an implicit reliance
on demons; a grudging recognition, fostered especially by the influx of
Arabic learning in the twelfth century, that much magic was in fact
natural; and a fear, stimulated in the later Middle Ages by the very real

exercise of necromancy, that magic involved an all too explicit invocation of demons even when it pretended to be innocent. But at this point we are getting ahead of our story.

PLAN FOR THIS BOOK

One of the clearest distinctions between high and popular culture in medieval Europe is that intellectuals derived many of their conceptions of magic from their reading of classical literature. Before we can understand how classical and medieval notions related to each other, and how writers around the thirteenth century began to cast off the classical mantle, or at least wear it differently, we must examine this inheritance from antiquity. That will be the task of Chapter 2, which will deal with the period up to about A.D. 500; the rest of the book will deal with magic in western and central Europe from about 500 to around 1500.

If the classical culture of the ancient Graeco-Roman world was one major source of medieval magic, the traditional culture of the Germanic and Celtic peoples was another, and we will turn to this in Chapter 3. Because we know much less about the magic of these northern European cultures, however, this presentation will be relatively brief.

Chapter 4 will argue that certain forms of magic were so widespread that they formed a "common tradition," found among both clergy and laity, among both nobles and commoners, among both men and women, and (with certain qualifications) among townspeople and country people, in later medieval Europe. This is not to say that such magic was always and everywhere the same, but its basic forms were essentially similar wherever it occurred.

In Chapter 5 we will look at the notions of magic prevalent in the courtly culture of later medieval Europe. The chronological focus here will be the twelfth through the fifteenth centuries, when courts had become established in many parts of Europe as major cultural centers. Geographically, this chapter will center mostly on France and on other countries influenced by French culture. The point, however, will not be simply to examine a particular region but to analyze a distinctive attitude toward magic that seems to have become prevalent around the twelfth century: a more or less romantic and at times quite fanciful notion of magic.

Something else was happening around the twelfth century: the importation of Arabic learning into western Europe, which brought with it new conceptions of the occult sciences, including astrology, alchemy, and related areas of natural magic. By the thirteenth century the material brought in from Arabic culture was so widespread and so influential that intellectuals had to undertake fundamental reconsideration of their views on magic. We will trace this development in Chapter 6.

Again, at about the same time a more sinister magic began to take hold in certain corners: the explicitly demonic magic of necromancy, which seems to have flourished mainly in a kind of clerical underworld. This will be the subject of Chapter 7. As we will see, this is not unrelated to the rise of the new learning derived from Muslim culture, yet it is not simply an offshoot of that development.

At every stage we will try to relate the theory and practice of magic to its various cultural contexts. Doing so will inevitably involve some artificiality, since society cannot be divided neatly into different cultural settings. The same individual might be a courtier and also a member of that intellectual avant-garde that was importing Muslim forms of magic. Or he might be a courtier and also a figure in that clerical underworld that practiced necromancy. Historians can set up all the conceptual walls they want, but they should not be surprised when medieval people pass through them freely, like ghosts. Nonetheless, the categories can prove useful even if they are not mutually exclusive.

Finally, in Chapter 8, we will see how Church and state reacted to all these forms of magic. We will survey the moral condemnations by theologians and preachers, the prohibitions enacted by legislators, and the prosecution by both ecclesiastical and secular courts. It might be interesting to deal with these matters within each chapter: to show how the authorities reacted first to the "common tradition" of magic, then to the each of the new developments in the twelfth and following centuries. Yet the authorities who condemned and prohibited magic tended in so doing to conflate its various forms, and the judges who prosecuted people for magic often charged them with different kinds of magical offense in the same trial. To see how different types of magic became confused with each other in condemnation, legislation, and prohibition we must reserve all this for the final chapter, which will serve to sum up what we have examined elsewhere.

2

THE CLASSICAL INHERITANCE

Archaeological evidence provides vivid details from the magic of antiquity. For example, in 1934 a lead plate dating from the era of the Roman Empire was unearthed in London. Someone had taken the trouble to rip it from a building, write an inscription on it, and pound seven nails through it. The inscription reads:

I curse Tretia Maria and her life and mind and memory and liver and lungs mixed up together, and her words, thoughts and memory; thus may she be unable to speak what things are concealed . . .[1]

One can only conjecture what sort of scandal lay behind this chilling curse. We do know, however, that it is not an isolated case. Through much of the Roman Empire people with enemies to dispatch might try doing so by writing a curse on some object, usually a small lead tablet. To heighten the magical efficacy they would often transfix the object with a nail and bury it or drop it into a well, where it could take its place amid the powers of the nether world.

Archaeologists have also turned up amulets made from magical gems, especially in Egypt. These present magic in a less obviously sinister form, since they could serve for protection or healing, but they could be put to other ends as well. One such gem (Figure 3a) has a picture of a mummy, with the inscription "Philippa's child Antipater sleeps." The person using the gem evidently wanted a certain Antipater to sleep like a mummy, which is a not very subtle way of saying he wanted Antipater dead. Another gem shows a female figure, possibly the goddess Isis, with a long

[1] R. G. Collingwood and R. P. Wright, *The Roman Inscriptions of Britain*, vol. 1 (Oxford: Clarendon, 1965), 3–4.

19

spiral of meaningless letters around her. On the reverse is an inscription asking that one Achillas be brought back to a certain Dionysias. In other words, a woman named Dionysias was using the gem for love magic, in hopes that it might bring Achillas to her. Evidently it failed, since a further inscription in a cruder hand reads "Bring him back or lay him low." If the gem would not work for love magic, perhaps it could work better for more sinister purposes.[2]

While these gems have short formulas inscribed on them, much fuller texts are to be found in the magical papyri: sheets of papyrus with magical writing on them in Greek or in the Demotic language of Egypt. The abundance and explicit character of these texts make them some of our most important sources for the magic of antiquity. Fourth- and fifth-century Egypt was rife with these papyri, though the oldest known example comes from the first century B.C. The general flavor is suggested by this formula for love magic:

I adjure you, demon of the dead . . . cause Sarapion to pine and melt away out of passion for Dioskorous, whom Tikoi bore. Inflame his heart, cause it to melt, and suck out his blood out of love, passion, and pain over me . . . And let him do all the things in my mind, and let him continue loving me, until he arrives in Hades.[3]

The papyrus goes on to list magical names and characters. Other such papyri sometimes repeat long magical words, progressively abridged with each repetition, such as:

> ablanathanablanamacharamaracharamarach
> ablanathanablanamacharamaracharamara
> ablanathanablanamacharamaracharamar
> ablanathanablanamacharamaracharama

And so forth, until nothing but the initial "A" remains. In the same era, magicians in the Mediterranean world were devising other magical words like "abracadabra" and "abraxas" to use on amulets or papyri. Still other papyri tell how to transfer insomnia from one person to another by writing an inscription on a seashell, or how to make a woman disclose her secrets while sleeping. For the latter purpose one takes a strip of hieratic papyrus, inscribes it with powerful names and characters, wraps it around a hoopoe's heart that has been marinated in myrrh, and puts it in an appropriate place on the sleeping woman's body. It is remarkable that any of this material has survived, considering that the Roman government took a dim view of such things; in a single year the emperor Augustus (63 B.C.–A.D. 14) is said to have had two thousand magical scrolls burned.

---

[2] Campbell Bonner, *Studies in Magical Amulets, Chiefly Graeco-Egyptian* (Ann Arbor: University of Michigan Press, 1950), nos. 151 and 156.

[3] *The Greek Magical Papyri in Translation*, PGM xvi, ed. Hans Dieter Betz (Chicago: University of Chicago Press, 1986), 252.

It would be difficult to distinguish here between magic and religion. The people who used these amulets and spells invoked all the powers they knew, and the strongest of these were the superhuman ones. Not only do the magical papyri and other sources contain endless appeal to the deities; they also ascribe their magical formulas to the kindness of those gods who have taught such things to mortals.

Christian authorities warned incessantly against this occultism, but their warnings went unheeded in many quarters, even within the Christian fold. The magical papyri often use Jewish and Christian names for God or Christ among their other magical formulas. One magical gem had "ho ōn" (Greek for "the Existing") inscribed on it, surely as an allusion to the God of Exodus 3:14, and an otherwise meaningless series of letters on this amulet discloses an echo of the Hebrew Tetragrammaton "YHWH", again a name for God (Fig. 3a). Far more explicit is a gem from around the third century that shows Christ crucified, with kneeling figures on either side of him, the inscription "Jesus M[essiah]" written in Aramaic, and magical characters on the reverse side (Fig. 3b). While it may be that non-Christian magicians were drawing on the power of the Christian God, it seems likely that Christians themselves were dabbling at times in magic.

All this material is available to us because of archaeologists' and antiquarians' diligence, but little of it was known in medieval Europe. What did survive above ground, in fair abundance, were the writings of Greeks, Egyptians, and Romans *about* magic, and these had profound influence in medieval culture. The scientific and philosophical literature of antiquity, even when it did not deal expressly with magic, helped to form medieval notions of what was possible and impossible in the physical world and thus contributed to medieval understanding of magic. Fictional literature in classical Greek and Latin provided stories about magic that could be cited, often as fact, in medieval writings. The Bible itself, and extrabiblical (or "apocryphal") literature similar to the books of the Bible, contributed further stories about magic. And Christian writers from the early centuries of the Church's history carried on a continuous diatribe of condemnations, interpretations, and prohibitions directed against magical practice, all of which helped to refine the notions of magic that persisted among churchmen throughout the Middle Ages. Medieval Europeans thus inherited a wealth of writings about magic; the way they used this inheritance depended on how they interpreted this mass of varied and often problematic material.

SCIENTIFIC AND PHILOSOPHICAL LITERATURE

The intellectuals of antiquity might look askance at magic, but their attitudes were usually ambivalent. One of the best examples is the *Natural*

History of Pliny the Elder (ca. A.D. 23–79), a compendious survey of all the sciences. Drawing from personal experience and from numerous earlier authorities, Pliny gives a picture of the heavens, Earth and its peoples, animals, plants, drugs, minerals, and metals. In his discussion of plants and their medicinal uses (books 20–7) he rarely includes magical cures, though he does occasionally tell of popular customs such as using a herb for an amulet. When he turns to the curative powers of animals and their effluvia (books 28–30), however, the picture changes. He starts by acknowledging that much of what he is going to tell will arouse disgust; he does not mind, since he is only interested in providing information that will help people. He proceeds to catalogue the curative and other powers of animal bodies, and in the process he often cites exotic and apparently senseless ingredients. He mentions eating spotted lizards, imported from abroad and boiled, as a cure for dysentery. The remedies he gives often seem to rely for their effect on hidden and symbolic powers; he does not refer to these powers as magical, but they are the sort that later writers would cite in discussing natural magic. Elsewhere he mentions a belief that the tongue of a live frog, set over the heart of a woman while she sleeps, will compel her to answer all questions truthfully. Dirt from a wheel rut can heal the bite of a shrew-mouse, because the effects of the bite, presumably like the mouse itself, "will not cross a wheel rut owing to a sort of natural torpor." Pliny clearly does not place equal faith in all such prescriptions. Often he hedges by ascribing them to the magi or to common lore: "they say" this and "they do" that. He reports that "hyena stones," taken from the eyes of hyenas, bestow prophetic gifts on a person if they are placed under the tongue, "if we can believe such a thing." It is even possible to read his entire section on the medicinal use of animals as essentially a catalogue of follies. Yet he takes the trouble to accumulate all this lore, allegedly as an aid to human health, and he seems unwilling to dismiss altogether even those formulas that he distrusts. In any event, later readers did not take him to be skeptical, but attached the authority of his name to every manner of marvel.

It is in his discussion of gems and their powers (books 38–7) that he is perhaps most wide-eyed. The diamond is so hard that nature's "most powerful substances," iron and fire, cannot break it, yet it can be shattered if soaked in warm goat's blood. Here more than anywhere else, he says, the principles of sympathy and antipathy can be seen at work, principles which lie at the heart of his science. He presumably means that the ignoble blood of the goat can undo the nobility of the diamond because of the antipathy of these two substances.

To whose researches or to what accident must we attribute this discovery? What inference could have led anyone to use the foulest of creatures for testing a priceless

Fig. 3(a and b). Magical gems from late antiquity

substance such as this? Surely it is to divinities that we must attribute such inventions and all such benefits.

When Pliny speaks expressly of magic he is referring not to his own methods but to those of the magi, and for these exotic charlatans he has nothing but contempt. If there were any value at all in their concoctions, the emperor Nero would have been a formidable figure indeed, since he studied the magical art with its best teachers, but in fact he was a man of little accomplishment. Magic has the shadow of truth only because it makes use of poisons. A magician may supplement his toxins with the mumbo-jumbo of rituals and spells, but it is the poisons themselves that have effect. No sooner has Pliny dismissed magic, however, than he again hedges: "There is no one who is not afraid of spells and incantations," evidently even scientists and philosophers.[4]

Much the same ambivalence shows in other scientific writers. Dioscorides (first century A.D.), whose work on the medicinal use of animals, plants, and minerals is a classic of early pharmacology, could not withhold his awe at the wondrous powers of certain stones. For this he was ridiculed by the famous physician Galen (ca. A.D. 130–ca. 200), who decried magic yet recommended gathering a herb with the left hand, preferably before sunrise, for maximum effect. More important for future development was Galen's notion that certain drugs work in a wondrous manner not because of any particular ingredient or quality in them but by virtue of their "whole substance." He did not yet speak explicitly of occult powers, but he laid the ground for this notion by suggesting that a plant or animal could have marvelous curative force not reducible to any specific property. Seneca (ca. 4 B.C.–A.D. 65), in his scientific writings, at times used Pliny's device of reporting marvels of nature as common belief rather than as truth. Yet he had profound confidence in the validity of divination: the movement of planets, the falling of meteors, the flight of birds, and especially the occurrence of thunder and lightning served for him as portents of future events. For these men the occult powers and signs within nature were not inherently magical. Magic was a parody of such things, the practice of the infamous magi. Yet their scientific writings provided material for what later writers would indeed call magic. The same is true of the "herbals," or books about medicinal herbs, which provided a lush growth of lore about the wondrous powers of plants.

The most important classical writings in this area, vital for their impact on occult science both in antiquity and in later ages, were works on

---

4 Quotation from *Natural History*, vol. 10, xxxvii.15, trans. D. E. Eichholz (Cambridge, Mass.: Harvard University Press, 1962), 211. Further material from Georg Luck, trans., *Arcana Mundi* (Baltimore: Johns Hopkins University Press, 1985), 38.

astrology. Scientific astronomy, which arose in Mesopotamia around the fifth century B.C., developed mainly in Greek culture. Astrology was built on the back of astronomy, somewhat later: the earliest surviving Babylonian horoscope is from 410 B.C., but the development of scientific astrology came later, again primarily within the Greek-speaking world. Of prime significance for this field were the writings of Aristotle (384–322 B.C.), not because he dealt explicitly with astrology but because his philosophy laid the foundations for later astrological science. He believed that the stars and planets were made of a "fifth essence," superior to the four essences (earth, air, fire, and water) found on Earth. He maintained that the revolution of these heavenly bodies was responsible for developing life and promoting action on Earth. And he saw the "prime mover," the ultimate divine being, as totally self-absorbed, remote from Earth, and exercising influence only through the mediation of these celestial bodies. This is not to say that he believed one could predict earthly affairs by observing the heavens. He did think that the motion of the heavens affected things below, however, and this premise was an important step toward justifying astrology on philosophical grounds.

The figure who took the further step of refining and defending astrological science was the Egyptian astronomer Ptolemy (second century A.D.). His impact on medieval science was far-reaching. Until Copernicus' heliocentric theory gained acceptance in the sixteenth century, it was Ptolemy's model of the cosmos that most intellectuals took for granted: a universe in which Earth was at the center, and the planets and stars revolved about it in complex patterns. In his *Tetrabiblos* he explained in detail how the heavenly bodies affect human life. Fully aware of objections to astrology, he gave reasoned replies to its critics. He did not believe the stars absolutely determine human conduct; their power could be resisted. (In this respect Ptolemy differed from certain Stoic philosophers, who believed human life was fully determined, and who saw astrology and other forms of divination as ways of knowing and thus bracing oneself for inevitable fate.) While Ptolemy's work was not available in Latin until the twelfth century, and before then was known in western Europe only indirectly, its eventual translation was a powerful stimulus to revived interest in astrology.

Medieval writers were indirectly influenced by early critics of astrology and divination, such as Carneades (219–126 B.C.) and Cicero (106–43 B.C.). In his treatise *On Divination*,[5] Cicero ridiculed the notion that the gods communicate messages in dreams, which are in fact merely confused

---

[5] Cicero, *De senectute, De amicitia, De divinatione*, trans. William Armistead Falconer (London: Heinemann; New York: Putnam, 1927), 214–537.

and ambiguous recollections from waking life. Besides, if the gods wanted to communicate their truths to mortals they could find some better and more dignified way than to "flit about" people's beds' and "when they find someone snoring, throw at him dark and twisted visions" which he has to take the next day to some interpreter. The diviners believe that Jupiter sends us warnings by means of thunderbolts. Why, then, does the god waste so many valuable thunderbolts by flinging them into the ocean, or on to deserts, or at people who pay them no heed? The defenders of divination claim that long and careful observation lies behind this science, but Cicero is doubtful. When and where have people systematically gathered data about the entrails from sacrificial animals, or the flight of birds, or the movements of the stars and planets? Other writers, such as Sextus Empiricus, tried to distinguish carefully those things which are determined in advance and those which are left to chance or free will. The former will occur in any event, whether foreseen or not, and in the nature of things the latter cannot be foreseen; thus there is little point in divination.

Skeptics like Cicero and Sextus might fulminate all they wanted; the crowds of people waiting for magicians' and diviners' services grew no thinner, and intellectuals would continue to find justification for their own practice of the occult arts. The Egyptian city of Alexandria, one of the largest and ethnically most diverse cities in the Roman Empire, was a focal point for the practice and development of magic and for its philosophical articulation. It was largely in Alexandria that cryptic and allegorical writings on certain crafts began to emerge – crafts such as metalworking and glassmaking, in which technical secrets were guarded jealously from outsiders – which laid the foundations for what would later be called alchemy. Also commonly associated with Alexandria, though in fact of uncertain provenance, is a body of second- and third-century Greek writings on philosophy, astrology, alchemy, and magic which posterity ascribed to "Hermes Trismegistus," or "Hermes the Thrice-Great." Hermes himself was a Greek god of cunning and invention, often identified with his Egyptian counterpart Thoth. When the treatises ascribed to this figure had gained renown, others were added to the collection, which over the centuries underwent revision and translation many times over. Readers disinclined to suppose that a real god wrote these works ascribed them instead to three "philosophers": the biblical Enoch, Noah, and an Egyptian king.

More important for philosophical development was Plotinus (ca. A.D. 205–70), founder of the Neoplatonic school of thought. His biographer tells how an envious rival tried to harm him by directing stellar rays against him, and Plotinus not only withstood these magical forces but actually deflected them on to the magician. Whether true or not, the story accords with the philosopher's own ideas. In his *Enneads* Plotinus explains both magic and prayer as working through natural sympathetic bonds within the universe. Beings on Earth are linked with each other and with the heavenly bodies in an intricate, living network of influences. Whether we know it or not, we are constantly subject to the tug of magical influences from everywhere in the cosmos: "every action has magic as its source, and the entire life of the practical man is a bewitchment." When people discover these forces they can employ them for their purposes. Thus, when a person prays to the gods, or to the divine heavenly bodies, the act takes automatic effect: "The prayer is answered by the mere fact that one part and the other part are wrought to one tone, like a musical string which, plucked at one end, vibrates at the other also."[6] Those who are truly wise, however, can cultivate the higher powers of the soul by turning inward in contemplation, and can thus become immune to magical forces directed at them. Such persons may still be affected by spells and incantations in their lower, unreasoning powers, and may in fact suffer death, disease, or other misfortune, but their true, essential selves will remain unaffected. This doctrine no doubt brought great consolation to a small philosophical elite.

Plotinus' followers Porphyry (ca. A.D. 233–ca. 304) and Iamblichus (d. ca. 330) further refined these theories. The Neoplatonists also worked out extravagant rituals for invoking the gods and heightening their own magical powers. Such philosophically grounded magic was known as "theurgy," and its practitioners fancied themselves far superior to the adepts of lower magic or "goetia." Many early Christian thinkers, such as Augustine, wrestled with Neoplatonic philosophy and derived much inspiration from it, but had little use for such notions and practices as these. Certain Neoplatonists of medieval Europe were fascinated by the notion of the cosmos as a great, harmonious, living organism, but not by Plotinus' theory of prayer and magic. It was only in the fifteenth century that Humanist proponents of Neoplatonism rediscovered Plotinus and again argued for this conception of magic.

The influence of classical authors on medieval culture was often more indirect than direct. Sometimes a classical author was better known through a later, derivative work. Often a scientist or philosopher of antiquity held such authority among later generations that much later works would capitalize on that authority by claiming him as their author. Thus we have works written centuries after Aristotle's death but claiming to be written by him, and other writings falsely ascribed to Pliny and other

---

[6] *The Enneads*, iv.4.41, trans. Stephen MacKenna, 3rd edn. (London: Faber & Faber, 1966), 323 (adapted).

authorities. This tradition of false ascription continued for centuries, so that a medieval library might be well stocked with the writings of Pseudo-Aristotle and other impostors. Among the works imputed to Aristotle were books of magical experiments, alchemical and astrological treatises, works on the hidden powers of gems and herbs, and manuals of chiromancy and physiognomy. Some of these writings were in fact ancient; others were medieval. Sometimes their authorial claims were based on some suggestive passage in the authentic writings of Aristotle, but often there was no such link.[7] One of the more frequently copied medical works of medieval Europe was a herbal falsely ascribed to "Apuleius the Platonist" of Madaura (2nd century). This work was often embellished with pictures of various plants, including the standard picture of a dog uprooting mandrake. Even when a work was correctly ascribed it might have undergone serious revision. Thus, Dioscorides was known to medieval readers specifically for the sections of his work dealing with plants, and even this material got handed down in a form that Dioscorides himself would not have recognized. One medieval charm even concludes with the preposterous claim, "This was used by Plato and me."[8]

Some of the works which had the strongest impact on medieval culture were writings of late antiquity which strike a modern reader as far more naïve than the works of Ptolemy, Plotinus, or even Pliny. Among these later authors, one of the more influential was Marcellus Empiricus of Bordeaux (ca. 400), who mingled fragments of earlier medicine with the folk traditions of Gaul. If some of his treatments involved Latin incantations, Marcellus had others in gibberish (*crissi crasi cancrasi*, or *sicy, cuma cucuma ucuma cuma uma maa*), or in Greek, or at least in Greek letters. He told how to transfer a toothache to a frog, and how to use the blood of various birds as a remedy for illness.

It is tempting, perhaps, to conclude that the standards of science were low in antiquity and sank still lower in late antiquity. This would be unfair for many reasons, mostly because the works mentioned here are chosen not to represent classical science at its best but for their impact on medieval magic. Medieval writers drew continually upon their ancient forebears for inspiration, but often they viewed the culture of antiquity through a glass darkly, and some of the classical writings they used seem mere parodies of better works. The task of medieval Europeans was not only to preserve classical culture but also at times to recover it, and at times to improve on it.

---

[7] Lynn Thorndike, "The Latin Pseudo-Aristotle and medieval occult science", *Journal of English and Germanic Philology*, 21 (1922), 229–58.

[8] Jerry Stannard, "Greco-Roman materia medica in medieval Germany", *Bulletin of the History of Medicine*, 46 (1972), 467.

FICTIONAL LITERATURE

The distinction between fictional and nonfictional literature may be misleading: apart from the borderline cases, or works in which fiction blends with or rests upon fact, there is the thorny problem of how a work was understood by its audience. Many a work of fiction has been taken as fact by later or even contemporary readers. Particularly the medieval readers of classical texts had a tendency to read them as "authorities" with a status not unlike that of the great philosophers or historians of antiquity. In medieval writings it is thus not uncommon to find the stories of Homer or of Apuleius cited as if they were events of history. This is not to say that medieval readers always read naïvely: while some conflated fiction with fact, others did not, and even those who did often had moral reasons for wanting to set aside the distinction and deal with fiction as if it were fact. In any case, the works of classical literature containing stories of magic are important for the influence they had on medieval understanding of magic. Indeed, they had greater impact on learned theories of magic than on medieval literature: medieval scholars, more than medieval story-tellers, were steeped in the classical tradition.

When medieval writers wanted to cite a classical example of magic, one of the tales they were most likely to recall was from Homer's *Odyssey* (eighth century B.C.). During his travels Odysseus lands on the island of the seductive sorceress Circe. She disposes of his companions by turning them into swine (Fig. 4). Odysseus protects himself by using a magic herb given him by the god Hermes. While he lingers on the island, Circe instructs him in the method for conjuring forth the shades of the dead. What he performs is necromancy, in the original sense of that term: he summons the spirits of the deceased to a trough in which he offers them sheep's blood to drink, and when they come to imbibe this life-giving fluid he has them foretell the future. This story was well known in medieval Europe, especially as retold by Ovid (43 B.C.–ca. A.D.17). Rabanus Maurus (ca. 780–856) argued that the transformation into swine could only be fiction because God alone can change things from one nature into another. But he had to *argue* this point; it did not seem self-evident. Indeed, his influential predecessor Isidore of Seville (ca. 560–636) seems to have taken the story of Circe as a factual account, and cited it alongside stories from history and the Bible. Reluctant to deny the factuality of the event, however, most theologians concluded that such incidents involved delusion of the senses. John of Frankfurt (d. 1440) advanced a different argument: if the poets speak of people being transformed into beasts, this is meant only metaphorically, the way one speaks of a glutton as a pig.

The literature of Greek and Roman antiquity often recounts the magic

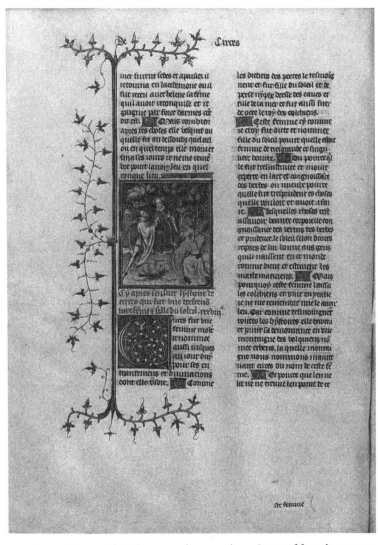

Fig. 4. Circe with Odysseus and companions, from a fifteenth-century manuscript

used by women against their unfaithful lovers, either to win them back or to destroy them. In some cases the woman seeks the aid of a known expert in magic. Virgil (70–19 B.C.), for example, shows Dido in the *Aeneid* soliciting the services of a famed priestess to work magic against Aeneas when he deserts her to sail off and found Rome. In one of his plays Seneca (ca. 4 B.C.–A.D. 65) depicts Heracles' wife using the services of a witch to form a love charm; thinking she has learned the art and can find magical plants on her own, the wife accidentally gives her husband poison. *The Witch* by Theocritus (third century B.C.) is a kind of incantatory lyric depicting a young woman of Alexandria, who tries by magical means to regain the lost affections of her lover. In the process she tells the story of their affair, and one can imagine her feverishly rubbing her hands together as she tells the panoply of magical devices she is using. Alas, her libations, herbs, pulverized lizards, and magic wheel all fail her, as does her invocation of the moon and its goddess Hecate. It is only in Virgil's retelling of the story in his eighth *Eclogue* that her magic succeeds in bringing back the lover.

While these abandoned women appear in a sympathetic light, other female magicians play the role of Evil Incarnate. The poets recount in detail the terrifying appearance, foul character, and unspeakable deeds of these hags. Lucan (A.D. 3–65) describes the witch Erictho as one whose awesome spells force the gods to heed her command:

Haggard and loathly with age is the face of the witch; her awful countenance, overcast with a hellish pallor and weighed down by uncombed locks, is never seen by the clear sky; but if storm and black clouds take away the stars, then she issues forth from rifled tombs and tries to catch the nocturnal lightnings.

She creates zombies for her service, feasts on the bodies of children, and snatches corpses from sepulchers for her enjoyment:

the witch eagerly vents her rage on all the limbs, thrusting her fingers into the eyes, scooping out gleefully the stiffened eyeballs, and gnawing the yellow nails on the withered hand.[9]

She even murders unborn babes "to offer them on a burning altar." Perhaps only Medea can rival her for sheer horror. Even Horace's witch Canidia, who buries a child alive and uses its liver for a love potion, is less monumentally evil than Erictho.

In quite a different vein, Roman literature sometimes presents magic from a satiric viewpoint. Horace (65–8 B.C.) recounts the disgusting nocturnal rituals of two hags in his *Satires*. They conjure the spirits of the

---

[9] *The Civil War*, vi. 515–20, 540–43, trans. J. D. Duff (Cambridge, Mass.: Harvard University Press, 1928), 343.

dead, and they use image magic. The god Priapus, embodied nearby in a wooden statue, has to put up with their repulsive behavior until he eventually puts an end to it by releasing an explosive burst of air from his posterior, whereupon the terrified witches scurry away so fast that one loses her false teeth and the other drops her wig. Even more bitingly satirical is Lucian of Samosata (A.D. 117–ca. 180), whose writings constitute a passionate crusade against superstition. He tells of a magician who, for a handsome fee, charms the moon down from the sky and brings a clay image of Cupid to life to win a woman's favors for his client. He succeeds, but we discover that the client might have accomplished the same end by giving the money directly to the lady. In another story Lucian provides the prototype of the sorcerer's apprentice: the magician's assistant who brings a pestle to life, only to find that he cannot control it, and that when chopped in two it becomes two uncontrollable pestles.

The Platonist Apuleius of Madaura (second century) – the "Apuleius the Platonist" to whom a herbal was pseudonymously ascribed in later centuries – was himself accused of magic and had to defend himself in court by ridiculing the very practices he was alleged to have engaged in. In his partly autobiographical story of *The Golden Ass*, however, magic plays a vital role. The main character is a young man who meets a seductive young witch and her more experienced mistress. They perform their magic with herbs and ointments, parts of human bodies taken from graves and gallows, metal plates with magical inscriptions, in short the standard materials for witchcraft. Not knowing better than to fall in with such folk, the hero finds himself transformed into an ass. It is only when he discovers the goddess Isis that she rescues him from this plight. The story lends itself to different readings: as an entertaining satire, or as a symbolic account of how a bumbling youth gets transformed into a real human being through the power of Isis. Medieval authors cited it as yet another classical authority, and had to deal with its evidence that magicians could transform people into animals. Was this metamorphosis real or only apparent? Augustine, who discussed this phenomenon at some length, refused to commit himself on the case of Apuleius, but shrugged his shoulders and remarked that the story might be fact or it might be fiction. Later theologians would agonize. They insisted that these metamorphoses could not be real, but they felt obliged to deal with the evidence they read in Apuleius. Johannes Vincentii (ca. 1475), for example, opined that Apuleius, like the companions of Odysseus, was a victim of diabolical machinations: the Devil lulled him into a deep sleep and he then had him dream about being transformed.

Doubtless this literature was originally intended to entertain but also to instruct. When it parodied magic it served as a kind of antimagical propaganda; deliberately or not, its authors were thus supporting the efforts of Roman authorities to curb the practice of magic, and it is not surprising to find that a writer such as Horace was closely linked with the emperor Augustus.

Conceived as contributions to Western culture, these writings are important perhaps most of all because they develop the stereotypes of the female magician or witch. In this early literature, as centuries later in trials for witchcraft, the witch tends to be either a young seductress using her magic to promote her amorous purposes or else an ugly hag with awesome and sinister power. Neither of these persistent stereotypes is designed to flatter women, even if the seduction motif could be more sympathetic in tone. If medieval Europeans had known no other sources for misogyny, they could easily have learned it from these texts.

THE BIBLE AND BIBLICAL APOCRYPHA

The Bible is replete with stories of wondrous events. For the most part these are miracles worked by divine power: miraculous escape from bondage, healing, or resurrection. Certain passages, however, are about magical wonders worked by powers other than God's. And even the miracle stories are sometimes reminiscent of magic in the outer details of what occurs, even if the underlying cause for these wonders is not magical.

When the Old Testament deals explicitly with magic, it is to condemn it. The biblical authors do so at times through straightforward command, as in the often-quoted text of Exodus 22:18, "You shall not permit a sorceress to live." Elsewhere the point is made through stories about the punishment for dabbling in magic. King Saul, who had banished all practitioners of the occult from his kingdom, nonetheless consulted the "witch" of Endor before going into battle against the Philistines (1 Samuel 28). This woman summoned the prophet Samuel from the dead, and Samuel grudgingly came forth, only to proclaim that because of Saul's misdeeds he would be defeated in battle and killed. Christian interpreters as early as Hippolytus (ca. 170–ca. 236) were sure that the spirit who appeared to Saul was not really the ghost of Samuel, but merely a demon posing as the prophet.

The most important set piece for biblical and later religious literature is the story of the wonder-working contest between the magicians and God's own agents. In Exodus 7:8–13, Aaron impresses Pharaoh with his power by throwing down his rod and having it turn into a serpent. Pharaoh's magicians do the same thing "by their secret arts": each of them casts down his rod, and all the rods become serpents. But to demonstrate the superior power of the Hebrews and their God, Aaron's rod then

devours all the other rods. Again when the prophet Elijah encounters the
pagan priests of Baal, he wins a miracle-working contest with them on
Mount Carmel (1 Kings 18). In medieval literature on magic, however, it
is the story of Pharaoh's magicians that figures prominently; Isidore of
Seville and other writers cite this as proof that God's miracles are superior
to the Devil's magic.

The New Testament presents one classic example of an evil magician,
Simon Magus of Samaria (Acts of the Apostles 8:9–24). Simon had
impressed the people with his wonder-working. Confronted with the
superior powers of the Christian apostles, however, he offered money for
a share in their power, but the apostle Peter, outraged by this offer, insisted
that such power could not be bought. By the second and third centuries,
Christian authors were elaborating at length upon this simple story and
converting Simon Magus into an arch-heretic and rival of Peter. (Because
the apostle Peter also bore the name Simon, the two figures were aptly
paired as foes: Simon Magus versus Simon Peter.) The apocryphal Acts of
Peter, a sort of novella purporting to tell the apostle's deeds not related in
the Bible, describes one miracle contest at length. Simon Magus feigns
revival of a dead man by using trickery to rouse a few feeble movements in
his body, but only Peter is genuinely able to bring the man back to life.
Frustrated and robbed of his following, the magus announces that he is
going to fly up to God. When he rises up, however, Peter's prayer brings
him crashing back down, and soon afterwards he dies. A similar version of
the story, which remained popular in medieval culture and became
enshrined in the influential *Golden Legend* of the thirteenth century, makes
it clear that when Simon Magus rises into the air he is borne aloft by
demons, and what Peter does is merely dispel them.

Another passage from the New Testament presents magicians in quite
a different light: the story of the magi who come to honor the newborn
Christ (Matthew 2:1–12). The gospel clearly represents them as honorable
figures, and medieval legend even represented them as kings. Defenders of
magic could thus argue that the magical arts hold a position of dignity,
since magicians were among the first to revere Christ. One response to this
argument, first made in the second century, was that while certain forms
of magic were legitimate under the Old Testament, the New Testament
had changed all that: the magi had submitted to Christ, symbolizing the
abdication of magic before Christ's power.

It could always be argued, of course, that Christ himself and his
followers performed magic. Indeed, this was a common theme in controversy between Christians and pagans as early as the second century. The
pagan writer Celsus (second century) claimed that Jesus had learned the
magical arts in Egypt: the techniques for "blowing away" illness, creating

the illusion of food, and making inanimate things seem to move as if alive. This argument could find support in the Gospels. When Jesus' power suffices to cure a woman who merely touches the fringe of his garment, and when Christ then exclaims, "Some one touched me, for I perceive that power has gone forth from me," one might well wonder what sort of power this is (Luke 9:43–8). When he cures a deaf-mute by putting his fingers in the man's ears, spitting, and touching his tongue (Mark 7:32–4), or when he heals a blind man by anointing his eyes with clay made with his own saliva (John 9:6ff.), these procedures could easily seem magical. Elsewhere, especially in Matthew's gospel, Christ is seen healing people without such techniques, merely by his word, with a simple command such as "be clean," "arise," or "rise, take up your pallet, and walk." Yet this lack of magical ritual did not dispel all suspicion of magic: some Jewish opponents even argued that Christ was a magician specifically because his words themselves had such power.

For the early Christians, Christ's miracles were important not only in themselves but for their broader religious significance. At times Jesus healed people and declared that he did so because of their faith. On occasion the physical healing was linked to spiritual cleansing: Christ cured both body and soul. Miracles are thus closely tied to the fundamental purposes of the Gospel, the kindling of faith and the preaching of repentance. They also have eschatological significance: they are part of a spiritual warfare between the kingdom of God and the rival kingdom of Satan. The paradigmatic miracles, especially in the Synoptic Gospels, are exorcisms, but even the healing of physical disease can be seen as involving conflict with the forces of evil, or with demons. When Jesus drives out demons or deprives them of their force, he is striking a blow on behalf of God's power in the world. As he says at one point, "if it is by the Spirit of God that I cast out demons, then the kingdom of God has come upon you" (Matthew 12:28; Luke 11.30). Yet a pagan or a Jew might respond that whatever broader or symbolic force it may claim, magic is still magic. Apuleius' transformation into an ass might also count as having symbolic meaning, but that does not exclude it from the category of magic.

Realizing that the techniques and the broader relevance of miracles were not decisive in this argument, early Christian writers did not usually focus on these matters. Instead they either made or presupposed one central, crucial point: that magic is the work of demons, while miracles are the work of God. What this amounted to, of course, was the claim that the Christian God is true and the pagan gods are false, which is precisely what the Christians were saying. The claim had social relevance: unlike the pagans and Jews, Christians had no ethnic cohesion, and they asserted their group identity not only by using mysterious rituals (like the mystery religions) but also by emphasizing strongly the distinctiveness of their God and their teachings about him. The Jews, too, asserted that their God was not simply one out of many gods, but it was the Christians who most vigorously *argued* the point. For them it was first of all a truth and secondly the sole basis for their existence as a group. And one clear corollary to this belief was the firm distinction: pagans worked magic, but Christ worked miracles. The two might appear to be alike, but just as a dog is different from a wolf and a tame pigeon differs from a wild one, "so also what is accomplished by God's power is nothing like what is done by sorcery.[10]

If the Gospels were problematic, the Acts of the Apostles must have been more so. This book of the Bible has several stories in which the apostles' power seems to resemble that of magic. Individuals who break the code of the early Christian community are suddenly struck dead (4:32–5:11). Peter's shadow has the power to cure (5:12–16), as do handkerchiefs and aprons that he has touched (19:11). The apostles overcome the power of other magicians on more than one occasion, and when magicians at Ephesus are converted they bring forth books of magic to be burned (19:13–19). Indeed, this book shows the apostles carrying out a systematic campaign against what they saw as magic. From the pagan or Jewish viewpoint, however, the apostles seemed merely to have a superior form of magic. Here again the sole Christian counterargument was that the Christian God was the true deity, and whatever the apostles accomplished, even if outwardly it resembled magic, was in fact a manifestation of God's power working through them.

MAGIC, EARLY CHRISTIANITY, AND THE GRAECO–ROMAN WORLD

The same arguments that were made about Christ and his apostles applied to later generations of Christians. They might readily be accused of magic because they ascribed power to an executed man, Christ, and to the cross on which he was executed. People in the Roman world often ascribed special power to those who had died violent or untimely deaths; the spirits of these victims were especially sought in necromancy. Apuleius mentions the belief that fingers and noses from crucified individuals have great power, and both he and Lucian refer to the notion that nails from a cross possess magical potency. Christian actions, as well as Christian symbols, could arouse distrust. Tertullian (ca. 160–ca. 225) warns Christian women that if they marry pagan husbands they are inviting trouble: "Shall you escape notice when you sign your bed, or your body; when you blow

---

[10] Origen, *Contra Celsum*, ii.51, trans. Henry Chadwick (Cambridge: Cambridge University Press, 1953), 105.

away some impurity; when even by night you rise to pray? Will you not be thought to be engaged in some sort of magic?"[11] Christian exorcists could command the demons by using powerful and secret names. Indeed, the name of Jesus held such power against demons that in the words of one Christian writer "there have been cases where it was effective even when pronounced by evil men."[12] Little wonder that when Christians were persecuted they were sometimes charged with magic. Yet Christians continued to insist that it was not they but the pagans who were the real magicians.

The conflict between Christians and pagans rested, finally, on their differing notions about magic and its place in society. For pagans who opposed magic, it was reprehensible because it was secret and antisocial. It was a force that worked against society, from within society itself, and for that reason it had to be uprooted. The pagans did not care what gods you venerated, so long as you did so openly and did not call on them for help in performing evil. If you did invoke the gods' help for evil, what you were doing was both religious and magical; the realms were not distinct, since magic relied on aid and instruction from the gods. For the Christians, magic was reprehensible because it was the work of demons. These were evil spirits, ultimately subject to God, but they paraded as gods and received veneration. Christians could not complain about secrecy because they themselves were secretive. But invocation of false gods, whether secret or open, was wrong no matter what its purposes. Veneration of these gods was inseparably bound up with magic and therefore was not authentic religion. By distinguishing sharply between Christianity (which alone was true religion) and paganism (which had magical reliance on demons at its heart), early Christian writers in effect introduced a distinction between religion and magic which had not previously been made and which was not easily understood except from a Christian viewpoint. It was a short step from saying that paganism was inauthentic religion to maintaining that it was no religion at all but mere idolatry and magic. This new way of disjoining magic from religion remained part of the Christian heritage for centuries to come, and was joined only around the thirteenth century by a new emphasis on specifically natural magic as a kind of third term.

In short, the pagan definition of magic had a moral and a theological dimension but was grounded in social concerns; the Christian definition had a moral and a social dimension but was explicitly centered on theological concerns. Between these two different models there was little

---

[11] *Ad uxorem*, ii.5, quoted in Stephen Benko, "Early Christian magical practices", *Society of Biblical Literature, Seminar Papers*, 21 (1982), 13.

[12] Pseudo-Clement, *De virginitate*, i.10, 12; quoted ibid.

room for discussion. The two sides might agree on their moral principles, since both pagans and Christians found the evil purposes of magic repugnant, but morality was not at the heart of the issue from either perspective.

Early Christian writers tended to see all forms of magic, even ostensibly harmless kinds, as relying on demons. Tatian (second century) viewed herbs, amulets, and other accoutrements of magic as having no power in themselves; they are nothing but a kind of signal-system devised by demons so that human beings can communicate their desires. Reading these signals, the demons act accordingly. Divination, too, is carried out only with the aid of demons. By pretending to serve human beings, the demons in fact ensnare them into their service. Clement of Alexandria (ca. 150–ca. 215) saw the pagan poets as largely responsible for trapping people into this service through the bewitchment of their song. Thus, when Christians converted others to the faith they conceived this as a victory over the forces of hell. St. Anthony of Egypt (ca. 251–356), a popular religious leader in one of the great centers of magic, is supposed to have declared, "Where the sign of the cross is made, magic loses its power and sorcery fails." Then according to his biographer, Anthony went on to taunt the pagans:

Tell me, therefore, where now are your oracles? Where are the incantations of the Egyptians? Where are the delusions of the magicians? When did all these lose their power and cease but at the coming of the cross of Christ?[13]

To grasp the force of this argument we must realize that demons were seen differently by pagans and by Christians. For pagans, *daimones* (Latin *daemones*) were neutral spirits, intermediate between gods and human beings and capable of serving either good or evil purposes. For Christians, as for most Jews, they were angels who had turned against their creator and turned wholly to evil.

The variations on this theme that had the greatest impact òn medieval culture were those by Augustine, particularly in his classic book *The City of God*.[14] Augustine wrote this work in response to the argument that the Roman Empire had declined after becoming Christian. It is Roman religion, he says, that is grounded in necromancy and other magical arts. Following earlier writers, Augustine insists that all magic is worked by demons. These evil spirits first instruct people how to perform magic

---

[13] St. Athanasius, "Life of St. Anthony", ch. 78ff., trans. Sister Mary Emily Keenan, in Roy J. Deferrari, ed., *Early Christian Biographies* ([New York]: Fathers of The Church, 1952), 203.

[14] Augustine, *Concerning the City of God, against the Pagans*, viii–x, trans. Henry Bettenson, new edn. (Harmondsworth: Penguin, 1984), 298–426.

rituals, and how to make use of magical stones, plants, animals, and incantations; when the magicians make use of these things, the demons come and carry out the desired deeds. Augustine does acknowledge certain marvelous powers in nature itself. He recognizes the mysterious qualities of the magnet, the power of goat's blood to shatter the otherwise indestructible adamant, and the salamander's capacity to survive fire. Furthermore, he concedes that certain powerful substances, perhaps medicinal herbs, may cure sick people if they are bound to their bodies or suspended over them. While he thus recognizes the efficacy of what would later be called natural magic, however, he does so grudgingly and always remains suspicious that demons are somehow at work in these matters. If magical images, words, or incantations come into play his suspicion is only confirmed.

Opposition to magic came partly from a sense that it posed an alternative to Christian prayers. It was a competing system of practice, a rival to Christian ways of coping with adversity. Thus, John Chrysostom (ca. 347–407) preached against women who use magic when their children are sick rather than using the one true Christian remedy, the sign of the cross. These women would never think of taking their children to the pagan temples in the hope of obtaining a cure through overt idolatry. Yet the Devil has deceived them into thinking that the magic they use at home is something other than idolatry. They use amulets and incantations; they bind to their children the names of rivers and other magical words, presumably written on slips of parchment. Rather than using properly Christian means they call on folk healers with their bags of magic tricks. "Christ is cast out, and a drunken and silly old woman is brought in."[15]

While there is no reason to think that women alone practiced magic, both pagan and Christian writers ascribed it primarily to them. Tertullian charged women generally with a propensity toward such things: fallen angels taught women the special and secret powers of herbs, because women more than men are subject to the deception of these evil spirits.

For some writers magic is more than merely an artificial system of signals worked out by demons. It is an objectively real system of powers which the demons know and teach. This is the thrust of Tertullian's notion that demons taught women about magical herbs; the magical powers were already there within the herbs, but it was through demons that women learned about them. For the Egyptian writer Origen (ca. 185–ca. 254) it is words that have magical power, and especially names. The names of demons, if pronounced in the right way, can be used to invoke them,

---

[15] Homily 8 on Colossians, in Philip Schaff, ed., *A Select Library of Nicene and Post-Nicene Fathers*, 13 (New York: Scribner, 1905), 298.

command them, or exorcise them. These names must be used in their
original forms; they cannot be translated into different languages or they
will lose their power. Various names for God and for Christ, too, have
prodigious force, as Origen's pagan compatriots knew when they invoked "the God of Abraham."

While most of these early Christian writers associated magic with
paganism, there were others who saw it as a craft exercised by heretical
Christians. Simon Magus was the prototype of the heretical magician;
when Irenaeus (ca. 130–ca. 200) wrote his voluminous attack on the
heresies of his day he recounted how Simon had learned all the magical
arts in his effort to rival the apostles, and how he and his disciples used
incantations and exorcisms in an effort to win a following. Occasionally
these attacks on heretics indicate specific forms of trickery used to deceive
people. To persuade the multitudes of their magical power, heretics use
chemicals to change the colors of liquids, or they speak through hidden
tubes to make people hear mysterious voices. Even if demons are involved, however, magic can still entail a kind of fraud: by duping people's
senses they make them think they see banquets spread before them when
in fact there is no real food, or they make inert matter appear to live and
move. So too, demons can persuade people that they have foreknowledge
of future events when they only rely on their cunning to make plausible
conjectures about the future.

While this is the general drift of early Christian thought regarding
magic, there are exceptions. Julius Africanus (ca. 160–ca. 240) recommended magical techniques for healing, for growing crops, even for
making love charms and destroying enemies in combat, without seeing
any of this as demonic. He was a Christian layman, writing for the high
society of imperial Rome rather than for the edification of fellow Christians. Even so, his views could hardly have won the approval of any
churchmen who might have seen them. Other Christian writers took
nuanced views regarding the occult. Firmicus Maternus (fourth century)
encouraged the Roman authorities to extirpate paganism and the magic
and divination linked with pagan temples, yet seems to have found
astrology a valid and legitimate science. These may appear to be isolated
and insignificant examples, but it is more likely that they spoke for untold
numbers of compromisers whose thought never found its way into
writing, or whose writings have not come down to us.

Furthermore, the Roman intellectual world was still by no means
wholly Christian even in the fourth and fifth centuries. Neoplatonist
writers like Martianus Capella (fourth century) were still interested in
philosophical interpretations of mythology, in which various types of
gods and other spirits function as the forces behind magic and divination.

And Macrobius (fifth century), whose major work seems to have preceded his conversion to Christianity, believed firmly in the occult powers of numbers, in the prophetic significance of dreams, and in the virtues hidden within nature. Their works might at times be found on the shelves of a medieval monastic library, alongside those of Augustine and other foes of magic. Yet the tendency was clear: as Christianity became dominant, magic fell ever more under suspicion.

The Church not only preached against magic but also passed ecclesiastical legislation against it. The decrees (or "canons") of regional assemblies (or "synods") eventually became the basis for the church's "canon law," which even in its early forms condemned magic. In 306 a synod in the Spanish town of Elvira proclaimed that people who had killed others by sorcery (*maleficium*) should not be allowed to receive communion on their own deathbeds, because such deeds could not be accomplished without "idolatry," which is to say the invocation of evil spirits. The synod of Ancyra in 314 required five years of penance for those guilty of divination and magical cures, and ten years for those who procured abortions by magical means. In 375 the council of Laodicaea forbade the clergy themselves to practice sorcery and related arts or to make magical amulets, while those who wore such amulets were to be excommunicated.

From the early fourth century, the Church had far greater influence because the emperors themselves were mostly Christian and subject to persuasion by the clergy. In earlier centuries Roman law had punished magic only when it was used to inflict harm. The laws of the Roman Republic had threatened severe punishment, possibly even death, for those who used magic to arouse storms, to steal crops, or to summon the deceased. Under the emperor Tiberius (reg. A.D. 14–37) provisions that had earlier applied to poisoners now were extended to magicians as well: all who endangered the life of others by magic could be punished by death. The same punishment later applied to those who used love magic. It was after the conversion of the emperors to Christianity, however, that magic of all kinds became a capital offense. In 357 Constantius threatened beheading for all those who used any form of magic or divination, and these severe measures were repeated in the codes of Theodosius II in 438 and Justinian in 529. Even people who wore magical amulets to ward off disease might now be executed. The pagan writer Ammianus Marcellinus (ca. 330–ca. 398) complained that anyone who consulted a soothsayer or used "some old wife's charm" to ease his pains was liable to capital punishment. The emperor Valentinian I (reg. 364–75) prescribed death for those who went out at night and engaged in "evil imprecations, magic rituals, or necromantic sacrifices," terms which a judge might construe either strictly or broadly. In 371 some people who used divination to predict the death of Valentinian and the name of his successor were brought to court in a sensational trial and later executed. Soon afterward, the censors' bonfires consumed massive piles of magical literature, and people who owned books that might be seen as even remotely offensive burned them in advance to avoid the scandal of public exposure.[16]

By the sixth century there was a new kind of society and a new culture in Europe which needed to take stock of the heritage bequeathed to it from antiquity. The Roman Empire had already become officially Christian, but then in the fifth century Germanic peoples from northern Europe had moved southward and westward and taken control of England, Gaul, Italy, Spain, even northern Africa. The lands that they conquered became effectively severed from the old Roman Empire; only the eastern part of the Empire survived this disintegration. The breakdown of central authority in the West meant also a change in the context for culture. Knowledge of Greek language and literature became rare in the West. As different vernacular languages evolved, command of Latin became the privilege of a clerical elite. Just when the old Roman cultured classes were becoming Christian, these classes lost the status they had previously held within society. New rulers, unfamiliar or only vaguely familiar with Roman traditions, governed the West. The first task confronting the Church was to convert these rulers and their subjects to the Christian and Catholic faith. In the process, not only the converts but the faith to which they were converted underwent a change, as elements of pre-Christian culture became grafted on to the new, medieval Christianity. However much churchmen repeated early prohibitions of magic, they now had to contend with new forms of magical belief and practice that took deep hold within Christian culture.

[16] A. A. Barb, "The survival of the magic arts", in Arnaldo Momigliano, ed., *The Conflict Between Paganism and Christianity in the Fourth Century* (Oxford: Clarendon, 1963), 110–25, with quotations translated.

3

THE TWILIGHT OF PAGANISM: MAGIC IN
NORSE AND IRISH CULTURE

·

Norse tradition tells of a conflict between two earls of tenth-century Norway in which both the parties, named Hakon and Thorleif, resorted to magic. Thorleif disguised himself as a beggar, went to the court of Hakon, and under the pretense of singing a poem in his honor recited a curse that caused Hakon to lose his beard and much of his hair, to itch uncontrollably between his legs, and to suffer a lingering illness. In revenge, Hakon invoked the goddesses Thorgerd and Irpa, who aided him with their "trollish and prophetic powers." They made a human figure out of driftwood, placed a heart inside it, and sent it to Thorleif, who promptly died.[1]

Our source for all this is a literary account, not a straightforward history. Indeed, the earliest recorded version of the tale is from the fourteenth century, and what it attests is not the actual practice of magic in pre-Christian Scandinavia but rather the recollection of that magic at a time when it could arouse a mixed reaction, combining horror with amusement. Precisely in this respect, however, the story gets to the heart of the problem in working with the pre-Christian magic of northern Europe: most of our information comes from after the conversion, and our fullest sources are fictional accounts that combine actual magical practice with fanciful embellishments. We know in principle that magic in later medieval Europe represented a fusion of diverse influences, some from Graeco-Roman antiquity and some from the early Germanic and Celtic culture. To get at the latter sources, however, we have to rely heavily on inference from late and problematic materials.

[1] Jacqueline Simpson, "Olaf Trygvason versus the powers of darkness", in Venetia Newall, ed., *The Witch Figure* (London: Routledge, 1973), 178ff. (Quotation translated by Simpson).

CONVERSION AND PAGAN SURVIVALS

The newly arrived peoples who now dominated western and central Europe eventually converted to Christianity, partly through assimilation to the Christian culture already present in the late Roman Empire, and partly through the efforts of foreign missionaries. The process took several generations, from about the fifth to around the tenth century. In bold outline: the Gauls and the Anglo-Saxons of England converted in the sixth and seventh centuries (partly through missionary efforts of the Irish, who had become Christian slightly earlier); in the seventh and eighth centuries, missionary monks from the British Isles preached to the Germanic peoples on the Continent; last to be included in the newly formed European Christendom were the Slavic peoples of eastern Europe and the Scandinavians the North, who joined this new cultural mainstream around the tenth century.

All of these dates, however, are approximations. Chroniclers usually took the year of a monarch's baptism as the official date for conversion of a kingdom. If we look more closely we will almost always find that there had been some Christians in the land beforehand, perhaps queens who had come from Christian countries and had brought their chaplains along, and perhaps also merchants from abroad. Nor did the rest of the country automatically follow the king's baptism. Indeed, effective conversion of the countryside might take several further generations. Yet if converting the monarch was neither the first nor the final step in Christianization, it was nonetheless a crucial step, which ensured the dominance of Christian institutions. Once the king was baptized a network of monasteries, bishoprics, and local churches would soon displace pagan temples, and Christian clergy would displace the pagan priesthood. Once the traditional structures dissolved, people would naturally turn to Christianity for their religious needs. The process did not occur overnight, however, and even when it was accomplished some elements of the earlier culture would inevitably survive.

Accommodation to certain elements of pagan culture was common (though not universal) missionary practice in the early Middle Ages. Pope Gregory the Great (reg. 590–604) told his missionaries to England that they should not demolish pagan temples but reconsecrate them and use them as Christian churches; they should endow pagan festivals with Christian meaning rather than prohibiting their observance. So too, the missionaries incorporated elements of what we are calling magic into their new cultural synthesis. Monks who traveled about as missionaries would often encounter magical charms, perhaps containing the names of Germanic gods; they would write them down so that other monks would know what to expect on the mission field, and perhaps they would devise Christianized versions of the same formulas. Thus, a famous early German charm tells how Woden was riding a horse through the woods when its leg was sprained and the god had to heal the afflicted limb. Later versions replace Woden with Christ, portrayed as riding his horse into Jerusalem, or with other Christian figures. While pagan priests were forbidden to continue their rites, it was harder to eradicate elements of pagan belief from the kings, who continued to be seen as descended from the gods and as sources of magical power and protection for their realms. There was little the Christian priest could do about these vestiges from the earlier culture.

Yet toleration had its limits. Monks and other churchmen usually drew the line at explicit veneration of the old gods, and they forbade practices that might be construed as involving such veneration. As an anonymous preacher in the early Middle Ages protested, "All those who believe they can prevent hail by means of inscribed lead tablets or charmed horns are no Christians, but rather pagans." Following early Christian writers, they identified the traditional gods as demons, and thus all magic that called on the services of these gods, explicitly or implicitly, was demonic magic.

The traditional cultures of northern Europe, like those of the Roman Empire, linked religion and magic without distinction. In Germanic mythology, for example, the god Woden (or Odin) was himself a master of magic who had gained power over the magical runic alphabet and could use its characters to perform wondrous deeds. An Anglo-Saxon healing charm might invoke the power of this god; indeed, an English book of charms from long after the conversion to Christianity still contained a spell referring to Woden. In early medieval Europe, therefore, the churchmen had to continue the fight begun by their predecessors in the Roman Empire, and the logic of their argument was essentially the same. In both eras orthodox opinion held that pagan religion was no true religion but mere demon-worship, and that magic was inseparably linked to this demonic cult.

People who had performed magic might repent of their misconduct, and might go to a priest for confession. If so, the priest would probably have a "penitential," or manual telling him what penances to impose for these and other sins. The early medieval penitentials furnish ample evidence for the varieties of magic priests expected to hear from the newly converted peoples of Europe. One such handbook has a section on the worship of pagan idols, and under this heading prescribes varying lengths of penance for those who have performed "diabolical incantations or divinations." The author continues, drawing in part upon a canon from the synod of Ancyra:

He who celebrates auguries, omens from birds, or dreams, or any divination according to the custom of the heathen, or introduces such people into his house, in seeking out any trick of the magicians – when these become penitents, if they belong to the clergy they shall be cast out; but if they are secular persons they shall do penance for five years.

The penitentials could be more specific: they condemned the use of magical potions to procure sterility, abortion, death, or love; they took seriously the belief that people can steal milk, honey, and other substances by magic, and kill animals with mere glances and words; according to these sources, women who boasted that they could arouse love or hatred, or that they could steal people's goods through magical means, were to be driven from their parishes. One penitential says that a person who "drives stakes into a man," meaning presumably an enemy's image, should fast for three years.[2]

Churchmen had occasion to condemn not only pagan practices but also pagan beliefs. Around 820, Bishop Agobard of Lyon wrote against the superstitious belief that sorcerers could arouse hail and thunderstorms; only God, he insisted, controls the weather. On one occasion the people of his region accused four unfortunate souls of having sailed about in the air on magical ships, from which they pilfered the fruits of the fields. Agobard concluded sadly that in his day folly had taken the upper hand, and Christians believed things which in better days even pagans would reject. An anonymous penitential, which got incorporated in Burchard of Worms' influential collection of canon law around 1020 and thus enjoyed wide circulation, rejected the belief that magic can disturb the weather, influence people's minds, or arouse love and hatred. The same source also dismisses the belief that people can be transformed into animals. All such notions seemed to infringe God's prerogative as creator. The canon *Episcopi*, probably from a ninth-century Frankish synod, condemned the belief of certain women that they rode through the air at night-time on the backs of animals, in the company of the goddess Diana. For believing in such things, rather than for participating in them, these churchmen prescribe penance. Yet most of the synodal and penitential literature concerned itself with what people did, not what they thought, and most churchmen railed against magic rather than the belief in magic.

When we attempt to analyze the actual magical practice of the northern European peoples, however, we are on treacherous ground. Apart from occasional references to very early customs in Roman historians such as Tacitus, and condemnations by early medieval monks, we have little in the

___

[2] John T. McNeill and Helena M. Gamer, trans., *Medieval Handbooks of Penance* (New York: Columbia University Press, 1938), especially 38–43, 198, 228ff., 305ff., 329–41, 349ff.

way of written record. The archaeological evidence usually tells us little: if excavation of a grave turns up a horse's tooth that has been pierced so it can be hung around a person's neck, is that an indication that this tooth once served as a magical amulet? If so, for what purpose? And why is it buried in the grave? Answers to these questions remain frustratingly speculative.

Two main areas for exploration nonetheless present themselves. First, while the pre-Christian cultures of northern Europe were for the most part illiterate, they were not entirely so. They had their own forms of writing, often used for magical inscriptions if not for literary composition. Most important in this regard are the runic inscriptions of the Norse culture that extended through Scandinavia and Iceland, gained a strong foothold in England, and made its mark on other parts of Europe through trade and looting. The Norsemen represent one branch of Germanic culture, and because they remained pagan longer than most other branches they left more vestiges of their pagan culture. Secondly, there are narrative sources from the time after the conversion which reflect the customs and the mentality of the pre-Christian era. The most important of these are again Norse, particularly the sagas from Iceland. Yet pagan motifs can be found elsewhere as well, even in the writings of the Irish, who had converted to Christianity much earlier. We cannot reconstruct an entire pagan culture from these remnants, but we can at least catch glimpses of what it must have been.

RUNIC INSCRIPTIONS

In a culture where writing is uncommon, it may well appear magical. Even ordinary script may seem to bear extraordinary power, and it is not surprising when people in search of magical weapons or magical protection seize upon the written word. The English chronicler Bede (ca. 673–735) tells of a Northumbrian captive whose brother, thinking him dead, had masses said for his soul. Wondrously, the prayers loosened the captive's fetters and set him free. His captors, however, not knowing the cause of this strange development, immediately asked if he was carrying magical writing on his person. For them, magic must have seemed intimately bound up with writing.

One of the clearest examples of this mentality is the use of the runes, the alphabet used in the Norse culture of Scandinavia and Iceland. The earliest known runes are from the third century. They are found among other early Germanic peoples, but it was the Norsemen who retained and used them well into the medieval era. Whether or not they were originally and essentially seen as magical is unclear, but clearly it did not take long for them to develop magical associations. We read in Norse stories about people who used runic inscriptions to work various types of magic: to gain victory in battle, to detect poison and split open a drinking-horn that contains a poisoned drink, to ensure fertility, to procure love, to affect the weather. One source speaks of the runes as having power even to revive the corpse of a hanged man. In *Egil's Saga* we hear of runes carved on whalebone to aid a sick woman. But they are, alas, the wrong runes, and when Egil finds them he comments sardonically that people who do not know their runes should leave this business alone. Then he carves the right ones, and the woman immediately revives.

Various objects bearing runic inscriptions have been found from Scandinavia, Iceland, and the part of England that was occupied by the Danes. It is not always possible to ascribe precise magical intent to the inscriptions, but sometimes magical effect was clearly intended. A sixth-century amulet made from the bone of a fish and discovered at Lindholm in Sweden bears the name of the god Týr, and also has combinations of runes that cannot have ordinary significance and probably are meant to convey magic power (Fig. 5). One portion of the inscription, for example, reads "aaaaaaaa*RRR*nnn"; repetition of magical runes in this manner seems to have been common. Such inscriptions also occur at burial sites as protective amulets: on stones inside or near the graves, to stave off evil powers or to bind the deceased to the grave and keep them from wandering.

THE NORSE SAGAS

Various genres of medieval literature make incidental reference to magic. *Beowulf*, for example, tells of a magical amulet set in a warrior's helmet as protection. For sustained and realistic depiction of early Germanic magic, however, there are few sources as revealing as the Norse sagas. To speak of these documents as realistic is not to say that they are faithful in every particular to real life, or that they were read in that way. More than most types of medieval literature, however, they depict magic as occurring amid realistic accounts of everyday situations: in the thick of family feuds, in the exercise of judicial business, in the ordinary grind of life, not in a fantasy world or an idealized or enchanted realm.

The verse sagas were written in Iceland around the thirteenth century, yet they are commonly set in a much earlier era, the period just after the conversion of Iceland to Christianity in A.D. 1000. The poets assume that the culture of their land has become at least nominally Christian, but they tell of people clinging to ancient beliefs and pagan practices. Thus they are a treasury of information, not so much for pre-Christian magic, but for Christian perception of that early magical practice.

Fig. 5. Lindholm wand-amulet, sixth century

The role of sorcery in this literature is manifest, for example, in *Grettir's Saga*, written in the fourteenth century but portraying events of the eleventh.[3] Like most sagas, this one is essentially a story of ruthless violence between families. The hero, Grettir, ends his days in exile on the lonely island of Drang, a rocky protrusion from the sea off the coast of Iceland. Before he goes to this refuge he bids his mother farewell. She warns him:

Be on your guard against treachery, but you will be slain by weapons. I have had some very strange dreams. Keep clear of sorcerers, for there are few things stronger than witchcraft.

The premonition turns out to be well grounded. Grettir's chief enemy, finding himself unable to attack Grettir on the island, solicits the aid of his old foster-mother, who practiced sorcery before the conversion and still remembers its secrets. Reluctantly, the feeble old woman agrees to help. She goes along with others to Drang in a boat, but Grettir recognizes her and hurls a stone that breaks her thigh. Eventually she recovers from this injury, and then proceeds against Grettir with savage cunning. Taking some men with her, she goes down to the coast and looks for driftwood. She finds a heavy tree-trunk, has the men scrape a smooth surface on it, then carves runes on it. She smears her own blood into the runes, chants a few spells, walks backwards and counterclockwise around the trunk, and

[3] *Grettir's Saga*, ch. 69, 78–80, trans. Denton Fox and Hermann Pálsson (Toronto: University of Toronto Press, 1974), 158–64.

has the men push it out into the sea. She puts a further spell on it, so that even though the wind is blowing toward land it drifts quickly out to Drang. The next day Grettir goes to look for firewood and finds this very tree, but rejects it as an "evil tree, sent to us by evil." The same thing happens the next day. The third day, however, a slave goes searching for wood, and unknowingly brings back the cursed trunk. Grettir begins chopping it before he recognizes it, but his axe glances off and strikes his leg, causing a deep wound. When the wound grows worse he knows he has been afflicted by sorcery. Weakened, he is unable to defend himself when his foes finally storm the island, and thus they are able to kill him with a blow to the head. When other people in Iceland learn what has happened, they hold Grettir's enemy guilty not for killing Grettir, but for having recourse to witchcraft, and thus they banish him from Iceland. "Then it was adopted as law," the saga tells us, "that all sorcerers should be outlawed."

In various ways the magic used against Grettir typifies the sorcery in the sagas. The magician is a specialist who performs services for others. She deploys ceremonies and magically charged objects, but her main source of power is the spoken and written word: the spells she chants over the tree-trunk and the runic inscription she carves on it. Others in her society find magic reprehensible not because it is violent but because it is unfair. One is supposed to kill enemies in honest combat, not through the furtive rituals of sorcery. Perhaps most importantly, the magic here and in other sagas takes place within the familiar context of Icelandic life. The witch is an old woman with special knowledge, but there is no suggestion that she is anything other than human, or that she is an outsider to Icelandic society. Nor is the situation that gives rise to magic anything out of the ordinary.

The effects of magic in the sagas are diverse. It may be offensive or defensive, but in either case it is almost always a means for confronting or evading one's enemies. It can kill them by ensuring they will be wounded in battle or by raising a storm while they are at sea. When accused of using magic, the magician can use further magic to kill the accuser. Short of bringing death, sorcery can make life miserable. It can keep a man from having intercourse with his wife. Magic can change people into animals so their enemies will not find them, or bring darkness and mist to confuse a pursuer. In a battle, a magician's glance can cause weapons to go blunt, a magical spell can prevent soldiers from protecting themselves, and a magically impenetrable shirt can make a warrior invincible. The evil eye is feared especially when the magician is apprehended; those who seize the sorcerer thus often put a sack over his head. Occasionally the sagas refer to healing magic, but even when someone claims to be using healing arts she may in fact have evil intent. *The Saga of Droplaug's Sons* tells of a fighter named Grim whose leg becomes wounded in combat and festers. A woman comes to him claiming skill in medicine. She bandages his leg, but it only grows worse, and soon he dies. It turns out that the woman is in fact a witch, the friend of a man Grim has killed, and now she has taken her revenge.

The magicians of the sagas are almost always thoroughly sinister characters, surly and unpopular, and sometimes they are explicitly connected with paganism. When they commit their foul deeds everyone agrees that they should suffer death or at least banishment. On occasion they are said to have learned their art from teachers, and small bands of assistants sometimes help by saying responses or chanting spells. One saga even refers to an entire family of sorcerers, "very skilled in magic," who have been driven from their home presumably because of this reputation. For the most part, however, they operate by themselves, whether for their own ends or on behalf of clients. Often they have animal spirits that aid them. At times they also keep visible animals; one had twenty large black cats to protect him, and because of his spells they scared all and sundry with their demonic glares and yowling. The magicians do not usually need elaborate equipment. A staff, a cloth or animal skin, a "troll's cloak," or a platform will suffice.

The role of spoken or chanted spells in the magic of the sagas can scarcely be exaggerated. An episode in the *Laxdaela Saga* demonstrates how incantation might work. An entire family of sorcerers approach their enemy's house at night and begin chanting. At first, the victims are merely confused, though the incantation sounds pleasant. Soon the householder realizes that a spell is being worked against someone in the family, and he cautions everyone to keep awake but not look outdoors. Nonetheless, everyone dozes off except a twelve-year-old boy at whom the spell is directed. He becomes restless, goes outdoors, walks toward the sorcerers, and immediately drops dead.

The relationship between sorcery and Norse paganism is somewhat elusive. The sorcerers' opponents typically see magic as a practice supposedly given up when Iceland converted to Christianity. Sorcery is part of a culture that Icelanders are supposed to have forsworn at baptism as one of the Devil's works. In that sense it is a "pagan survival." Yet there is no hint that it is part of an organized pagan religion that has gone underground; neither here nor elsewhere is there evidence for persistence of a pagan cultural system. Nor does the magic of the sagas seem to be connected integrally with veneration of the Norse gods. While the sorcerers' magic may sometimes make reference to the gods, and may sometimes resemble the magic practiced by the gods, it seldom involves appeal to the gods. As elsewhere in Christianized Scandinavia, sorcery and heathen worship seem to have been seen as essentially different things, even if they might overlap at points. It was Christian writers who conflated these categories, telling stories about pagan deities who aid magicians with their "trollish powers," and it was later preachers who popularized that conflation.

While much of the magical lore in these tales can be traced to Germanic antiquity, and sometimes there are echoes of the magical power ascribed to the Norse god Odin, there is also evidence for absorption of non-Germanic beliefs. In some ways the magic of Iceland resembles that of the Lapps and other Arctic peoples. Like the shamans of the far North, Icelandic magicians are sometimes portrayed as having special psychic powers while asleep or in trance. Like Siberian magicians they can transform people into unexpected shapes to prevent their detection. Like Lapp wizards they can attack their enemies in the form of animals such as the walrus, and in Icelandic as in other northern stories the magicians in animal form are sometimes confused with the animal spirits that protect them. There are parallels even among Eskimo shamans, who are known to enter ecstasy while lying on platforms and covered with skins: practices found or at least suggested in the sagas.[4] Yet another pathway, that of Arctic cultural systems, thus converges with those we have already located in our study of magic.

In other ways, however, the sagas represent a situation distinctive to Iceland. The society that they reflect, built on small-scale farming and fishing, is far more settled than it had been prior to conversion. Despite its geographical isolation, Iceland had cultural and ecclesiastical links with Scandinavia and with Europe generally. It had vernacular translations of essential Latin literature. Perhaps precisely because of its geographical isolation, however, its cultural elite had to remind people of the need to keep up the ties with civilization. The sagas, written down after several generations of oral transmission, reminded people of a heroic but not a romantic past. Parts of the old Scandinavian tradition are darkly portrayed. Much as Horace and Lucian poked fun at sorceresses in an age when the Roman authorities were campaigning against real-life sorcery, so now the writers of the sagas depicted the unsavory powers of magic as a reminder of those bad old days to which Iceland should not return. In the process, these authors left a lively record of how sorcery was thought to work. They were writing stories about a particular kind of social turmoil, and the magic they depicted was part of the shading they used in painting this canvas.

[4] H. R. Ellis Davidson, "Hostile magic in the Icelandic sagas", in Venetia Newall, ed., *The Witch Figure* (London: Routledge, 1973), 37–8.

Quite different are the magical motifs in the "eddas," which preserve much more of Norse mythology than do the sagas: while the distinction is by no means absolute, it is fair to say that the sagas deal more with human beings, and the eddas are our chief source for the gods. For the history of magic as it actually was practiced in human society, the eddas are thus the less important documents, yet it is important to bear in mind that the eddas also refer to magic and that the magical themes here are not altogether distinct from those in the sagas. Perhaps the most famous tale from the eddas, and for our purposes the most important, is that of how the god Odin hung on a tree, fasting and exposed to the elements, until he was rewarded by gaining mastery of the runes and their magical powers. For a divine as well as for a human magician, then, magic is a force closely linked with writing. What this myth conveys more vividly than the sagas is a sense of how magic assumes ascetic preparation: here as in other early European cultures, magical force issues from one who has performed heroic disciplines, mastered the body and strengthened the soul, and with intense effort of will has gained access to otherwise hidden energies.[5]

IRISH LITERATURE

Celtic literature also contains magical themes, generally closer to those of the eddas than to those of the sagas. Like Norse literature, that of Ireland and other Celtic lands comes down to us primarily in later medieval redactions, from the twelfth and later centuries, and its pagan elements are reminiscences of an earlier culture, but the pre-Christian past was a much more distant memory for the Irish. Furthermore, the vestiges in Irish literature come more from mythology than from popular conceptions of how magic was actually performed; in that respect the Irish materials resemble the eddas more than the sagas.

The link between fairies and human beings is a prominent motif in the Irish tradition. One twelfth-century Irish work, for example, tells how hunters come upon a Fairy Hill, inhabited by twenty-eight warriors, each with a charming woman. Accepting their hospitality, the hunters spend the night in the hill. An earlier Irish source tells how Conle the Redhaired begins to hear the voice of a love-struck and alluring fairy. She invites him to join her in the Fairy Hill, where there are everlasting feasts, no cares, and no death. Fearing her enchantment, Conle obtains from a druid a musical charm with which he can ward off her allurement. She goes away for a time, but as she departs she throws him an apple which nourishes him for an entire month. Then she returns, warns Conle against the demonic

[5] A. G. van Hamel, "Oðinn hanging on the tree", *Acta Philologica Scandinavica*, 7 (1932–33), 260–88.

power of the druids, prophesies the coming of St. Patrick to convert the Irish, and beckons for Conle to come away in a crystal boat. At last he succumbs to her entreaties and is never again seen among mortals. What we have here is clearly a Christianized version of earlier lore; fairies are more often interpreted in medieval Christendom as demons, but here the fairy allies herself with the forces of goodness and faith against the pagan druids.[6] As we shall see (in Chapter 5), the same ambivalence can be found in Continental romances as well: fairies have both good and evil sides, and while they can represent primal paganism they can also be said to hold the Christian faith.

Themes that appear in secular Celtic literature often show up in saints' lives as well. These texts, too, survive mostly in high medieval versions from well after the conversion. Both secular and saintly heroes, for example, were able to survive long periods beneath water. St. Colman mac Luachain once remained submerged for an entire day and night, while the aquatic fauna amused him by running races. Borrowing perhaps from early Celtic stories of gods and heroes, the biographers of Irish saints often told wondrous tales of their power over fire as well as water: they could produce fire from their fingertips, or carry it their hands. They could also inflict curses on their foes, and often used this power against thieves, druids, and other enemies of all that was good and holy.[7] When a druid confronted St. Patrick (ca. 390–ca. 460?), for example, the saint raised him high in the air and then let him dash upon the rocks, like Simon Magus. Patrick also challenged the druids to wonder-working contests: in one tale, a druid put into a hut made of green wood was burned alive, while Patrick remained unharmed when fire was set to his hut of dry wood. Doubtless it is possible to represent such stories as exercises in divine righteousness. If it is easier to see the saints as magicians casting spells on their adversaries, we must remember that for the writers and readers of this literature the saints were not magicians precisely because they worked with divine aid. We are constantly reminded in certain texts that Patrick's miracles redounded to his glory and to God's. The druids, like the priests of Baal and like Simon Magus, are the true magicians because their power comes not from God but from demons.

Both Norse and Irish literature – and more broadly, Germanic and Celtic tradition – demonstrate that the beliefs of early Christian writers remained very much alive in medieval Europe. When medieval authors condemned magic as demonic, their perceptions were rooted in the

[6] Kennneth Hurlstone Jackson, ed., A Celtic Miscellany: Translations from the Celtic Literature, rev. edn (Harmondsworth: Penguin, 1971), 143–5, 164–5.

[7] Carolus Plummer, ed., Vitae sanctorum Hiberniae, vol. 1 (Oxford: Clarendon, 1910), introduction, cxxix–clxxxviii.

experience of missionaries, propagandists, and other churchmen. In some cases the magic of the Germanic and Celtic peoples made explicit appeal to the traditional deities. Even when it did not, Christian critics tended to assume an implicit link to pagan worship, and thus veneration of demons, simply because this magic was rooted in the same pre-Christian culture that had fostered veneration of the old gods. Those who contended that all magic is demonic would have met little argument from the missionaries of early medieval Europe.

4

THE COMMON TRADITION OF MEDIEVAL MAGIC

Part of the inheritance passed down from classical antiquity to medieval and modern Western culture is the notion of magic as something performed by special individuals. It is the magi, or magicians, who perform magic. Whatever similarities their operations may have to the work of others around them, "magic" remains a negative term associated with a suspicious class of practitioners.

When we look at the people who were in fact using varieties of magic in medieval Europe, however, it becomes hard to sustain the stereotype. Instead of finding a single, readily identifiable class of magicians we find various types of people involved in diverse magical activities: monks, parish priests, physicians, surgeon-barbers, midwives, folk healers and diviners with no formal training, and even ordinary women and men who, without claiming special knowledge or competence, used whatever magic they happened to know. The monks and priests who practiced magic were able to write much earlier and more widely than laypeople, and left more records of their magic, but this does not mean that they engaged in these activities more often.

Nor is there reason to think that these various practitioners engaged in wholly different kinds of magic. There is every indication that monks learned about medicinal and magic herbs from laypeople as well as from classical authors, that lay practitioners learned healing charms from monks and priests, and that before medicine became a university subject there was little to distinguish physicians from lay healers. One can thus speak of a "common tradition" of medieval magic. The term should not mislead: it does not mean that specific types of magic were found universally in medieval society, or that they persisted wholly unchanged through the centuries. What does seem to have been true is that much of the magic in medieval Europe was distributed widely, and that it was not regularly limited to any specific group. It was not always in the hands of the monks, or the women, or the physicians. In later chapters we will examine other types of magic that were somewhat more specialized, but first we must survey this common magical tradition.

This chapter will deal mainly with materials from the twelfth through fifteenth centuries: a time when Christianity, pervaded with accretions from folk culture, was accepted throughout Europe. Numerous manuscripts have survived from throughout this period, most especially from the fifteenth century, and from them we are richly informed about the magic of the age. We will also look at some earlier materials which show how magical beliefs and practices evolved and fit into the culture of medieval Europe.

PRACTITIONERS OF MAGIC: HEALERS AND DIVINERS

There is ample evidence that monks studied medicine within their monasteries and did what they could to absorb and transmit the medical knowledge of antiquity. When Cassiodorus (487–583) laid out a curriculum of studies for monks he recommended the herbal ascribed to Dioscorides, the works of Hippocrates, Galen, and other Greek or Latin medical writers. During the early medieval centuries it was the monks who copied out manuscripts of these and other classical authors. This is not to say that monks were training to become physicians. Rather, medical knowledge was a small part of the general education that they were expected to obtain; it was one portion of their inheritance from antiquity. Each monastery was expected to have an infirmary for its ailing and aged members, and in it the monks were most likely to apply whatever medical learning they had acquired. They might also provide medical aid for the poor, for travelers, and for pilgrims who came visiting at their monasteries. In many cases the care of such outsiders gave rise to early hospitals distinct from the monks' own infirmaries; around 940, for example, a hospital was founded at Flixton in Yorkshire for the care of these lay patients. Some monks gained such skill as healers that they were sought outside the monasteries by lay patients, even by royalty.[1]

To the extent that classical medicine entailed magical elements, or that the monks picked up new forms of medical magic from the culture

[1] For both clerical and lay healers, especially in England, see C. H. Talbot, *Medicine in Medieval England* (London: Oldbourne, 1967), and Stanley Rubin, *Medieval English Medicine* (London: Newton Abbot, 1974). For France, Danielle Jacquart, *Le milieu médical en France du XIIe au XVe siècle* (Geneva: Droz, 1981).

around them, they would be practicing magical cures. Or rather, they would be using what later authors called magic. The early medieval monks would not have thought of themselves as dabbling in the magical arts. Without scruples, however, they would use mandrake for its mysterious curative powers, and they might also use charms to drive away the "elves" that were causing sickness.

Monks were not the only healers in early medieval Europe. There were also lay practitioners, known in England as "leeches," though we know little about them. Evidently some of them were itinerant. They had some kind of training, probably more practical than theoretical, and probably amounting to a kind of apprenticeship. They too might have some access to the medical writings of antiquity, though they did not have the systematic education of the monasteries available to them, and must have relied all the more on folk medicine and informal observation. While it is difficult to make comparisons, they even more than the monks probably used forms of medicine that later writers would call magical.

What applied to monks would apply as well to some of the diocesan clergy, at least those priests who had some kind of systematic education. Rabanus Maurus proposed that all such clerics should have medical knowledge, but realities fell short of this ideal, and indeed only a minority of the clergy would have any formal education at all. At least up to the thirteenth century, rural priests seem to have been essentially grass-roots purveyors of ritual, happy to oblige their parishioners with uncritical use of such rites as they could perform. Typically they came from village families, and might have minimal education beyond a wobbly command of Latin. Their training, much like that of informal healers, was essentially a kind of apprenticeship. Bishops of the thirteenth and following centuries tried to amend the situation: they tried to enforce higher standards of education for local clergy and to eradicate magical and superstitious use of rituals, but they were struggling against deeply ingrained custom.

While ordinary parish priests may have dabbled in medicine, they were more likely to practice other forms of magic. The sort of duty a village priest might be expected to perform is clear from a twelfth-century ritual for infertile fields. The ceremony extends through an entire day, starting before sunrise with the digging of four clumps of earth from the four sides of the affected land. It is presumably the local priest who is supposed to sprinkle these clumps with a mixture of holy water, oil, milk and honey, and fragments of trees and herbs, while reciting in Latin the words that God said to Adam and Eve, "Be fruitful and multiply, and fill the earth" (Genesis 1:28), followed by further prayers. The clumps are then carried to church, where the priest sings four masses over them. Before sunset the clumps are taken back out to the fields, where, fortified with a day's worth of ritual, they will spread the power for growth to all the land.[2] Homespun ceremonies of this kind might remain purely religious, with no admixture of magic, but the possibilities for combining the two were always present.

If the leeches and the parish priests had only meager education, there were other practitioners in medieval society with even less formal training. Most societies have informal healers and diviners recognized as such by their clients but not by any sort of certifying authorities or official teachers. Different people can adopt this role. Folklore researchers in modern times have found that the rules regarding the practice of popular healing vary widely from place to place even within Europe. In some areas the healers are mostly women; in others they are predominantly men. Sometimes the secrets of healing can be passed only from women to women or from men to men, but in other regions the gender must alternate with each transmission. In some places the healers are thought to possess inherited powers, and if charms are passed to people without these gifts they will have no force, but elsewhere there are recognized procedures for acquiring the powers without inheritance.[3] We have no reports from systematic field workers in medieval Europe, but the situation then is not likely to have been less varied.

If it is impossible to generalize about the sort of people who became unofficial healers, it is equally hopeless to generalize about the techniques they used. Some of the possibilities, however, are clear from the story of Matteuccia Francisci, a woman of Todi who was tried in 1428 because of the sorts of magic she was using. She taught people to cure illness by taking a bone from an unbaptized baby out to a crossroad, burying it there, and saying various prayers and formulas on that spot over nine days. She knew how to counteract curses. When a man found a strange feather in his pillow and suspected it had been put there to cast a spell on him, he took it to Matteuccia, who destroyed the spell by means of an incantation, then told the man to take the feather home and burn it. Matteuccia could also transfer ailments, and did so on one occasion to cure a client's lameness: she took a potion with thirty different herbs, enhanced its power with an incantation, and cast it out on to the street so that the lameness might be transferred from the client to an unsuspecting passerby. She gave a contraceptive formula to a priest's mistress: she was to take ashes from the burnt hoof of a female mule, mix them with wine, and drink them. But Matteuccia's real specialty was love magic. She recited incantations over

---

[2] G. Storms, *Anglo-Saxon Magic* (The Hague: Nijhoff, 1948), 172–87. Storms suggests that the priest was pagan, but this seems unlikely.

[3] Irmgard Hampp, *Beschwörung, Segen, Gebet: Untersuchungen zum Zauberspruch aus dem Bereich der Volksheilkunde* (Stuttgart: Silberburg, 1961), 15–17.

herbs, then gave them to women as love potions. She gave women lotions
for their hands and faces which would arouse men's affections. When the
mistress of a priest complained that he had not had relations with her for a
long time, but beat her, Matteuccia took a wax image and placed in on a
fire, while the client recited words comparing the wax to the priest's heart;
after this ceremony the priest loved the woman passionately and did her
bidding.[4]

Matteuccia was obviously a professional. Clients came to her, sometimes from out of town, to obtain various kinds of magic in exchange for
money. Not all folk practitioners would have been as bold as she was:
some might have been wary of using overtly magical techniques, and
some might have been more scrupulous about the purposes they served.
Yet others may have been even more daring than she: unofficial exorcists,
for example, who would go about driving demons out of people to cure
their ailments. The theologian John of Frankfurt had little patience with
such vigilante attacks on demons. Popular exorcists, he complained, take
hold of people with natural illness and try to cure them with savage rituals,
torturing them with cold water, strangling them, and beating them with
switches. If the victims are not mad already they can be driven mad with
such treatment.[5] We know of one such exorcist who competed with the
local clergy around Florence. By using strange rituals with a candle and
incantations he managed to cure a ten-year-old girl, though she was left
weak after the rigors of his exorcism.[6]

If some people were known as healers, others were known as diviners
or fortune-tellers. No doubt these categories overlapped, and no doubt
there were monks and priests who engaged in divination as well. We have
manuals for fortune-telling that may have been written by monks, either
for fellow monks or for lay readers, though both the authorship and the
audience are often obscure. When the duchess of Gloucester wanted
assurance of her husband's future good fortune in 1441, one of the people
she went to was Margery Jourdemayne, who was known as a "witch" but
seems to have been known especially for her divination. Along with two
distinguished scholars from Oxford, one a noted astrologer and the other
an eminent physician, Margery aided the duchess in foretelling the duke's
future and in working image magic to ensure an heir. This, at any rate, is
what the defendants admitted when they were brought to trial; whether
they performed further magic is unclear.

4 Candida Peruzzi, "Un processo di stregoneria a Todi nel 400", *Lares: Organo della Società di Etnografia Italiana-Roma*, 21 (1955), fasc. I–II, 1–17.
5 Joseph Hansen, ed., *Quellen und Untersuchungen zur Geschichte des Hexenwahns und der Hexenverfolgung im Mittelalter* (Bonn: Georgi, 1901), 79.
6 Gene A. Brucker, "Sorcery in early Renaissance Florence", *Studies in the Renaissance*, 10 (1963), 13–16.

Some of the business of these folk practitioners – the healing if not the divining – must have been siphoned off by the rise of university-trained physicians around the twelfth century.[7] There had been places where one could obtain scientific medical education in earlier years: medical study had been available at Salerno as early as the tenth century. The growth of universities in the thirteenth century brought more systematic medical training, integrated into the curriculum of scholastic education then emerging. After taking several years of formal coursework and passing examinations, the physician would be formally certified as such. It might be pleasant to report that the rise of the medical profession brought about the abolition of magical techniques, but since classical writings were still the foundation of medical education, the distinction between medicine and magic remained no clearer than it had been in antiquity.

The earlier types of practitioner remained in demand, especially among poor folk who could not afford the fees of university-trained doctors. It was not long before physicians with official credentials began challenging the right of other healers to practice their arts. Articulate medical writers steeped in formal medical theory would rail against those with merely empirical command of the healing arts. Popes in the second quarter of the fourteenth century supported the physicians' efforts to suppress medical care by uneducated practitioners. English physicians tried in the 1420s to secure an Act of Parliament prohibiting the practice of medicine without a university education, and specifically excluding women from all medical practice, though these efforts were in vain.

The distinction between physicians and surgeons emerged fitfully in medieval culture. Often the terms were interchangeable. When medicine became a subject for study at the universities, however, the dirty work of surgery remained at first outside the curriculum in many places, and thus a clearer distinction emerged: physicians were university-educated men who practiced internal medicine, while surgeons had less exalted credentials and cut into people. Physicians in the thirteenth and following centuries did their best to secure control over surgeons (and apothecaries as well); the surgeons responded by setting up their own schools and attempting to gain professional recognition in their own right.

Further down the social ladder were barber-surgeons, whose business was not simply cutting hair but also bleeding people and performing other routine medical care. Much of medieval medicine was based on the notion that bodily humors must be kept in proper balance; to relieve people of excessive blood, it was common to bleed them regularly. Such operations might be routine and minor, but they still required knowledge of where

---

[7] Vern L. Bullough, *The Development of Medicine as a Profession: The Contribution of the Medieval University to Modern Medicine* (New York: Hafner, 1966).

to puncture the skin, how much blood to withdraw, and how to stop the flow. Preventing infection was not yet a subject for systematic study, but the trained barber-surgeon would have known that there are certain times of the month or of the year when a patient should not be bled, and would have observed these strictures.

Surgeons and barber-surgeons may have been less inclined toward magic than other practitioners. Their hands-on approach to health precluded some of the more exotic remedies that prevailed in internal medicine. Yet they were not wholly immune to the allure of magic. The biography of Antoninus Pierozzi (d. 1459), archbishop of Florence, tells that he once went to a local barber-surgeon, and while the man was taking care of him the prelate asked how he had gained medical knowledge without command of Latin. The man replied in all innocence that a monk had given him a book from which he learned all he needed to know. The archbishop asked to see the book, and the barber-surgeon happily complied. To his astonishment, Antoninus found the manuscript filled with incantations "and things and signs pertaining to the evil and magical arts." It is difficult to know how to interpret this description. It might have applied quite literally to a compilation such as the Munich handbook, though the barber-surgeon would not have been likely to mistake that for anything else. More probably it contained prescriptions like those in the Wolfsthurn handbook, in which case the archbishop's reaction was overstated.[8]

Medical manuals from medieval Europe often have gynecological and obstetric information alongside other material, which suggests that general practitioners (to use modern parlance) might deal with these matters. For aid in childbirth, however, most people would go not to physicians but to midwives. They too might engage in practices that others would call magical: there is ample evidence, for example, that amulets of various kinds were used to aid in childbirth, and a midwife might be expected to know and use such techniques. In the later medieval centuries, when medicine had taken steps toward professional status and the notion of legal control had been established, midwives in some parts of Europe were officially licensed. Yet their training remained practical rather than theoretical or academic, and people with higher education no doubt saw them as unsophisticated. Not surprisingly, this unprestigious career was left to women, and this was virtually the only sort of health care that women were widely and officially allowed to provide in these later centuries.

The practice of midwifery could at times involve serious forms of magic. In the early fifteenth century a woman of Paris named Perrette was

<hr>

[8] *Acta sanctorum*, May, vol. 2 (Paris and Rome: Palmé, 1866), 339.

practicing as a licensed midwife with clients even from the aristocracy. Against her better judgment she became involved in a scheme to cure a certain nobleman of leprosy by irregular means: in exchange for a sum of money she was to obtain the body of a stillborn infant, whose fat would be used for an unguent. After great hesitation she procured the needed corpse, only to find herself incarcerated under suspicion of witchcraft. Eventually her friends appealed to the king for a pardon, which she obtained.[9]

There were also outright quacks who claimed medical competence they did not have. One in London in 1382 tried to cure a woman by giving her a piece of parchment with a prayer on it, which he alleged had special medicinal value. Another, earlier in the century, had been importing spoiled wolves' meat for its curative virtues. In both cases the authorities made a point of showing that the culprits were in fact neither physicians nor surgeons. Apart from practicing unorthodox medicine, they were guilty of impersonation. [10]

Physicians soon found themselves competing not only with the earlier, traditional practitioners, but with a new sort as well: the occasional mendicant friar who developed skill in medicine. The mendicant (or "begging") orders, such as the Franciscans and Dominicans, arose in the thirteenth century. They distinguished themselves for their preaching and other religious service, especially in the towns, and became immensely popular and influential. Many of them went to the universities for their education, and before long they became prominent as scholars. Those who had studied the liberal arts might in the process obtain at least some a smattering of medical knowledge, and some made it a special interest, even though they were forbidden to obtain medical degrees. There is evidence of Dominicans and Franciscans who provided medical care, especially for those who could not afford professional physicians. One medical treatise, ascribed to a Friar Randolf (or sometimes Friar Roland), is explicitly intended as a guide to those who would "help poor folk that fall into sickness and do not have the knowledge to help themselves or the ability to hire physicians." Drawing on the most authoritative sources, this author laid out systematically all the basic principles of medicine.

There were, finally, the nonspecialists: people such as the compiler of the Wolfsthurn handbook, who probably had no special competence, but would gladly make use of magical techniques helpful in coping with the problems of daily life. In the fourteenth and fifteenth centuries, partly because literacy was increasingly common among the laity and partly

---

[9] Thomas Rogers Forbes, *The Midwife and the Witch* (New Haven: Yale University Press, 1966), 13–38. [10] Bullough, *The Development of Medicine*, 104–5.

because paper was beginning to become available (as an alternative to the more expensive parchment) as a material for books, European towns were flooded with popular writings on all topics. Medical writings taught people how to heal themselves: how to let their own blood, how to examine their own urine, what herbs to use in treating their ailments. Books of charms proliferated. Manuals for divination, long known in monastic and clerical circles, became common now among the laity. These and other materials, which had previously circulated for the most part in Latin, were increasingly available in the various vernacular languages. If the late Middle Ages saw a flowering of popular education generally, they were also a golden age for magic. Now one no longer needed to be a specialist. Anyone could learn the magical arts, and many people evidently did so.

These, then, are the *dramatis personae*, the characters we will see on the stage of medieval magic. They are a diverse company, and their interaction was unpredictable. Yet they did interact: scarcely any form of magic was the exclusive preserve of any of these groups. It was a monk who gave the Florentine barber-surgeon his book of magic. Margery Jourdemayne had a record of collaborating with clerics in the occult arts. Professionals might be jealous of nonprofessionals, but that was all the more reason for the latter to plunder the medical knowledge of the former via popular manuals that disseminated up-to-date medical techniques. The culture of the age was by no means uniform, but the distinctions that did exist – social, professional, and geographical – were remarkably fluid.

MEDICAL MAGIC: HERBS AND ANIMALS

The varieties of medical practice in medieval Europe can already be gleaned from two Anglo-Saxon manuals, both of which show how the pre-Christian culture of northern Europe became grafted on to Graeco-Roman tradition.[11]. The first is generally known as the leechbook (or "doctor-book") of Bald, because a poem incorporated in it refers to a man named Bald as having it written out for him. Living well before the rise of universities, Bald must have been an informally trained leech. The use of the vernacular Anglo-Saxon language suggests that he was a layman, though the occasional use of Latin indicates that he was a man of some culture. On the other hand, some of his formulas require either saying masses or having masses said over the healing herbs; these materials probably came from a clerical or monastic setting. His book dates from the tenth century, though it includes much earlier material, some of it classical. It cites the authority of "Pliny the great physician" for some of its

[11] For both see Storms, *Anglo-Saxon Magic*.

prescriptions, it takes over bodily a treatise by Alexander of Tralles (ca. 525–ca. 605), and it also draws from Marcellus Empiricus. It starts in orderly fashion, dealing first with ailments on the outside of the body from head to foot, then covering internal illnesses. Then it adds a jumble of prescriptions that borrow heavily from Christian ritual: such things as incense, holy water, and prayers figure prominently in this third section.

The character of this leechbook is difficult to indicate, since it is a collection from various sources. On the whole it is a reasonably sober distillation of classical medicine, yet it did not lack elements of what later authors would call natural magic. Consider, for example, its prescription for skin disease:

> Take goose-fat, and the lower part of elecampane and viper's bugloss, bishop's wort, and cleavers. Pound the four herbs together well, squeeze them out, and add a spoonful of old soap. If you have a little oil, mix it in thoroughly and lather it on at night. Scratch the neck after sunset, and silently pour the blood into running water, spit three times after it, then say, "Take this disease and depart with it." Go back to the house by an open road, and go each way in silence.[12]

The first part of the prescription is ordinary herbal medicine, but the procedure for transferring illness to running water, with its attendant rituals and taboos, is clearly magical.

The second of these compilations, the *Lacnunga*, is from the eleventh century, and has a much stronger leaning toward magic. Many of its prescriptions are from European folk culture: that of the Anglo-Saxons themselves, or of the Celts or the Norsemen, all of which traditions would have been familiar in Britain. Intermingled are remedies taken from the ancient culture of the Greeks, Romans, and Hebrews. While the *Lacnunga* is anything but a coherent treatise on medicine, there are recurrent themes that afford insight into the compiler's view of diseases, their causes and their cures. One of the most important sources of illness is the mischief making of elves, whom Christian theologians and moralists would identify with demons. The book tells how to cure "elf-shot", meaning disease caused by the invisible but all too perceptible assault of these elves. More than many leechbooks, the *Lacnunga* prescribes Christian prayers to be recited in Latin over the ingredients used for medicine. One healing salve, for example, is made of butter from a completely red or completely white cow, to which fifty-seven specified herbs are added. The mixture must be stirred with a stick on which the names "Matthew, Mark, Luke, and John" are inscribed in Latin. Several charms or incantations are then sung over the salve. Most of them are Latin, though one is gibberish possibly derived from some foreign language: "Acre arcre arnem nona aernem

---

[12] Storms, *Anglo-Saxon Magic*, 165 (adapted).

beoðor aernem nidren acrun cunað ele harassan fidine." This book may also be the work of a lay leech, though the heavy influence of Christian liturgy points perhaps to monastic influence.

The same kind of material found in these two books can be read in later works as well, and most of it can be found on the Continent as well as in England. The materials prescribed in this literature tend to be quite simple, at least until they are compounded by the healer: herbs and other plants, portions of animal bodies, and the effluvia of animals are the stock ingredients for drugs. While some of these medicines are specifics, any given plant is likely to have multiple uses. Thus, mandrake is recommended for afflictions of the eyes, wounds, snakebite, earache, gout, baldness, and numerous other complaints.[13] The oak and vervain had diverse magical uses, and merited separate treatises outlining their wondrous properties.[14] If healing virtue was sought from animal bodies, each organ was likely to have its special function. Thus, a short treatise on the uses of the vulture, which has survived in a manuscript from Gaul around the year 800 and in many other versions, gives minute instructions on how to use each portion of the bird. The skull, wrapped in the skin of a deer, cures headaches. Its brains, mixed with unguent and stuffed into the nose, are effective against head ailments. The kidneys and testicles cure impotence if they are dried out, pulverized, and administered in wine.[15]

The authors of these materials do not reflect explicitly on the relationship between medicine and magic, nor do they indicate which of their cures have "occult" as opposed to ordinary power. Doubtless they would have argued that the curative value of all their remedies was borne out by experience. Even modern pharmacology often relies more on trial and error than on theoretical notions of how chemicals will work, and medieval healers seem to have worked essentially the same way. If they claimed that cat faeces could cure baldness or a quartan fever,[16] they would support this claim not so much with theoretical explanation as with appeal to their own experience. "An experienced woman told me," says the compiler of one work, "that after she had been weighed down by frequent childbearing she ate a bee, and after that she no longer conceived."[17] Precisely why this or that remedy worked was not the healer's concern. Given this apparent indifference to causes, the distinction be-

---

[13] E.g. British Library, MS Harley 5294, fol. 43^{v-r}.

[14] Jerry Stannard, "Magiferous plants and magic in medieval medical botany", *Maryland Historian*, 8 (1977), no. 2, 33–46.

[15] Loren C. MacKinnery, "An unpublished treatise on medicine and magic from the age of Charlemagne" (with translation), *Speculum*, 18 (1943), 494–6; cf. A. A. Barb, "Birds and medical magic", *Journal of the Warburg and Courtauld Institutes*, 13 (1950), 316–22.

[16] British Library, MS Harley 1585, fol. 74^r.

[17] British Library, MS Sloane 3132, fol. 57^v.

tween occult and manifest power seems perhaps beside the point: what mattered was whether a remedy worked, not how.

Without doing violence to the mentality of the healers, however, we can identify certain features of their work that do point in the direction of magic, or what later writers would refer to as such.

First, the preparation of the drug often involves observance of taboos; though these may strike us as having no obvious role in the healing process, they are important for maintaining the purity of the healing substance, or for enhancing the power of the healer. The ashes from burnt ravens are effective against gout and epilepsy, for example, but only if the birds are taken live from their nest, carried without touching the ground or entering into a house, and burned in a new pot.[18] One should go out barefoot, or in silence, to pick a herb; or one should abstain from sexual contact before gathering herbs. One should dig a herb from the ground without using an iron implement: a common requirement, perhaps showing that the magic in question predates the use of iron in prehistoric Europe. The killing of magical animals, too, can involve such taboos: the vulture should be killed with a sharp reed, not a sword, and before its decapitation the killer should say, "Angel Adonai Abraham, on your account the work is completed."

Secondly, the choice of healing ingredients was sometimes dictated by the symbolic considerations of sympathetic magic. Thus, animals known for their strength, their speed, or their ferocity are preferred over gentler beasts, and often a male animal such as a bull, a hart, or a ram is indicated because it is physically stronger than the female and thus by extension has greater healing potency. Patients with jaundice are to be given earthworms to drink in stale ale, but the worms must be the sort with "yellow knots" to counteract the yellowness of jaundice. In this case the author insists on grinding the worms so small that the patient will not recognize them, "for loathing," but this is merely an element of common sense in an otherwise magical prescription.[19]

Thirdly, even apart from the rise of systematic astrology, medical procedures often involve explicit or implicit attention to the effects of the heavenly bodies. Certain plants can cure lunacy if they are wrapped in red cloth and tied around the lunatic's head under a specified astrological sign while the moon is waxing. One should go out before sunrise to pluck a herb. Fragments of bark are more potent if they come from the eastern side of the tree, where they can absorb the rays of the rising sun.

---

[18] Henry Ellis, "Extracts in prose and verse from an old English medical manuscript, preserved in the Royal Library at Stockholm", *Archaeologia*, 30 (1844), 397.

[19] Warren R. Dawson, ed. and trans., *A Leechbook or Collection of Medical Recipes of the Fifteenth Century* (London: Macmillan, 1934), 154–5.

Fourthly, use of arcane language, whatever other significance it has, at least suggests that the cure involves mysterious ingredients or processes. Thus, one recipe for sciatica and other diseases reads merely, "Dialanga dracumino diazinsebri, equally much." The modern editor proposes that the words come from alchemy, but it is more likely that they are garbled echoes of some foreign tongue, or perhaps ordinary words in cipher.[20]

These ways of approaching the healing process seem to have been common to healers of all sorts, not just the monks and priests, or the lay practitioners, or members of any other group. Even if such factors were of less importance in the medicine of the universities, they were not uprooted altogether: as we will see in a later chapter, astrological considerations became if anything more important in formal medical study. The people who used these magical cures may not have reflected deeply on the causes they were invoking or the philosophical implications of these causes, but when later writers decreed that certain cures appealed to "occult powers" in nature they were not seriously distorting the realities of medical practice.

A further complicating factor is that the use of herbal magic, if it cannot be rigorously distinguished on one hand from science, has links on the other hand to religion. Herbs and ointment were often compounded with holy water, and it becomes artificial to distinguish between its function as "holy" and its role as "water." Popular and monastic manuals for healing, at least, not infrequently encouraged their readers to say prayers over the herbs. One prayer written specifically for this purpose is quite straightforwardly religious rather than magical:

O God, who at the beginning of the world commanded the verdant plants . . . to grow and multiply, we offer humble and suppliant prayers that you may bless and consecrate in your name these herbs, gathered for medicinal use, so that all who take potions or unguents made from them, or apply them to their wounds, may deserve to obtain health of mind and body.[21]

The same essential notion is conveyed graphically by a herbal that depicts Christ and Mary standing beside a large cluster of foliage; Christ has his hand extended in a gesture of blessing (Fig. 6). The meaning would have been clear to any medieval reader: Christ's blessing is what bestows or enhances the healing power of the herbs.[22]

[20] Ibid., 318–19.
[21] British Library, MS Sloane 783B, fol. 214ᵛ.
[22] Cf. the apocryphal legend about Jesus collecting herbs for Mary, in A. Vögtlin, ed., *Vita beate virginis Marie et salvatoris rhythmica* (Tübingen: Litterarischer Verein in Stuttgart, 1887), 94–5.

Fig. 6. Christ blessing the herbs, with Mary, from a fourteenth-century herbal

CHARMS: PRAYERS, BLESSINGS, AND ADJURATIONS

If the boundary between natural magic and religion is elusive in the case of medicinal herbs, it is all the harder to distinguish the magical from the religious in verbal formulas. These are of three basic types. First there are *prayers*, which have the form of requests and are directed to God, Christ, Mary, or a saint. Second there are *blessings*, which have the form of wishes and are addressed to the patients. Third there are *adjurations or exorcisms*,

which have the form of commands and are directed to the sickness itself or
to the worm, demon, elf, or other agent responsible for it. The term
"exorcism" is usually reserved for an extended ritual expressly directed
against demons, but the border between these and adjurations is fluid.[23]

It is clear even from the Wolfsthurn manual how prayers can play a role
in otherwise magical practices. Often these are snippets from the Christian
liturgy, removed from their context and used without any sense of their
meaning. The standard prayers known throughout Christian society are
also used: the Lord's Prayer, the Hail Mary, sometimes the Creed. To keep
cattle from harm, one is advised to sing the liturgical "Agios, Agios,
Agios" around them every evening. If such prayers were used by themselves, there would be no reason to refer to them as magical. When a
charm for toothache begins with an appeal to "Lady Moon," what we
have is evidently a vestige of pagan religion, but in most cases the prayers
used are clearly Christian. Often the manuals advise saying these prayers
three times, and it is tempting to read magical significance into that fact,
but of course the number three stood for the Trinity, and in healing as in
the liturgy threefold repetition of a prayer could be in honor of the
Trinity. At times the prayers are linked with magical rites or taboos, as in a
twelfth-century manuscript, evidently from Germany, which gives a
prayer to be written out on five wafers. The patient, who must be
barefoot, removes the wafers and eats them, then says a further prayer.[24]
When linked with explicitly magical embellishments of this sort, the
prayers themselves seem to take on a magical character – not because of
their intended force (which we cannot judge) but because emphasis
appears to lie on the observance of religiously irrelevant conditions
surrounding the formula.

Much the same can be said about blessings, which take the general form
"May God bless you . . ." or "May God heal you . . ." If these were used by
themselves they would be clearly religious and not magical. The explicitly
religious character of these formulas becomes especially clear when the
manuals suggest saying further prayers *after* one has been cured. There is
no suggestion in that case that the prayers are intended for direct practical
effect; rather, they express gratitude to God or to his saints. In short,
prayers and blessings can be used alongside magic and can be integrated
with magic, but they are not inherently magical.[25]

Adjurations are more problematic and require closer scrutiny. Some-

---

[23] Hampp, *Beschwörung, Segen, Gebet*, 136–40.
[24] Lynn Thorndike, *The History of Magic and Experimental Science*, vol. 1 (New York:
Macmillan, 1923), 729–30. Another prayer is meant to be written on a piece of bread,
which should then be crumbled and fed to hogs for their protection.
[25] Klapper, "Das Gebet im Zauberglauben des Mittelalters, aus schlesischen Quellen",
Mitteilungen der schlesischen Gesellschaft für Volkskunde, 9 (1907), pt. 18, 5–41.

times they involve simple commands, repeated perhaps three times. One brief Anglo-Saxon charm goes, "Fly, devil; Christ pursues you. When Christ is born the pain will go." A German adjuration addressed to a worm enjoins it to "go out" from the patient's marrow into his veins, then from his veins into his flesh, and so forth until it is outside the body altogether. The same progressive weakening of the illness is found in a charm for a cyst:

> May you be consumed as coal upon the hearth. May you shrink as dung upon a wall. And may you dry up as water in a pail. May you become as small as a linseed grain, and much smaller than the hipbone of an itch-mite, and may you become so small that you become nothing.[26]

Often the power of an adjuration is enhanced by appeal to persons, things, or events that are sacred and therefore powerful. The disease or the demon is adjured by the cross or the blood of Christ, or by his burial, or by the Last Judgment. The adjuration is still addressed to the sickness or its cause rather than to God or a saint, but the sickness is commanded "in the name" or "by the power" of someone or something holy. This does not necessarily mean that either the disease or the holy person is being coerced, or that the ritual is seen as having mechanical or binding effect. A command leaves open the possibility of refusal; the sickness or demon may not depart. The healer is locked in a kind of combat with the evil power of the disease, and relies on sacred powers as aids in this battle.

In both blessings and adjurations the sacred events of the Bible or of Christian legend might be more than simple sources of power: they could serve as archetypal events, directly analogous to the healing process itself. Just as the spear of Longinus pierced Christ's side and then came out, so too may some iron implement come out of a wounded patient. Just as Mary suffered anguish when she saw Christ hanging on the cross, so too "must you suffer, O worm!". One of the most popular instances of this formula was the Jordan charm, found as early as the ninth or tenth century. The original version tells how Christ and St. John were approaching the river Jordan, and Christ told the waters to stop flowing. Later variants refer to the baptism of Christ in the Jordan, or to an apocryphal tale of how Christ and John (or Mary) stopped the torrent so they could pass over to the other bank. In any case, the stopping of the water becomes an archetype for the clotting of blood. The formula may be a blessing, in which case the key notion is: "Just as the Jordan stopped, so may your blood stop flowing." Or it may be an adjuration addressed directly to the blood. In some later versions this charm is made into an adjuration against disease, weapons, fire, animals, even thieves, all of which are commanded, like the Jordan, to stand still in one or another sense.

---

[26] Storms, *Anglo-Saxon Magic*, 155 (with translation).

The authority of the charms is sometimes enhanced by ascription to a saint. The "charm of St. William", for example, was allegedly given to the holy man by Christ himself as a remedy for worms, cankers, festers, and various forms of gout. Another charm was said to have been devised by St. Eustace for the benefit of a woman in great pain. A common variation on this theme is the blessing or adjuration woven into an apocryphal story, with a character in the legend actually speaking the healing words. In these cases the legend itself becomes the charm, and the words ascribed to the holy person are the operative portion. The charm for toothache from the Wolfsthurn book is a case in point. When Christ finds Peter sitting on a rock and holding his jaw because a worm is rotting his tooth, Christ himself in most versions adjures the worm or the toothache to depart. A charm that derives from early Jewish and Byzantine sources is that of three angels who, while walking on Mount Sinai, encounter a demon. They ask where he is going, and he says he is off to inflict pain on a certain person. The angels then adjure him by the Father, Son, and Holy Spirit, and by Abraham, Isaac, Jacob, all the patriarchs, prophets, apostles, martyrs, confessors, virgins, and all saints of God, not to harm that person. The earliest Western version of this charm is a Latin text from the tenth century. Some later examples have multiple demons, who recite a long list of bodily organs they intend to afflict when they attack their victim.

As we have seen, early charms were found among the pagans of northern Europe, and got written down and adapted when these areas were converted. At a later stage, perhaps beginning around the eleventh century, Christian monks and priests began writing new charms that were not derived from pagan models. Many of these appear in similar form through much of Europe, apparently sent or taken from one monastery to another. Originally in Latin, they were translated sooner or later into the vernacular languages. A still later phase in the evolution of charms came around the fourteenth and fifteenth centuries, when lay influence asserted itself once more. Certain formulas were now composed originally in the vernacular, or at least expressed in poetic forms long popular in the vernacular languages. Thus the three-flower charm, first found in a French Swiss manuscript from 1429, tells of three roses planted in a garden, or perhaps by Christ's tomb. In some versions this charm begins in the first person singular: "I went to a garden . . ." In any case, the names of the three roses are given, the third usually being "Blood-Stand-Still" or some variation. The folk poem itself ends up as a healing charm.

While rooted in popular culture and developed by monks, charms could be used by physicians as well. John of Gaddesden (ca. 1280–1361), who was court physician under Edward II and was mentioned by Chaucer as an eminent medical authority, recommended the use of such methods, and while John of Mirfeld of St. Bartholomew's Hospital expressed some skepticism in these matters he nonetheless copied out several charms for whatever benefit they might provide.[27]

Exorcisms, which tend to be much longer than charms, often involve a complex mixture of liturgical and folkloric elements. There was no firm distinction between official exorcisms used by the higher clergy and popular exorcisms devised by lower clergy or even laypeople. The Church did not yet have fixed rituals for universal use in expelling demons, and in the nature of things exorcisms were put together *ad hoc* or else borrowed from someone else's invention. In some cases they might be reminiscent of standard Christian rites, even if elements of folklore intrude:

> In the name of the Father, and of the Son, and of the Holy Spirit, amen. I conjure you, O elves and all sorts of demons, whether of the day or of the night, by the Father, and the Son, and the Holy Spirit, and the undivided Trinity, and by the intercession of the most blessed and glorious Mary ever Virgin, by the prayers of the prophets, by the merits of the patriarchs, by the supplication of the angels and archangels, by the intercession of the apostles, by the passion of the martyrs, by the faith of the confessors, by the chastity of the virgins, by the intercession of all the saints, and by the Seven Sleepers, whose names are Malchus, Maximianus, Dionysius, John, Constantine, Seraphion, and Martimanus, and by the name of the Lord + a + g + l + a +, which is blessed unto all ages, that you should not harm nor do or inflict anything evil against this servant of God N., whether sleeping or waking. + Christ conquers + Christ reigns + Christ commands + May Christ bless us + [and] defend us from all evil + Amen.

Each time the exorcist finds the cross marked on the page he is to make the sign of the cross over the afflicted person. Elsewhere the formula of exorcism draws more heavily from folklore, as in one which begins by "conjuring" and "adjuring" the elves and all diabolical enemies that they may have no more power over the patient. (The words *coniuro* and *adiuro* are used interchangeably for "command".) The exorcist calls on all God's saints to cast these "accursed elves" into the eternal hellfire that is prepared for them. He implores Jesus to send his blessing so that these wretched elves will no longer harm the patient in head or brain, nose, neck, mouth, eyes, hands, and so forth through the various members and organs of the body. He commands Heradiana, the "deaf-mute mother of malignant elves," to depart. As the exorcism progresses it shifts at random, addressing now the patient, now the elves, and now the heavenly powers.[28]

---

[27] H. P. Cholmeley, *John of Gaddesden and the Rosa medicinae* (Oxford: Clarendon, 1912), 48–52; Percival Horton-Smith Hartley, *Johannes de Mirfeld of St. Bartholomew's Smithfield: His Life and Works* (Cambridge University Press, 1936), 44.

[28] British Library, MS Sloane 962, fols. 9ᵛ–10ʳ, and MS Sloane 963, fols. 15ʳ–16ᵛ.

If both those exorcisms seem only marginally magical, a third one steps unquestionably across the border. If you see a man or woman seized by a demon, the manuscript in question instructs, you should take a piece of parchment and write on it the sign of the cross and the opening of the gospel according to John. Then you should scrape the words off the parchment into a bowl, and give these scrapings to the afflicted person to drink, along with holy water. If the first potion does not work, a second or even third application may be necessary. This "charm" is given on the best authority: a demon taught it to a possessed person, and it is tried and proven.[29]

While adjurations and exorcisms were usually intended for individuals suffering bodily or mental affliction, they could be put to other purposes as well. Thieves and soldiers might be adjured. Demons responsible for hail, likewise, could be addressed, as in an eleventh-century charm: "I adjure you, O Devil, and your angels . . . I adjure you, O Mermeut, with your companions, you who have power over tempests." While such formulas normally sought to drive evil beings away, the same language could also be used to keep helpful beings from leaving. Thus, one fourteenth-century Continental manuscript has a charm addressed to bees: "I conjure you in the name of the Father, and of the Son, and of the Holy Spirit, O you handmaids of God who produce wax for God's service, not to withdraw or flee from me . . ."[30]

While most charms fall into the three categories we have been discussing, there is a fourth type that is less common but more explicitly magical: incantations articulating the meaning of sympathetic magic. A pregnant woman who fears miscarriage or misshapen offspring is instructed to step three times over a grave. If there were no charm for her to use, we might be able to conjecture that she is performing sympathetic magic expressing victory over death. The point is made explicit, however, by a charm she is supposed to say in the process: "This as my help against the evil late birth, this as my help against the grievous dismal birth, this as my help against the evil lame birth."[31]

If we ask what it is that qualifies the first three categories of charm as magic from a medieval perspective, we find that they are for the most part borderline cases. When speculative minds in the later medieval centuries began reflecting on natural magic, one of the questions that they considered was whether words by themselves, just like certain herbs and other

[29] Bodleian Library, Oxford, MS e Mus. 219, fol. 187^{r-v}.
[30] Max Siller, "Zauberspruch und Hexenprozess: Die Rolle des Zauberspruchs in den Zauber- und Hexenprozessen Tirols", in Werner M. Bauer et al., eds., *Tradition und Entwicklung: Festschrift Eugen Thurnher* (Innsbruck: Institut für Germanistik der Universität Innsbruck, 1982), 129; Hampp, *Beschwörung, Segen, Gebet*, 125.
[31] Storms, *Anglo-Saxon Magic*, 197.

objects of nature, held special powers. Many people believed that verbal formulas could have such inherent power, and these charms would be prime examples. Thus, for *some* medieval people charms would count as magic. Other people would have been hard pressed to distinguish between them and purely religious prayers. And perhaps the majority of users would simply not have reflected on the question: if the charms worked, that was more important than how they worked.

PROTECTIVE AMULETS AND TALISMANS

Herbs, animal remedies, and charms were used mostly to cure diseases that had already set in. Amulets, on the other hand, were typically meant as protective devices. Unlike the other forms of magic we have discussed, amulets served psychological purposes somewhat more than physical ones: they ensured health of the mind more than that of the body. They could ward off disease, to be sure, but more often they protected their bearers against the attacks of visible and invisible enemies. Whereas herbal and animal cures were usually ingested or applied directly to the body, amulets worked through mere proximity. A potion would be swallowed and an unguent was for anointing, but an amulet was merely to be carried about on one's person. Herbal and animal cures were depleted with use, but amulets could be retained for long or repeated deployment.

Nonetheless, the use of amulets represents essentially a variation on these other forms of magic. This is clear from the nature of the objects used as amulets, which for the most part fall into two categories: plants and parts of animals' bodies. The materials used are essentially the same as those we have already examined, but the way they are applied differs. And the mode of employment usually indicates that occult virtues are assumed to lie within these objects. A hare's foot, bound to the left arm, will enable a person to go anywhere without danger. The right foot of a hare, or the heart of a dog, will keep dogs from barking. Sprigs of rosemary, put at a person's door, will keep venomous snakes away. Carried on one's person, rosemary keeps evil spirits at bay, and a spoon made of its wood has power against poisons. If five leaves of a nettle plant are held in the hand they will ensure safety from all fear and fantasy. Heliotrope, gathered under the sign of Virgo and wrapped in laurel leaves along with the tooth of a wolf, will keep people from saying anything bad about its bearer. If mistletoe is carried on one's person one will not be condemned in court. If a person goes out in the sign of Virgo before sunrise, collects various herbs, says three Pater Nosters and three Ave Marias, then carries the herbs on his person, no one will be able to speak evil against him, or if they do he will overcome them. If heliotrope is placed at the entrance to a church where

Fig. 7. Augustine recommending a herb for exorcism, from a fourteenth-century herbal

adulteresses are present, they will be unable to leave the building until it is removed. The list could be extended indefinitely.[32]

Even in their mode of employment and in their purpose, amulets do not differ absolutely from other magical substances. For example, unguents as well as amulets can serve for prevention: by anointing yourself with the blood of a lion you can keep yourself safe from all other beasts, and if you smear lion fat over your body you will be secure from snakebite.[33] When herbs are used for ligatures or suspensions, bound to or hung from the body, they became similar to amulets. Indeed, the distinction breaks down altogether in a prescription given for demonic possession. In discussion of one plant that goes by various names, including "the herb of Solomon," the author of a herbal tells how St. Augustine learned of its power to expel evil spirits. The saint had learned this lore from an anonymous philosopher. He had occasion to use this knowledge when a

---

[32] Bodleian Library, Oxford, MS Wood empt. 18, fols. 32ʳ, 34ʳ; MS e Mus. 219, fol. 187ᵛ. British Library, MS Sloane 3132, fol. 56ʳ; MS Sloane 3564, fols. 34ᵛ–35ʳ, 37ʳ–ᵛ. Ellis, "Extracts in prose and verse", 396.
[33] British Library, MS Harley 1585, fol. 66ᵛ.

noble and pious woman complained to him that her daughter and son were both troubled by demons. He recommended that she take this herb and suspend it around their necks, and when she tried the remedy it worked. The cure is even more dramatic in the accompanying drawing (Fig. 7), which shows the herb – magnified to enormous dimensions, presumably for identification – being held up to the possessed youths, who are so far beside themselves that attendants must hold them up from behind. The herb is, however, doing its job, and demons are flying from the victims' mouths.

While talismans are generally similar to amulets in purpose and in mode of employment, historians sometimes treat them separately. The distinguishing feature is that talismans, unlike amulets, have written words or at least letters inscribed on them. The power of such inscriptions is at least as great as that of plants and animals. Many in medieval society, including the noted medical authority Bernard Gordon (d. ca. 1320), believed one could ward off epileptic attacks by carrying the names of the biblical magi on one's person, written on a slip of parchment. One manuscript gives series of letters from the alphabet which, if written out and carried, will have wondrous effect: one series, to be hidden under the right foot, will silence the bearer's enemies; another, to be held in the left hand, will win favors from potential benefactors. Another manuscript gives a series of names for God which, if borne on one's person, will protect against fire, water, arms, and poison. If a pregnant woman has this formula on her she will not die in childbirth. Then the author hedges, adding a condition: whoever carries such a sequence of divine names *and looks at them each day* will not die by sword, fire, or water, and will remain unvanquished in battle.[34]

Perhaps the most famous device used on talismans was the magic square with the SATOR–AREPO formula:

```
S A T O R
A R E P O
T E N E T
O P E R A
R O T A S
```

These words make little sense in themselves. Their interest lies largely in the fact that the square reads the same four ways: from top to bottom, from left to right, from bottom to top backward, and from right to left backward. More to the point, while the origin of the square has been disputed, it seems to be an anagram for the opening words of the Lord's

34 Bodleian Library, Oxford, MS e Mus. 219, fol. 186ᵛ; MS Wood empt. 18, fol. 9ʳ ᵛ.

Prayer in Latin, laid out as a cross, with a double "A" and "O" for Christ the Alpha and Omega (Revelation 1:8):

```
                P
                A
        A       T       O
                E
                R
P A T E R N O S T E R
                O
                S
        A       T       O
                E
                R
```

The earliest known occurrence of the square is in a first-century Christian house at Pompeii. In medieval Europe it served various magical purposes. It could be inscribed on cloth and placed over the womb to aid a woman in childbirth, and if carried on one's person it could win the favor of all those one met.[35]

What connection did these amulets and talismans have with the Church's sacramentals? The question is not easy to answer. Certainly some of the holy objects provided or sanctioned by churchmen seem reminiscent of amulets. Wax blessed on the feast of the Purification was thought effective against thunderbolts. Ringing of church bells could safeguard the parish from storms. The *Salernitan Regimen*, a popular medical compilation, recommended the "Agnus Dei" (a wax lamb blessed, in principle, by the pope) as protection against various evils, including death by lightning. Long sheets of parchment or paper, inscribed with prayers and then rolled up, could protect their bearers against sudden death, wounding by weapons, the slander of false witnesses, evil spirits, tribulation, illness, danger in childbirth, and other afflictions.[36]

The relics of saints also seem at times to have served as amulets. When Count Rudolf of Pfullendorf brought relics of the biblical patriarchs back from the Holy Land they imparted peace, fertility, and good weather everywhere he took them. Wax taken from the tomb of St. Martin of Tours and placed atop a tree could protect the surrounding vineyard from hail. Carried into battle, relics could secure victory over the foe. Yet it is dangerous to focus on such reports in isolation from other factors in the

---

[35] Storms, *Anglo-Saxon Magic*, 281; Bodleian MS Wood empt. 18, fol. 32ʳ.
[36] Keith Thomas, *Religion and the Decline of Magic* (London: Weidenfeld & Nicolson, 1971), ch. 1; Curt F. Bühler, "Prayers and charms in certain Middle English scrolls", *Speculum*, 39 (1964), 270–8.

veneration of saints. These holy persons might work on earth through their physical remains, but their devotees knew that their souls were in heaven interceding before God. They had annual feast days that would be celebrated; in the meantime they could be addressed in prayer. Their deeds on earth were recorded in legend and recalled in preaching. They had personalities, specific desires, and the ability to punish those who offended them. It is thus misleading to assume that their relics were seen as having *inherent* power, only loosely connected to their spiritual presence. Even the unsophisticated in medieval Europe seem to have had a lively sense that the saints were real persons, subjects for both imitation and awe. They may still on occasion have treated their relics as magical amulets, but concrete evidence for this is rare. The danger for the historian lies in the temptation to strip away the religious context by a process of abstraction and then take the magical remainder as the essence of popular piety.

Similar difficulty surrounds popular veneration of the eucharist. The twelfth and thirteenth centuries saw escalating devotion to the eucharist, or to the host that the priest consecrated during the mass. This was the age when the theological doctrine of transubstantiation was being refined: no longer content with the vague assurance that Christ was somehow present in the consecrated host, theologians now proposed that the "substance" of bread was miraculously replaced with that of Christ each time the priest pronounced the words of consecration, despite the remaining "accidents" or appearances of bread. Fortified by this doctrine, popular piety now demanded to *see* this miraculously transubstantiated host, and the custom spread of having the priest elevate it over his head after the consecration so that people at mass could behold it. Popular belief soon held that a person who saw the consecrated host during mass would be safe from harm for the rest of the day. On the feast of Corpus Christi the host would be carried in procession through town and then out to the fields to ensure fertility of the crops. Laypeople allegedly carried the process further, stealing or otherwise obtaining consecrated hosts to protect themselves against wounding or drowning, to cure their diseases or procure fertility, to prevent storms or to gain riches. At times they might heighten the power of the host by writing Bible verses or magical charms on it. From one source we learn that peasants were using the eucharist to protect their livestock: a twelfth-century nun told how Christ came to her in a dream and complained, "They have made me into a swineherd and concealed my body in the stall so their cattle will not succumb to the plague."[37]

In short, the eucharist lent itself at least as much as saints' relics to use as a magical amulet. This form of abuse may in fact have been easier, since the

[37] Peter Browe, "Die Eucharistie als Zaubermittel im Mittelalter", *Archiv für Kulturgeschichte*, 20 (1930), 134–54.

connection between the consecrated host and Christ's historical life was less apparent, and for that reason it may have been easier to conceive the host as having inherent power. Reformers in the fifteenth century complained that people who were venerating the consecrated host seemed little interested in receiving the same host in communion; this is not quite the same as saying that they viewed it as a magical amulet, but it is a related complaint, based on the observation that people were missing the authentic significance of the eucharist.

People in medieval Europe who noted and protested against these abuses were not likely to call them magic, but rather superstition, which in this context meant the improper use of a holy object. One corollary to the intellectuals' ways of defining magic is that they had little reason to reflect on the similarities between what they called magic and what they termed superstition. They would scarcely have said that improper use of relics or the eucharist was an example of *demonic* magic. Demons might tempt people to such abuse, but the abuse itself did not involve the conjuring of demons, even implicitly. Nor was it a case of natural magic when the power being used came from God and the saints. From the theologians' and preachers' viewpoint, relics and hosts were not *natural* repositories for occult power; they were not analogous to sprigs of rosemary or organs from vultures.

These distinctions surely corresponded in some measure to the sensibilities of ordinary people. It was not just the theologians who recognized the saints as personal beings, or who knew that the Christ who came in the form of a wafer was the same as the Christ who would come one day as judge. Yet for many people the practical implications of this theology seem to have been less straightforward. Whatever religious meaning these holy objects had, they were immediate sources of potential power. If one could ask the peasant whether the host that he concealed in his stable was similar to some herb that might have served to protect his horses, he might well have said that of course it was not: it had far greater power, and that is why he used it. Practically, however, he was using the host as if it were an amulet. The theoretical difference in the nature of the objects was overshadowed by the practical similarity in the way he used them.

SORCERY: THE MISUSE OF MEDICAL AND PROTECTIVE MAGIC

If it is difficult at times to distinguish magic from science or from religion, it is all the more difficult to separate "white" (helpful) magic from "black" (harmful) magic, or medical and protective magic from sorcery. Much depends on one's point of view, and while it is not customary to speak of "gray magic," there are indeed gray areas between these categories. What if a healer attempts a cure and the patient only grows worse?

Some may assume that the healer was in fact trying to harm the patient. Someone with special knowledge of healing herbs may, after all, know other herbs that can bring sickness and death – or so people in premodern Europe seem often to have reasoned. Apart from the healer's intentions, the remedy may have been the wrong one, and if a magical cure backfires it may count as sorcery by virtue of its effect. Different but equally great problems arise with love magic. If a magician uses magic to inspire adultery, a God-fearing Christian may easily brand this as sorcery. But what if the same magician uses love magic to help a woman regain her husband's affections? Is this too a form of sorcery? Many in medieval society would have assumed so.

Much of our information about sorcery comes from the records of prosecution: we hear from some disgruntled peasant, for example, that an old woman who lives near him has bewitched his cows or his children. The most common allegation when people are brought to court for magic is that they have caused bodily harm or even death. In some places, particularly Italy, love magic is also a frequent basis for prosecution. In theologians' and lawyers' eyes love magic seems to have counted as sorcery even if used by a wife to regain her husband's affections; it was a means for constraining the will, and that in itself was evil. Elsewhere, especially in and around Switzerland, we find people taken to court for magically inducing storms to destroy their neighbors' crops. A German charm of the tenth century enjoined the Devil in Christ's name not to cause any harm "through destructive rain, through frost, through storms, or through the murmured incantations of sorcerers." Sorcery itself must have appeared as a force of nature, focused in individual agents yet linking them with cosmic powers. On a smaller scale, theft was also punished at times as an act of sorcery, on the assumption that the thief had broken in or removed an object by magical means.

The techniques for sorcery were essentially the same as those for medical or protective magic: potions, charms, and amulets, often with accompanying rituals. The difference between positive and negative magic lay not in their basic conception but in the purposes they served. Sorcerers who gave people food and drink to do them harm might be accused of "poisoning" them, the distinction between normal and occult powers being as difficult to define here as elsewhere. Thus, a Swiss woman in the early fifteenth century allegedly killed a man by giving him a "poisoned" apple, but she was being tried as a sorceress, not simply as a murderer. Love potions might include herbs, ashes, and other materials. Like Heracles' wife in the play by Seneca, women who used love magic at times confused lethal poisons with aphrodisiacs. A woman at Lucerne in the mid-fifteenth century, for example, was accused of making this mistake and was punished by banishment from town. Another woman confessed that she had given a man her menstrual blood as a love potion, but when he died soon afterward she refused to believe her magic was the cause.

Charms used with evil intent are usually known as "curses." Such a formula was often simply an inverted blessing or adjuration, and had the same structure as these. Like a blessing or adjuration, a curse might make appeal to the events of sacred history or religious legend. At Innsbruck in 1485 a baptized Jewish woman was accused of reciting a blasphemous spell to arouse as much pain in her enemy's head as Mary had in her body when she bore Jesus. Better attested is the used of a charm for love magic: "May N. love me as much as Mary loved her Son when she gave him birth."

Because these curses would be uttered in secrecy, the victim would have little reason to know what they were or even that they had been uttered, and for that reason they probably show up in the court records much less often than they were actually used. For different but equally obvious reasons the victims of sorcery could not present as evidence potions that had been consumed. What the accusers did have to show the judges were magical amulets that had been left under their thresholds or beds to do them harm. Often these amulets were bundles of noxious powders, human faeces, wood from a gallows, or other such materials. One sick woman checked under the threshold of her home and discovered the bodies of three small black animals, like mice, wrapped in cloth.

The rituals used for sorcery typically involved sympathetic magic. Thus, a witness at Lucerne in 1486 told that she had seen two neighbors performing a strange ritual at a well: one of them reached behind herself into the well and drew water over her head three times, and soon it began to hail. If sorceresses stole milk from cows, it might be by "milking" a knife stuck into a wall. Or physical harm could by worked by image magic, the most notorious of sympathetic techniques: when a person's image is pierced with pins or otherwise afflicted, the symbolic harm to the image causes real harm to the victim. Thus, a sorcerer in fourteenth-century Coventry experimented with a wax image of a neighbor. When he drove a lead spike into the image's forehead, the neighbor went mad and began shrieking with pain. After several weeks of this agony the sorcerer drove the spike into the image's heart and the neighbor died.

Not surprisingly, sorcerers were often thought to use the Church's holy objects and rituals for their transgressions. Seeking supernatural power wherever it was to be found, they would not scruple to bend holy things to their purposes. Fear of such sacrilege might arise in anti-Jewish propaganda. An epidemic that spread through Aquitaine in 1321 led to the rumor that lepers and Jews had poisoned the wells with a magical mixture of blood, urine, plants, and the consecrated host. As early as 1130, when the archbishop of Trier gave the Jews of his archdiocese the choice of converting to Christianity or being banished, he died soon afterward, and Jews were charged with having had a wax statue of him baptized, then slowly melting it over a fire to cause his death. Heightened veneration for the eucharist in the thirteenth and following centuries brought intense fear that the consecrated host would be stolen from churches and used for sorcery. Stories were told of how a woman might kiss a man while holding the host in her mouth to increase his love for her. In one famous case a woman who did this was punished with inability to see the consecrated host even when it was elevated during the mass. Only when she touched a relic of St. Bridget of Sweden was she released from this affliction. Such stories tend to have a breathless, legendary air about them, but there is nothing inherently implausible about the fear that holy things might get used for unholy ends.

Manuscripts with formulas for medical magic sometimes include material that a theologian or judge would consider as sorcery. The procedures recommended in these manuscripts do not seem different in principle from those hinted at in court records, but because we have further detail it becomes easier to see how this magic resembles the herbal concoctions used for healing.[38]

These manuscripts often prescribe aphrodisiacs, which would have been seen by outsiders as means for love magic. To arouse a woman's lust, one manuscript advises soaking wool in the blood of a bat and putting it under her head while she is sleeping. The testicles of a stag or bull, or the tail of a fox, will arouse a woman to sexual desire. Putting ants' eggs in her bath will arouse her so violently that willy-nilly she will seek intercourse.[39] More questionable still is the advice of one compiler that if you write "pax + pix + abyra + syth + samasic" on a hazel stick and hit a woman on the head with it three times, then immediately kiss her, you will be assured of her love. A woman, on the other hand, can arouse her husband to love by mixing a herb with earthworms and giving it to him in his food.

Herbs can serve for other kinds of sorcery as well. If teasel is given in food or drink along with a tooth, presumably ground up, it will cause all who ingest it to fight with each other until they consume the juice of

---

[38] British Library, MSS Sloane 3132 and 3564; Bodleian Library, MSS e Mus. 219 and Wood empt. 18.

[39] W. L. Wardale, "A Low German–Latin miscellany of the early fourteenth century", *Niederdeutsche Mitteilungen*, 8 (1952), 5–22. The prescription concludes with the instruction to write "amet lamet te misael," of which only *amet* ("may she love") and *te* ("you") are intelligible. The same manuscript has other counsel for heightening sexual pleasure and for quelling passion.

another herb. There are many kinds of potion that can make a man impotent or at least diminish his sexual desire. Eating the flowers of the willow or poplar can do so, "as is proved from long experience". Indeed, a man could be rendered impotent for the rest of his life by being so careless as to imbibe forty ants boiled in daffodil juice. Perhaps the most extravagant claim is that sage, allowed to decay while surrounded by dung, will give rise to a bird with a serpent-like tail; if people are touched with the blood of this bird they will lose their senses for at least fifteen days, while if the serpent is burned and then the ashes are cast into a fire there will at once be terrible thunder.

We need not assume that all such instructions were penned with an equally straight face. Medieval people did seriously believe, however, that bewitchment could cause impotence, and when King Lothar II was unable to consummate his marriage because he was magically impeded, Archbishop Hincmar of Rheims (806–82) was called on to decide whether the affliction was sufficient grounds for the king to dismiss his bride and marry a different woman. The question arose again later, absorbing the attention of leading canon lawyers and other churchmen in the eleventh and twelfth centuries. The solution to the problem was that separation from the bride was allowed if remedies had failed, and remarriage was permitted if the cause of the first failure was clearly magical. In short, sorcery was serious business indeed.

For sorcery as for healing magic, the power of herbs might be enhanced by use of charms. One fourteenth-century formula, superficially Christian, is addressed to a plant:

In the name of Christ, amen. I conjure you, O herb, that I may conquer by Lord Peter . . . by the moon and stars . . . and may you conquer all my enemies, pontiffs and priests and all laymen and all women and all lawyers who are working against me . . .[40]

If the same basic techniques were used for both positive and negative magic, it is not surprising that these techniques could also be used as protection against sorcery, or as countermagic for use against a curse that someone was inflicting. One formula from 1475 is explicitly identified as a charm for use against "a wicked witch." While worded as a charm, it is intended as a talisman: it is to be written out and carried on one's person, for protection "in sleeping, in waking, in drinking, and especially in dreaming." It reads:

In nomine Patris, etc. By the power of the Lord, may the cross + and passion of Christ + be a medicine for me. May the five wounds of the Lord be my

---

[40] Thorndike, *History of Magic*, vol. 1, 598 n. 1 (with translation of quotation).

medicine +. May the Virgin Mary aid and defend me from every malign demon and from every malign spirit, amen. + A + G + L + A + Tetragrammaton + Alpha + O . . .[41]

The physician Arnold of Villanova wrote a treatise *On Bewitchments* around 1300 in which he gave numerous remedies for impotence caused by magic. In some cases, he says, men who are unable to have sexual relations with their wives can be cured by human means; in other cases divine aid is necessary. Sometimes the bewitchment is caused by use of some object which can simply be removed: the testicles of a rooster placed under the bed of the married couple, or an inscription with characters written in bat's blood. There are further natural expedients to use: fumigation of the bedchamber with the bile of a fish will counteract the bewitchment (cf. Tobit 6:16–17 and 8:4, in the Old Testament apocrypha), as will smearing or sprinkling the walls with the blood of a black dog. For more difficult cases Arnold prescribes an elaborate exorcism in which the opening verses from the Gospel of John are written and immersed in a liquid, which the couple drinks. Leaves, flowers, and fruit are placed over burning coals to drive away the meddling demon. The assumption here seems to be that the magic in question can be either natural or demonic: in the former case natural countermagic will suffice, but in the latter one must resort to an exorcism.[42]

DIVINATION AND POPULAR ASTROLOGY

The forms of magic so far examined were ways of manipulating nature to affect one's destiny. Divination was a means for knowing a destiny that was foreordained. As we have seen, early medieval writers thought of magic primarily as a series of divinatory techniques, all of which, like the rest of magic, relied on demonic inspiration. Roughly half of Isidore of Seville's section on magicians deals with diviners, and his schema had lasting influence. While other forms of magic attracted increasing attention in later medieval Europe, divination lost nothing of its appeal for the populace or its horror for moralists.

The varieties of divination were legion. "Oneiromancy" or interpretation of dreams remained popular, as did treatises suggesting how to interpret them. Popular oneiromancy might involve simple equation of dream content with future events: dreams about water, for example, might signal death by drowning. On a more sophisticated level, the

[41] John Brand, *Popular Antiquities of Great Britain*, ed. W. Carew Hazlitt, vol. 3 (London: Smith, 1870), 73.
[42] Hansen, *Quellen und Untersuchungen*, 44–7. Cf. British Library, MS Sloane 3132, fol. 56ʳ.

"dream books" of writers such as Hans Lobenzweig (mid-fifteenth century) made careful allowance for the social status and physical condition of the dreamer, and contained complex rules for interpreting dreams. Observation of signs in nature seems also to have retained its importance. The elaborate norms that the Romans had developed for augury may have been lost, but a primitive sort of popular augury could discern the future from the calls of birds. The number of croaks uttered by a raven could be a sign of changes in the weather, because that bird was so sensitive to conditions of the air. One woman, we are told, asked a cuckoo how long she would live, and when the bird cried five times she concluded she had five more years, but of course this story was told to debunk the superstition, and we cannot assume it is a fair report of something that actually happened. Chiromancers made more show of subtlety, with their claim that they could read on people's hands how many spouses they would have, what promotions lay in store for them, or whether they were fated to die on the gallows.

Scientific astrology, based on detailed observation of the heavens, seems to have been rare in Europe until the twelfth century, but popular astrology was perennial. Usually the popular form referred more to phases of the moon than to motions of the other heavenly bodies, for the fairly simple reason that the moon could more easily be seen and its movements more readily understood. Detailed charts told which days of the lunar cycle were good or bad for various activities. Such written material may have originated among people with some education, but the mentality was not specifically learned.

Other signs of the future could be detected in the skies as well, and they were often treated in the same kind of mock-systematic fashion. One of the more common means of prognostication was interpretation of thunder. The direction it came from might be significant: if it sounded in the east, for example, it portended great bloodshed in the coming year. Even more important, perhaps especially in regions where thunderstorms are relatively rare and might not occur in most months of the year, was the month in which the thunder was heard. A chart from the fourteenth century shows "what thunder signifies in each month," complete with simple drawings that make the future clear (Fig. 8). If it thunders in January there will be strong winds, abundance of fruit, and war. Thunder in February means death for many people, especially the rich. The most cheering prospect on this generally bleak chart is reserved for the end of the year: if thunder occurs in December it portends a rich harvest in the land and peace and concord among the people.

Certain days of the month are more propitious than others, and certain days of the year are exceptionally unlucky. Murders, battles, and other

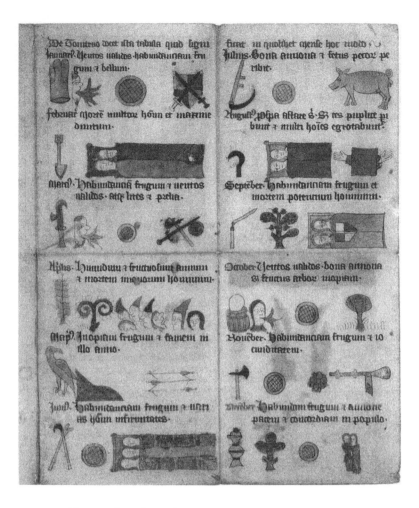

Fig. 8. Chart for divination by thunder, fourteenth century

misfortunes are especially likely to occur on the "Egyptian days," though by knowing these in advance one can take precautions. One leechbook says there are thirty-two evil days in the year, apart from local variations:

Whoever weds a wife on any of these days, he shall not long have joy of her. And whoever undertakes any great journey shall never come back again, or some misfortune shall befall him. And he that begins any great work shall never make an end thereof. And he that has his blood let shall soon die, or never be well.[43]

Casual superstitions of all sorts were used to foretell one's fate. Those who found halfpennies or needles could congratulate themselves on their good luck, unless they were so foolish as to dispose of these discovered objects, in which case the luck would turn against them. It was lucky to find a horseshoe or an iron nail, or to meet a hare as it was escaping from hounds. To encounter a raven or an ass was unlucky. Some people believed it could be bad luck to meet a monk or priest unless one made the sign of the cross; a favorite anecdote for preachers told how a woman took this precaution to avert misfortune on meeting a priest, but the cleric cast her into a muddy ditch and thus proved her superstition ineffective. Whether such beliefs fall within the realm of magic, however, even on medieval terms, is doubtful. Early medieval authors who spoke of "the magical arts" would have reserved the term for divinatory or other practices that involved some measure of systematic correlation between signs and future events. The term "art" in this context referred to a systematic body of knowledge, and few would have accorded the dignity of this title to a casual superstition.

Not all forms of divination were passive, or required mere observation of signs present in the world. Certain forms, which seem to have become especially popular in the fifteenth century but could be found much earlier, required active operation of the person foretelling the future. These varieties of divination might be referred to as "experimental." Opening a book at random and reading the passage that first meets one's eyes is a time-honored method. Another means of prognostication, found in antiquity and developed in medieval sources, involves rolling of dice. One late medieval manual instructs its user on how to roll dice as a key to whether they will obtain some desire.[44] For the lucky person who rolls three sixes, the book gives this verse:

You that have cast three sixes here
Shall have your desire this same year.
Hold you stable and worry you not,
For you shall have the desire that is in your thought.

The player who casts two sixes and a two will also have the desired object, but much adversity along with it. Those who roll a six and two fours are told to give up their notions. Such techniques could always be used for serious divination, but perhaps lent themselves better to use as party games. Sometimes the techniques involved are extremely elaborate, with several charts to consult and movable pointers to turn before one receives counsel. One German example is intended for lovers, but could also be

[43] Dawson, A Leechbook, 328–9.
[44] W. L. Braekman, "Fortune-telling by the casting of dice: a Middle English poem and its background", Studia Neophilologica, 52 (1980), 3–29.

meant as light entertainment, even if its tone is at times sober. The hopeful young lady is told in one scenario, "Your love is wasted on the young man you have chosen. Although he is very friendly to you it is someone else who pleases him. You love him and he does not love you, no matter how much he pretends to."

Certain techniques of experimental divination make use of the same kinds of objects that are used in manipulative magic; these techniques typically occur in the same manuscripts as other forms of magic. Herbs, for example, can aid in the detection of a thief: if heliotrope is placed under the head of a sleeping person from whom something has been stolen, that person will be able to see the thief and his whereabouts in his dreams.

Such techniques can also serve the purposes of medical prognosis. If a healer holds vervain against a sick person's hand and asks how he fares, the vervain will enable the person to give a correct answer; the patient will live or die, according to the answer he or she gives. The physician John of Mirfeld gives a series of techniques combining prognosis with prognostication, including one specimen of "onomancy", or divination through calculations based on names:

> take the name of the patient, the name of the messenger sent to summon the physician, and the name of the day upon which the messenger first came to you; join [the numerical values of] all their letters together, and if an even number result, the patient will not escape; if the number be odd, then he will recover.[45]

It is not surprising to read such techniques, but to find them in the work of a leading and generally hard-headed practitioner gives one pause.

The manuscripts containing divinatory procedures sometimes include elaborate techniques to detect a thief. Write the formula "+ Agios crux | Agios Crux + Agios Crux Domini" on virgin wax and hold it over your head with your left hand, and in your sleep you will see the thief. If you suspect someone, write certain letters on a piece of bread and give it to the suspect to eat, and if he is guilty he will be unable to swallow it. If there are several suspects, one manuscript recommends inscribing elaborate formulas on a piece of bread, reciting various prayers, and then administering the bread to the suspects. Alternatively, one can draw a picture of an eye on the wall, gather all the suspects, and watch to see which one weeps from his right eye. If he denies having stolen the missing object, drive a copper nail into the eye on the wall, and when you strike the nail the guilty person will cry out as if he himself had been struck: a clear case of sympathetic magic.

Detection of a thief or location of stolen goods might be linked to magic that would restore the lost property. A fourteenth-century Flemish manuscript, for example, uses a kind of sympathetic magic as a way to

---

[45] Aldridge, *Johannes de Mirfeld*, 71 (with translation).

discover and regain a stolen object. It is based on the legend that after Christ's crucifixion his cross was buried until St. Helen sought and discovered it. Just as the earth yielded this holy relic, so too the earth itself should now disclose the stolen goods. To invoke the power of the cross itself, the diviner lies four times on the ground, once in each of the compass directions, with arms stretched out in the form of a cross, and each time recites a formula commanding the cross of Christ to fetch back the thief and the stolen goods.

Magical procedures can also be used to obtain secret information directly from another person, and since the goal here is to gain knowledge one might class these operations as forms of experimental divination. If you put the heart and left foot of a toad over the mouth of a sleeping man, for example, he will immediately reveal to you whatever you ask him.

It is reasonably clear how divination might be taken for a species of demonic magic. Augustine had explained in his treatise *On the Divination of Demons* that, while evil spirits do not have truly prophetic knowledge of the future, they can make conjectures that are informed by their keen perception, their ability to move about quickly, and their rich store of experience, and it is these conjectures that are communicated to human beings in divination. What was less obvious was how divination could count as natural magic. The people who spoke of occult virtues in nature were usually thinking of powers that could be put to use, rather than natural signs of future events. Yet they were not wholly inattentive to prognostication. William of Auvergne, for example, speaks of a "sense of nature," a kind of extrasensory perception that enables a person, for example, to detect the presence of a burglar. Animals can also have this sense, according to William. Sheep use it to guard against wolves, and by means of it vultures know when there is going to be a battle (and thus, for them, a feast). Still other authors ascribed prognosticatory signs to God, who has bestowed them on humankind to help people brace themselves for future misfortune. The Flemish writer Venancius of Moerbeke catalogues numerous forms of divination ("the varieties of prognostication are practically infinite," he says), and laments that God's efforts to warn people meet all too often with unconcern or incomprehension.[46] But to view divination in these terms is to take it clearly outside the realm of magic and place it within the sphere of religion.

THE ART OF TRICKERY

Not all magic in medieval culture was serious. Just as there were forms of divination intended for entertainment, so too there was other magic that

---

[46] Roger A. Pack, "A treatise on prognostications by Venancius of Moerbeke", *Archives d'Histoire Doctrinale et Littéraire du Moyen Age*, 43 (1976), 311–22.

aimed to amuse: performative magic that would arouse wonder at the magician's virtuosity, and practical jokes that would give amusement at least to the one who played them.

The notebook of Thomas Betson (late fifteenth century) is instructive in this regard.[47] Betson was a monk at Syon Abbey in Middlesex. He seems to have been a pious man, but also a prankster and a dabbler in magic, and his notebook includes instructions on how to perform various tricks. Take a fine hair from the head of a woman, for example, and attach it to a hollowed-out egg. You will be able to move the egg about, holding the other end of the hair in your hand, and no one will see the hair because of its thinness. You can even hang the egg in a house, and "many people will think it is being held up by nothing at all." Or use a bit of wax to attach one end of a hair to a coin; pull on the other end of the hair, and the coin will move, and "many people will think it is done by magical art." Put a beetle inside an apple with a hole in its center, and when the beetle rocks the apple people will think the fruit is moving by itself. Was Betson counting on an exceptionally gullible audience? Not necessarily. Presumably he performed for people who wanted to be entertained, were willing to suspend their disbelief, and could be amused by even a simple "magic" trick if it was executed with panache. Betson also copied down instructions for much more sophisticated operations, for making images appear by elaborate arrangement of mirrors, or for producing interesting optical effects with a coin and a dish of water, and thus it seems he was not merely a buffoon.

Betson's moving apple finds its analogue in several other objects made to appear self-moved: loaves of bread that dance about on a table or leap through the house, dead fish that jump out of a pan, hollow rings and eggs that seem to roll about of their own accord. Numerous manuscripts tell how to perform tricks with fire: how to make a candle that cannot be extinguished; how to cause a great flame to rise up from a pan full of water. Likewise there are formulas for creating special light effects that will create illusions, such as making men appear headless, or making people appear so large that their heads seem to be in the heavens while their feet remain on earth. Often these "experiments" require basic knowledge of chemistry, though the last of them calls for simpler ingredients: oil, centaury, and blood from a female hoopoe. Any well-stocked kitchen would have had the onion juice required for secret writing or the strong red wine whose vapor could turn a white rose red.

Other forms of entertainment required equipment and manual dexterity. For example, the magicians' instructions tell how to release tied hands

---

[47] St. John's College, Cambridge, MS E.6. For other materials here cited, see Bodleian Library, MS e Mus. 219, MS Wood empt. 18, and MS Ashm. 1393; British Library, MSS Sloane 121 (a particularly rich source) and Sloane 3564.

by cutting the rope with a concealed knife. From artistic evidence we know that certain tricksters used the classic ball-and-cups game to deceive onlookers by sleight of hand. The subject is common in fifteenth-century German art; late in the century Hieronymus Bosch (ca. 1450–1516) did a drawing of this motif, and early in the following century he executed a painting of it. Like earlier artists, Bosch pokes fun at the folly of the spectators who are duped by the clever illusionist.[48]

In other cases the tricks that later medieval magicians had up their sleeves were examples of pure mischief, inflicted on unsuspecting victims. The manuscripts tell how to frighten a companion by making a torch explode in his face, how to make people itch in their beds, how to turn them black as they bathe, how to make their dinner meat appear raw or wormy, and so forth ad infinitum and, no doubt, ad nauseam.

Magic of this kind might find its way into various sorts of manuscript. Sometimes it appears in collections of medical material or in general potpourris of magical lore. One medical miscellany from Germany contains a great deal of straightforward medical lore but mixes in with it prescriptions for invisibility ("take two eyes from a black frog . . ."), for making people appear headless, for finding stolen goods in one's dreams, and so forth.[49] There were special compilations devoted specifically to magical tricks, of which The Supplement to Solomon is one of the better known. It would be difficult to say who would have used this material. A monk might, but so might a physician. Professional qualifications were clearly less important than a stage personality and a desire to entertain.

Almost all of the surviving sources for such magic date from the fourteenth and fifteenth centuries. It may be that the vogue did not set in until that late. What is perhaps more likely is that similar tricks were known much earlier but that they did not get widely recorded until the fourteenth and fifteenth centuries with their proliferation of popular written material. Some evidence of earlier practice does survive: William of Auvergne tells how a magician can make a house appear full of snakes by burning a snakeskin in a place filled with sticks or rushes, so that the flickering of the flame makes these things appear to be writhing serpents. Indeed, many of the tricks with fire seem inspired by Byzantine experiments with "Greek fire," intended primarily for military use.

What historical significance, if any, attaches to this trickery? For various reasons we must at least take passing cognizance of such stuff even if we do not dwell upon it. It is, first of all, one element in the medieval

---

[48] Kurt Volkmann, The Oldest Deception: Cups and Balls in the 15th and 16th Centuries, trans. Barrows Mussey (Minneapolis: Jones, 1956).
[49] Wardale, "A Low German–Latin miscellany".

complex of notions associated with magic, and if we do not take it into account our notions of what medieval people meant by magic will be incomplete. This side of magic may not be primary in medieval culture, as it is in modern culture; when fifteenth-century townspeople thought of magicians they probably did not think first of all about stage performers pulling rabbits out of hats. Yet the performative element is one component of medieval magic. Furthermore, it became linked in complex ways with other, more sophisticated or more sinister forms of magic, as we will see. Joachim Ringelberg in the sixteenth century referred to such tricks as entertaining diversion from otherwise taxing studies, and perhaps they served this function in earlier centuries as well. There is no reason to think this trickery was exclusively a learned craft, but when taken over by scholars it might well provide light distraction from their study of astrology, alchemy, and other heady pursuits.

Magical tricks were also the stuff of literature, particularly the fabliaux: short, often bawdy tales of the high and late Middle Ages, usually telling the exploits of those lower classes that were presumed incapable of noble conduct. In one fabliau a swindling enchanter is said to be able to transform a cow into a bear, and another can create coins out of little fragments of debris. A peasant taken in by such tricks sets out to make a fortune by such means, but ends by giving his soul to the Devil. Elsewhere the authors play upon the double sense of the word "enchant": the magician is one who can enchant the audience itself with his deceiving tongue. Yet another fabliau tells of a peasant from whom two thieves steal a ham, whereupon the peasant regains the meat by trickery. Both the original theft and the subsequent recovery are said to be cases of "enchant-ment." An English poem of the fifteenth century, "Jack and His Stepdame," follows in the tradition of the fabliaux. A stranger gives Jack various magical favors, including a pipe that causes its hearers to dance about madly. Taken to court as a "great necromancer" and a "witch" for this and other pranks, Jack begins playing his pipe and causes everyone present to dance and tumble until they promise to let him go free.[50]

The power of Jack's magical pipe might be mysterious, but most magical trickery, even in the fabliaux, worked in natural ways – like the other forms of magic we have surveyed in this chapter. The powers in question were occult in only a crude sense: the magician knew them full well, but tried to keep them hidden from the audience or the victims. What we have here is thus, in a sense, a parody of natural magic. Thomas

---

[50] Raleigh Morgan, Jr., "Old French *jogleor* and kindred terms: studies in mediaeval Romance Lexicology", *Romance Philology*, 7 (1954), 301–14; Melissa M. Furrow, ed., *Ten Fifteenth-Century Comic Poems* (New York: Garland, 1985), 67–153.

Betson does not say that the effects of his simple tricks will *be* magic, but that many people will *think* they are magic. Or perhaps we should say that for lack of an immediate explanation people who wished to be entertained would suspend their disbelief and pretend for the moment that the magician had awesome powers over nature. For the bulk of the populace, however, this distinction would have been a fine point.

5

THE ROMANCE OF MAGIC IN COURTLY CULTURE

•

The word "magic", like many related words, began as a term of abuse but has taken on more positive connotations. Particularly the adjectival forms of these words, "magical," "enchanting," "charming," "fascinating," and even "bewitching," now stand for objects and experiences that are out of the ordinary but alluring and attractive.[1] This shift in usage came after the Middle Ages, but for background to it we must turn to the portrayal of magic in medieval courtly culture, and especially in the literary romances written for that culture. People at court clearly recognized that certain magical practices could be sinister and destructive; there is ample evidence that kings and courtiers feared sorcery at least as much as commoners did. In their imaginative literature, however, they were willing to accord it a different status and to consider without horror the symbolic uses of magical motifs. Even sorcerers in courtly literature were figures in an enchanted realm. On one level this literature offered escape from the humdrum realities of life, but on a deeper level it reflected the social and psychological complexities of courtly society, and made possible for medieval and for modern readers a richer understanding of that life.

The court as an institution and a cultural center had existed well before the twelfth century – the court of Charlemagne (reg. 768–814) at Aachen is a classic instance – but it was during that century in particular that rulers of all sorts began rivaling each other to establish glamorous and impressive courts as tokens of their own splendor. Not only kings had magnificent courts, but also dukes and counts, popes and bishops, and lesser rulers. Women might exercise political and cultural dominance at certain courts,

---

[1] For parallel cases, cf. the nouns "glamor" and "prestige." I owe this list and the observation about it to Barbara Newman.

as did Eleanor of Aquitaine (ca. 1122–1204) and her daughter Marie of Champagne (1145–98). Clerics left a profound mark on some courts, but rulers elsewhere prided themselves on their freedom from clerical influence. In any case, rulers surrounded themselves with officials, advisers, servants, physicians, relatives, and friends. Among their advisers and aides might be astrologers and magicians. And among the entertainers who came to court there might be minstrels to celebrate the exploits of fictional courtiers in a world charged with enchantment.

MAGICIANS AT COURT

It has been argued that the medieval court, particularly from the thirteenth century on, was an especially good breeding-ground for magic. The main reason for this, it is suggested, is the disparity between two levels of power at court. On the one hand there are the officials formally invested with power by the lord: chancellors and chamberlains, treasurers, ambassadors, and others. On the other hand there are the throngs of courtiers who have no formal claim to power but who for various reasons nonetheless wield informal power: relatives and friends of the lord, clerics and mistresses, poets and physicians, and a coterie of servants. Individuals in both groups could rise meteorically to high favor and then plummet. Apart from the inevitable rivalries *within* each of these groups, there was more basic tension *between* them. To the extent that those with unofficial power sought to displace those with official power, the two classes would hold each other in constant suspicion. Those seeking royal favor might use sorcery in doing so. As we will see more fully in a later chapter, there were methods prescribed specifically for gaining favor at court. Love magic could be used by a prospective wife or mistress. And various forms of magic could dispose of rivals and other enemies. Foreigners at court, such as monarchs' mothers-in-law, might have dynastic and other interests different from those of other courtiers, and they might be unscrupulous and surreptitious in their pursuit of those interests. Even when magic was not actually used, the tensions at court could easily lead to suspicion of its employment. In brief, courtly society was ridden with magic and fear of magic.[2]

There is much substance to this picture. Magical assassination and love magic were common allegations in the French court during the early fourteenth century, and they were not uncommon in the English court throughout the late Middle Ages. In 1316 a sorceress who was being interrogated accused Mahaut of Artois, mother-in-law of Philip V of

---

[2] Edward Peters, *The Magician, the Witch, and the Law* (Philadelphia: University of Pennsylvania Press, 1978), 110–37.

France (reg. 1316–22), of using magic to reconcile the king with her daughter. More seriously, she had supposedly used poison (whether magical or ordinary) to kill Louis X (reg. 1314–16) and secure Philip's succession as monarch. In 1441 the duchess of Gloucester was charged with using image magic against Henry VI of England so that her husband the duke might rise in power and perhaps gain the throne. Nor was the papal court immune from such intrigue. Perhaps the best-known cases in which magic was suspected in the papal curia come from the pontificate of John XXII (1316–34). The most celebrated instance of all was that of 1317, in which the bishop of Cahors was executed for involvement with an alleged Jewish magician and other shadowy figures in an attempt on John's life. Not content with poisons, the conspirators allegedly tried to smuggle into the papal palace magical images, with inscriptions attached to them, concealed in loaves of bread.

Yet it is misleading to portray the situation at court as different in principle from that elsewhere. There were rivalries and animosities in all walks of life that led to the use and suspicion of magic; the historical record gives little warrant for taking the courts as distinctive in this regard. We know more about magic at court than in many settings because the records are much more ample. Magic in a rural village might pass unnoticed, but magic at court was likely to arouse the interests of chroniclers and other writers. In many cases – indeed, in all the cases cited above – even when courtiers were charged with magic it was not they but outsiders, common people brought in *ad hoc* from the towns or villages, who are actually supposed to have done the deed.

Within courtly society itself, diviners seem to have been very much in demand. This is the burden of the complaint by John of Salisbury (ca. 1115–80): in a long section of his *Policraticus* he deplores the various magical arts to which courtiers are tempted, but when he turns to specific forms and examples what he delivers is in effect a treatise on divination. His references are almost entirely to the literature of antiquity, and readers who hope to find in his work details about the practice of magic or divination at court will be disappointed. Yet he clearly feels it important, in giving moral guidance for courtiers, to expose the ways and errors of augurs, astrologers, chiromancers, interpreters of dreams, crystal-gazers, and diviners of every stripe. From other sources as well we know there were often astrologers at court, and (as we shall see in a later chapter) they gained special popularity there in the twelfth century.

Apart from diviners and astrologers, rulers might find employment for other specialists in occult practices. Johannes Trithemius (1462–1516), though not the most reliable of witnesses, tells of an archbishop of Trier who depleted his treasury in buying books of alchemy and hiring alchemists. One of his successors retained his own alchemist for twelve years, until the alchemist went off to serve the duke of Württemberg. The case of Conrad Kyeser is instructive. Evidently a physician by training, Kyeser did service on the battlefield and as a diplomat, for Duke Stephan III of Bavaria-Ingolstadt among others. He fell from favor, first because of his role in the crusade that terminated in disaster at Nicopolis in 1396, and secondly because he took the wrong side in imperial politics at the turn of the century. To satisfy his ambition and regain favor, he decided to write a great work on warfare, his *Bellifortis*, which he dedicated to the emperor Rupert. The work is replete with descriptions and pictures of marvelous, fanciful engines of war, torches that cannot be extinguished (thanks to technology borrowed from Byzantine sources), and various kinds of herbal and animal magic. The hide from the breast of a deer, he says, will give special protection against wounds in battle, and feathers or hairs from animals killed in the hunt will guide arrows to their goal. Perhaps the most remarkable feature of the collection is that the text is all put into elaborate and often dense Latin verse. One of the most perplexing sections is one where Kyeser recommends making a candle out of used wax, tow, and the brine from the umbilicus of a new-born baby. "You can carry it where you will, on a moon-lit night, and you will see its effect." Then he adds that a lantern can be made if fat from a hanged man is added to the concoction. The text is accompanied by a picture showing a castle (probably Karlstein, outside of Prague) with a trumpeter on a tower, a new moon in the sky, a naked impish figure riding toward the castle on a long stick, and another such figure carrying a candle (Fig. 9). Was this simply another recipe for a magical light, or did Kyeser intend some other effect? The author was a man of considerable education and some practical skill as a physician and engineer, but he was also fond of covering his practical counsel with a dark cloak of mystery. Did he hope to impress the emperor more effectively in that way? If so, we have no indication whether he succeeded.

Royal and aristocratic courts were also graced with various kinds of entertainers whose repertoire might include performative magic. Chrétien de Troyes (ca. 1140–ca. 1190), describing the fictional marriage of Erec and Enide, tells how minstrels from all over the countryside came to provide entertainment for the occasion: "one leaps, another does acrobatics and another performs magic tricks; one tells tales, one sings, others play on the harp," and so forth.[3] Another fictional work recounts how a magician renowned for his feats of "necromancy," "enchantment," and "conjuration" is brought to court to entertain the hero. He

---

[3] Chrétien de Troyes, *Arthurian Romances*, trans. D. D. R. Owen (London: Dent, 1987), 27.

Fig. 9. Magical activities at a castle, from Conrad Kyeser's *Bellifortis*

can turn stones into cheese, cause oxen to fly, or have asses play on harps, or so it seems to his astonished audience. He appears to cut off someone's head, but the severed head turns out to be a lizard or a snake.[4] Other magicians in literature can turn animals into knights, make water run uphill, increase the size of rooms, or conjure forth hundreds of knights to joust with each other. Their accomplishments may have exceeded those of

[4] For this and numerous other examples, see DeLaWarr Benjamin Easter, *A Study of the Magic Elements in the Romans d'Aventure and the Romans Bretons* (Baltimore: Furst, 1906). I have also used extensively Easter's dissertation, from Johns Hopkins University, of which his published book is a portion.

real-life magicians, but they provided a high standard for emulation. Nonfictional accounts sometimes wrote disparagingly of such magic: Roger Bacon and Marsilio Ficino both expressed disdain for the sleight of hand, ventriloquism, and illusions of performative magicians. Neither Bacon nor Ficino was writing specifically about magicians at court, and we can perhaps assume that the peformers who did go to court had more sophisticated versions of the tricks performed in the marketplace. The less accomplished magicians, like most popular performers, could expect only revilement from respectable society. At times, indeed, the "illusions" enacted at court seem to have involved elaborate and expensive staging of entertainments, done very much by craft rather than through necromancy.[5]

One might suppose that there were two distinct categories: astrologers and other diviners to serve as advisers at court and provide serious counsel for practical use, and minstrels and mimes who could lighten the life at court with their stories about magic and displays of magic. The case of Conrad Kyeser, however, should caution us against such a simple distinction. He sought to win favor at court with a book that mixed hard-headed technology with an air of fantasy. In this respect he was probably not exceptional. Magicians who could do extraordinary things and astrologers who claimed to read the future in the stars were individuals who could arouse wonder. Their skills might also have practical relevance, but in any event the state of wonder would in itself be gratifying. They could be both counselors and entertainers. Their counsel was probably taken with selective seriousness, heeded when their courtly patron found it plausible and prudent, but otherwise taken – in both senses of the word – lightly.

MAGICAL OBJECTS: AUTOMATONS AND GEMS

When literary texts spoke of magical spectacles provided for the entertainment of courtly audiences, the wonders they recounted had their counterpart in the real life of the courts. The technology for creating mechanical men and beasts had been known since antiquity: Philo of Byzantium and Hero of Alexandria had written treatises on such things. In the early medieval centuries this technology was better preserved in the Byzantine and Muslim worlds than in Western Europe. When traveling Westerners encountered mechanical angels that blew trumpets, or clocks on which mechanical horsemen signaled the passing hours, they were understandably awestruck. In the tenth century Liutprand of Cremona

[5] Laura H. Loomis, "Secular dramatics in the royal palace, Paris, 1378, 1389, and Chaucer's 'tregetoures'", *Speculum*, 33 (1958), 242–55.

visited the imperial court at Constantinople and reported on the marvelous Throne of Solomon displayed there:

Before the emperor's seat stood a tree, made of bronze gilded over, whose branches were filled with birds, also made of gilded bronze, which uttered different cries, each according to its varying species. The throne itself was so marvelously fashioned that at one moment it seemed a low structure, and at another it rose high into the air. It was of immense size and was guarded by lions, made either of bronze or of wood covered over with gold, who beat the ground with their tails and give a dreadful roar with open mouth and quivering tongue.[6]

By the thirteenth century the technology for such devices had become widely known in the West. All that was required to build them was money, which meant that they were typically playthings for the nobility. In the late thirteenth century the count of Artois fitted out a palace at Hesdin with automatons, a room equipped to create the illusion of thunderstorms, and, among many other such curiosities, "eight pipes for wetting ladies from below and three pipes by which, when people stop in front of them, they are whitened and covered with flour."[7]

To appreciate the fascination with these devices we must bear in mind that major advances were occurring in mechanics and engineering in and around the thirteenth century. This was the age that saw the birth of windmills, the rebirth of stone bridges, and numerous other developments. It comes as no surprise to find Roger Bacon stimulated to speculation that must have struck most contemporaries as wild-eyed: sea-going ships can be made which a single man can steer, and which move more rapidly than if propelled by oarsmen; a fast-moving vehicle can be constructed that goes without being pulled by any living being; a flying machine can perhaps be made, with artificial wings moved by a crank; optical devices might strike terror into an army by creating the illusion of a great opposing force. Bacon's readers might be impatient for such developments, but in the meantime they at least had mechanical birds and illusions of thunderstorms to keep them enchanted.

No matter how well known these mechanisms became, writers of fiction persisted in teasing their readers with the suggestion that such things were done by "necromancy." But it was not only in the realm of fiction that mechanical wonders might seem magical: when the fifteenth-century physician Giovanni da Fontana laid out schemes for making clocks, mechanical carriages, combination locks, alchemical furnaces, and many more such devices, he evidently took pride in the reputation he gained as a demon-conjuring magician. Similarly, when Conrad Kyeser

⁶ William Eamon, "Technology as magic in the late Middle Ages and Renaissance", *Janus*, 70 (1983), 175 (with translations of quotations).   ⁷ Ibid., 176.

devised military machines in the early fifteenth century he took no pains
to distinguish his skill in engineering from his fascination with magic: one
of his battle wagons took the form of a giant cat with its claws outstretched
in a threatening gesture. One scarcely knows whether medieval people
beholding such wonders did so in a spirit of awestruck terror, in a mood of
playful fascination, or with a mixture of both.

It was probably a different combination of attitudes that inspired the
collection of magical gems. There is little about these that one could call
playful; rather, they were marks of that sumptuous magnificence in which
courtiers would rival each other. Royalty and nobility had no exclusive
hold on precious gems, not even on those with magical power. A grocer
named Richard de Preston, for example, is known to have donated to St.
Paul's at London a sapphire with virtue to cure ailments of the eyes, and
doubtless there were other commoners who obtained and kept such items.
In the nature of things, however, those with political power had more
wealth than most people to spend on these jewels, and their life at court
called for a habit of extravagance which made the display of gems normal.
All the better if a precious stone not only looked beautiful and advertised
its bearer's magnificence but also cured diseases and performed other
wonders.

It is not surprising, then, that most of the magical gems for which we
have evidence were found at court. Inventories of royal or aristocratic
treasuries afford numerous examples. A ring from the late fourteenth
century, discovered at the Palace of Eltham, is set with five diamonds and a
ruby, and has an inscription promising luck to its wearer. Charles V of
France (reg. 1364–80) had a stone which could aid women in childbirth,
and an inventory of the ducal treasury of Burgundy in 1455 lists a similar
item. Hubert de Burgh was accused in 1232 of having taken a gem from
the king's treasury which bestowed invincibility in combat; allegedly he
had given it to one of the king's enemies. Various kinds of stone were
prized for their ability to detect poison, a function that would always
prove helpful at court. One chronicle suggests that when gems were in
proximity to poison they would break out in a kind of sweat. Such notions
may seem fanciful, but clearly they were meant seriously. Thus, in 1408
the duke of Burgundy had a stone set in a ring as a means for detecting
poison.

Quite often the magical power of the stone itself was enhanced by that
of inscriptions. One example which in many ways typifies the tendency is
a fourteenth-century ring from Italy (Fig. 10a). The ring itself is gold. It is
set with a "toadstone." This stone, which counted as precious, allegedly
came from the head of a toad, though actually it was a fossil derived from a
certain kind of fish. The ring is inscribed with two lines from the Gospels,

Iesus autem transiens per medium illorum ibat (Latin for Luke 4:30, "But Jesus passed through their midst") and *Et verbum caro factum est* (John 1:14, "And the Word became flesh"). There is precedent for use of both these texts on talismans.[8] Similar examples can be found from many parts of Europe from the thirteenth century onward.

In more than one way the power of gems could be linked with that of the saints. Reliquaries with saints' bones in them were sometimes set with gems, presumably to render honor to the saints thus enshrined, but perhaps also to heighten the wonder-working power of the relics. A different kind of link is to be found in legend: St. Edward the Confessor (reg. 1042–66) was said to have given a ring to a beggar, who took it with him to Rome and brought it back just before the monarch died (Fig. 10b). The ring, thus sanctified, was enclosed in Edward's coffin until 1163, when it was removed and used to cure epilepsy. In a case like this religion fuses altogether with natural magic.

Books called "lapidaries" set out in detail the wondrous properties of gems. The genre was known even in antiquity, but for medieval Europe the classic was the *Book of Stones* by Bishop Marbode of Rennes, from the late eleventh century. Marbode claims no originality for the contents of his work, but says that he is putting a previous collection into verse form for the reading of a small circle of friends, presumably people close to the episcopal court. God himself, Marbode affirms, has endowed precious stones with singular power. While herbs contain great strength, that of jewels is far greater. The sapphire, for instance, has a wide range of physical effects. Being inherently "cold," it can counterbalance excessive bodily heat and reduce perspiration. If pulverized and administered in milk it is good for ulcers, headaches, and other ailments. Furthermore, it has spiritual and moral powers. It dispels envy and terror, induces peacefulness, and even renders God favorable to supplication.

Other lapidaries, mostly following Marbode's, further disseminated such lore, telling the magical uses of each precious stone: one could cure gout and eye diseases, another could defend against madness and wild beasts, yet another could render a garment fireproof. Several stones were prized for their luminosity. Stones can even aid in theft: a burglar need only sprinkle a crushed magnet over hot coals, and the occupants of the house will mysteriously depart, leaving the place easy prey for burglary. Certain gems aid in "prophecy": placed presumably in the speaker's mouth, they educe truths that would otherwise remain hidden. Or they can be used to compel others to divulge the truth. A man who doubts the chastity of his wife, for example, can place a magnet against her head while

[8] O. M. Dalton, *Franks Bequest: Catalogue of the Finger Rings, Early Christian, Byzantine, Teutonic, Mediaeval and Later . . . in the Museum* (London: British Museum, 1912), 142.

Fig. 10a. Italian ring, fourteenth century

Fig. 10b. Edward the Confessor giving a ring to a peasant, from a thirteenth-
century manuscript

she is lying in bed, and if she has been unfaithful she will fall on to the floor. There were some who doubted these wondrous powers, but others vigorously defended such notions. Gervase of Tilbury (ca. 1152–ca. 1220) ridiculed the scoffers, and told how Solomon himself was the first to perceive the magical virtues of gems.

While the lapidary was never exclusively a courtly genre, medieval lapidaries seem to been especially popular at court. One such work was even ascribed to a monarch, Alfonso the Wise of Castile and León (reg. 1252–4), and the printed editions of one French lapidary say that it was translated from Latin for the sake of René of Anjou (1408–80). In the later Middle Ages it is likely that the genre had a far wider audience, and even works written originally for courtly consumption might reach noncourtly readers, as did other, more specifically courtly forms of literature. It is tempting to see the lapidary as a kind of user's manual for the wonder-working gems found in the royal or aristocratic treasury, but there is only rough correspondence between the gems listed in the lapidaries and those known to have been worn or otherwise used at court. One can imagine a courtier delighting in the knowledge that the sapphire induces prophecy. One can even imagine the courtier experimenting, with results we can only conjecture, to test the truth of this knowledge. It is difficult not to suppose, however, that we have once again come upon the border between instruction and entertainment. Much as a faithful Christian would listen with awestruck belief or suspended disbelief to reports of miracle working relics, so too a medieval European might read with awe this information about magical gems. In both cases, the sensation of wonder would be reason enough for listening or reading, and wonder is a state that seldom notes carefully the bounds between fiction and fact.

Further ambiguity surrounds these magical gems: we can assume that their powers were usually seen as natural, but some authors toyed with the notion that they might be repositories of demonic power. One lapidary advises that by pulverizing a gem called diadochos and sprinkling it in water one can evoke the forms of demons and of the dead.

MAGIC IN THE ROMANCES AND RELATED LITERATURE

Even explicitly fictional writings would of course reflect certain realities of courtly culture: they are unhelpful as sources for events, but invaluable as guides to attitudes and values.

French poets of the twelfth century composed extended verse narrations, which were most often based on the chivalrous adventures of King Arthur and his circle. Their stories provided common stock for later romances as well, in France, Germany, and England. While they were set in the immemorial past, in the fantasy world of Arthur's court, they often projected on to that setting the customs of the author's own day: knights in these romances met at tournaments, fought in battles, and went to court more or less the way the author and his audience might do. Yet the Arthurian world of the romances was less predictable than the familiar world of ordinary experience. It was inhabited by monsters of popular mythology, occasionally by angels and demons of Christian lore, and quite regularly by fairies borrowed from Celtic literature.

We know little about most of the authors of these romances. One of the most important, Chrétien de Troyes, wrote in the second half of the twelfth century and was patronized by Countess Marie of Champagne (1145–98) and by the count of Flanders, in whose courts he evidently composed his romances for oral reading. Other writers of romances also seem also to have been patronized by rulers, though there is ample evidence that the genre soon moved outward to noncourtly settings: that people in the towns, for example, were reading romances originally written for courtiers, or else adaptations or translations of these romances.[9] The border between "courtly" and "popular" romances is difficult to define with any clarity. What is clear is that even when the romances were not written for a courtly audience they remained courtly in their content, portraying and glamorizing the lives and adventures of kings, knights, and others at court.

The romances differ strikingly from the sagas in their conception of the foci for magical power. In the sagas, power inheres mainly in words; in the romances it resides more in objects. First, when characters have been wounded they are healed by wondrous herbs and unguents, usually administered by women: not necessarily major figures in the stories, but nurturing and kindly souls who happen to be on hand when a character needs magical refreshment. Secondly there are love potions, such as Tristan and Iseult accidentally drank. Thirdly, the romances abound in luminous and otherwise magical gems, often set in rings, generally used to preserve the characters from danger. One such gem proves its ability to protect the hero from water, fire, and weapons when he has himself thrown into a river with a millstone tied to himself, then walks into a raging fire, and finally enters a duel.[10] Fourthly there are artifacts with marvelous properties: serving dishes that present themselves for use; mechanical birds, lions, chessmen, and angels that appear alive; mechanical heads that talk with their makers; swords that bring sure victory; boats

[9] John Lough, *Writer and Public in France, from the Middle Ages to the Present Day* (Oxford: Clarendon, 1978), 7–30.

[10] Gautier d'Arras, *Eracle*, lines 981–1132, ed. Guy Raynaud de Lage (Paris: Champion, 1976), 31–6.

that sail of their own accord to wondrous harbors unknown to their hapless riders. The world of the romances seems at times a vast toy shop stocked with magical delights. Magical objects of this fourth variety often resemble the automatons and other mechanical wonders actually manufactured for courtly entertainment, and doubtless the fictional and real examples appealed to courtiers for the same mixture of motives: the allure of machines combined with the mystery of the unexplained. Chaucer (ca. 1340–1400) set forth an array of such marvels in *The Squire's Tale*, which is clearly indebted to the romance tradition.

The romances sometimes describe marvelous objects with an element of humor, irony, even self-parody. Luminous gems, for example, may not be an unmixed blessing. If they are set in a bed and blaze brightly through the night, it may be necessary to cover them up if anyone wishes to sleep. And magical unguents may have power that is wondrous to the point of comic effect. Thomas Malory (ca. 1400–71) tells how Sir Gareth beheads another knight and Dame Lynet anoints his severed head and trunk, puts them back together, and thus in effect glues his head back onto his body. Gareth then cuts the knight's head off again, chops it into a hundred pieces, and throws the fragments out the window into the castle moat. Even so, Lynet glues the pieces back together with her extraordinary ointment and revives the victim.[11]

The romances often lay down conditions for use of these objects. A magic bridge may be crossable only by those who possess all knightly and godly graces. A boat may give passage only to riders innocent of treachery, treason, and boasting; a passenger who utters a boast may be plunged immediately into the water. A gate may close on a knight who is proud, until he humbles himself in prayer. A magic castle may be invisible to cowards. The Siege Perilous, or "dangerous chair," may only be sat upon by a paragon of all knightly virtues. A magical sword may bring unfailing victory, but only for one who uses it in a righteous cause. An extension of this notion is that of the magical object that only a true ruler can use: Authur shows himself as heir to the throne of Britain by drawing the sword Excalibur from a stone, and Havelok the Dane proves himself ruler of Denmark by blowing a magic horn.

The purveyors of magical objects are often fairies, immortal beings who live in the "Land of Fairy" but occasionally enter the world of mortals and favor certain individuals with magical gifts. The romance *Escanor* bristles with magical objects made by fairies: an entire castle full of them, including a wondrous bed with shining jewels. Elsewhere the fairies provide magical boats, a marvelous tent made of silk, gold, and cypress, or

[11] Sir Thomas Malory, *Le Morte d'Arthur*, vii. 22–3, ed. Janet Cowan, vol. 1 (Harmondsworth: Penguin, 1969), 272–5.

a soft coverlet that protects people from harm, even from harmful thoughts. They may fall in love with human males and attempt to seduce them away to their own world. When they wish to enter the human realm they typically do so at night. They wander in forests and linger by fountains. The ambivalence regarding fairies sometimes found in Irish literature can be seen in the romances as well: they have both good and evil sides, and while they can represent primal paganism they can also be spoken of as "good Christians." They can bestow favors or destruction, according to their individual character, whim, or purpose. They serve other purposes as well, but one of their main functions is to keep the romances well stocked with magical paraphernalia.

Secular magic blends at times into religious observance. Things that are holy in Christian cult can substitute for magical objects, and things that are inherently powerful can have their power enhanced through sacred names or rituals. A sword may have the name of Jesus inscribed on it or relics placed on its pommel. Certain romances tell of people anointed with the very unguent used on Christ's body; one tells how Perceval uses such an unguent to heal his own wounds, to resuscitate his horse, to revive a dead enemy (whom he kills again as soon as the experiment has worked), and then to cure other warriors.[12] When the romances are reworked by clerical or monastic authors these religious elements come much more clearly to the fore. The classic case is *The Quest of the Holy Grail* (early thirteenth century), which takes the theme of then wonder-working chalice of the Last Supper as its central motif, rich with theological and liturgical associations.

Some writers feared that these magical motifs were too superstitious to be redeemed. In the fifteenth century, John Gerson complained that the French passion for romances had accustomed people to all sorts of fabulous and superstitious beliefs. Doubtless he was right in seeing the fascination for romances as one part of a broader interest in fabulous lore, though it seems less obvious that these poems were in themselves the cause of this preoccupation.

In many romances magic is central to the plot. The entire story may revolve about relations between lovers whose fate has been sealed by a magic love potion, or a hero may find himself besotted with love for a fairy who has enchanted him. Magical healing, resuscitation, and shape-shifting may be integral to the plot, or the narration may hinge on magical distortions of time, as when a hero spends a few moments in an enchanted castle and emerges to find that winter has turned to spring.

---

[12] Chrétien de Troyes, *Perceval: The Story of the Grail*, trans. Nigel Bryant (Cambridge: Brewer, 1982), 222–5.

Often, however, magic is less important in itself than as a symbol or indicator of some psychological state. Indeed, the same instance of magic may function differently in different versions of the same story. For one author, the love potion that Tristan and Iseult drink magically and irreversibly seals their fate; for another, the magical character of the potion is unclear, and the potion serves as a symbol or pointer, calling attention to the psychological interaction between the lovers. Similar variation can be seen in the romances of King Horn. When Horn goes into battle all he needs to conquer his enemy is a glance at a ring given him by his beloved. In popular versions of the romance it is clear that the ring is exerting magical force, but the courtly Anglo-Norman *King Horn* is more subtle, and leaves open the possibility that the moving force is in fact the hero's love. Again, when a magician makes the dangerous coastal rocks of Brittany seem to disappear in Chaucer's *Franklin's Tale*, the event itself is not as important as reactions to it: no one even goes to the coast to verify that the magic has occurred, but the reported success of the magician's power sets in motion a series of crises in the characters' lives. Pliny and other sources relate the notion that leprosy can be cured with the blood of an innocent person; what is distinctive about the story of *Poor Henry*, by Hartman von Aue (ca. 1200), is that the patient is cured of his moral flaws – and thus also of the leprosy that symbolizes those flaws – not by the actual use of a young girl's blood but by the realization that she is willing to be sacrificed for his sake.[13] In all of these cases it would be misleading to say that because magic occurs in the story, the tale is one about magic. In the more subtle and skilfully crafted romances the focus is usually on inward states of mind and soul, which may be just as mysterious as any magic, and the magical motifs function as ploys for developing the inner lives of the characters.

The subordination of magic to psychology is especially clear when the plot hinges precisely on the non-use of a magical object. In *The Two Lovers*, a story by Marie de France (late twelfth century), the suitor is required to carry his beloved up a high mountain before he can marry her. He is too proud to drink the magic potion that will enable him to do so, and though his love is thus shown to be as strong as magic, his exertions kill him. Chrétien de Troyes also plays upon the non-use of magic in *Yvain*. The hero goes in search of adventures, equipped with a ring from his bride that will protect him from all adversity. In a year he is to return to her, but a year passes and he fails to return. In the meantime he has not used his ring, but his possession of it tells us something important: it is not

---

[13] Saul Nathaniel Brody, *The Disease of the Soul: Leprosy in Medieval Literature* (Ithaca, NY: Cornell University Press, 1974).

Fig. 11. Lancelot releasing captives from a magic dance, from a fourteenth-
century manuscript

adversity that has held him back, but his inability to balance his quest for adventure with commitment to his bride.[14]

The plot of a romance often presents magic as part of a preestablished situation: a castle has been enchanted, or a sword has had a spell cast on it, at some time prior to the action in the romance, whether by a human adversary or by a fairy. The adventure now narrated involves the *disenchantment* of the place or object, the undoing of the original enchantment. In *The Book of Lancelot of the Lake*, the hero enters a wood and discovers a band of knights and damsels singing and dancing around a chair that bears a golden crown. As soon as he joins them he loses all memory and is trapped in the dance. When he sits on the chair and has the crown placed on his head, however, the enchantment is broken. He then learns how the dancers were enchanted, many years beforehand, and how they could not be released until the "best and handsomest knight in the world" sat on the chair and wore the crown (Fig. 11). The hero works the disenchantment without intending or even knowing how to do so. He simply pursues adventure into an unknown realm where the magical power of his very person suffices to break the enchantment. (There are other romances in which disenchantment requires some heroic effort.) Only afterward do hero and reader learn the background to the original spell; the romances delight in presenting their heroes with mysterious situations and pitting them against disguised adversaries, and their willingness to undertake adventures without key knowledge is one test of their prowess.[15]

The magicians depicted in the romances are almost always secondary figures, foils for the heroes. Whether allies or antagonists, they serve mainly to aid or challenge the heroes in their quest for adventure and in their attainment of knightly virtue. Merlin, tutor of King Arthur, is the offspring of a demon father who raped his human mother, and from his father he inherits magical and prophetic powers. He aids Arthur by casting a spell on enemy troops, causing them to fall asleep, and he prophesies the outcome of future combat. In the major Arthurian sources – from Geoffrey of Monmouth's fanciful but seminal *History of the Kings of Britain* (twelfth century) to Thomas Malory's grand summation of Arthurian lore in the *Morte Darthur* (fifteenth century) – Merlin demonstrates his wondrous powers early on and then is quickly dispatched, allowing Arthur to mature on his own without preternatural help. Arthur's sister Morgan le Fay (i.e. "the Fairy"), at times nurturing and helpful, is nonetheless mainly a thorn in Arthur's side. According to Malory she

---

[14] Helen Cooper, "Magic that does not work", *Medievalia et Humanistica*, n.s., 7 (1976), 131–46, used here extensively.
[15] *The Vulgate Version of the Arthurian Romances*, ed. H. Oskar Sommer, vol. 5 (Washington: Carnegie Institute, 1912), 120–4, 148–52, with English glosses.

learned "necromancy" in a nunnery where she was sent as a girl. She has learned her lessons well: she provides healing unguents; to evade capture she transforms herself, her horse, and her companions into marble blocks; she devises a splendid jewel-studded mantle which bursts into flame when worn; and out of love for Lancelot she kidnaps him with an enchantment that puts him to sleep. At one juncture a foreign king solicits the aid of Morgan and a friend of hers, asking them to "set all the country in fire with ladies that [are] enchantresses." In case after case, her mischief serves not merely for incidental interest but as provocation to the heroes, who must exercise their own cunning to evade her traps. In other romances as well, the heroes' knightly prowess is tested, proved, and reinforced by conflict with magicians. Gawan, in Wolfram von Eschenbach's *Parzival* (early thirteenth century), heroically withstands a series of ordeals, culminating in hand-to-paw struggle with a hungry lion, and his success breaks the spell by which the wizard Clinschor holds a castle full of hapless captives. Clinschor himself, however, does not even appear in the romance: his story is told by other characters, but he remains mysteriously in the wings, leaving the stage to Gawan.

Is the magic of the romances natural or demonic? Generally the question is not addressed explicitly, even if there are clues pointing in one direction or another. When the visiting knight in Chaucer's *Squire's Tale* appears with a complement of magical artifacts, bystanders immediately begin speculating on possible natural causes for their wondrous powers. If a sword can slice through thickest armor and inflict incurable wounds, perhaps that is because it has been tempered in some special way with the proper chemicals. Elsewhere the reader or audience is teased with deliberate uncertainty about a magical device, which may be fashioned by "craft" (natural means) or "necromancy" (diabolical agency). Clinschor may be intended as a demonic magician, but Wolfram gives only indirect suggestions to that effect.

In the romance of *Wigalois* (thirteenth century) the pagan magician Roaz of Glois appears as an explicitly demonic magician. Early in the work we are told that he has given himself to the Devil, who in return performs wonders and secures land for him. In the end, however, the hero Wigalois defeats him in single combat. Wigalois himself is protected by a slip of parchment with a prayer written on it, and by the sign of the cross which he has made on approaching the castle. As the hero fights with his heathen foe, Roaz' richly adorned wife looks on from her high seat, flanked by maidens who illuminate the scene with tall candles. The presence of these women, and the recollection of Wigalois' own beloved, has a powerful effect on the fighters, giving them strength for their combat. A manuscript of this romance, copied and illustrated in 1372 by a

Cistercian monk under the patronage of the duke of Brunswick-Grubenhagen, depicts this scene with a vivid splendor designed to evoke a sense of enchantment (Fig. 12a).

Even when magic was most explicitly demonic, then, it held a kind of romantic fascination. The demons themselves may not be glamorized, but their magical effects do take on a wondrous aura. The rulers and courtiers for whom such material was originally written would surely not have been dazzled and entertained by genuine demonic magic in their midst, but within the realm of imaginative literature they were willing to take a more nuanced view. Magic might be evil, but it had its allurements. The magic dance in *The Book of Lancelot* was originally devised by a clever cleric as an entertainment for a lady whose favors he sought. The cleric's ruse may have been worked by necromancy, and it may eventually have palled, but the reader can understand why the lady would succumb to this temptation. It would be too much to suggest that the romances portray demonic magic sympathetically, but not too much to say that they make its dangerous attractions clear.

It was not only the Arthurian tradition that provided magical lore for writers of romances. During the twelfth and thirteenth centuries the ancient poet Virgil, long revered for his great learning, came to be seen as a maker of magical artifacts, as an adept of the magical arts, and finally as a servant of the Devil. One legend, reminiscent of the story of Aladdin, told how he gained his knowledge of the occult arts from twelve demons whom he had released from a bottle in which they were trapped (Fig. 12b). To some extent the legend of Virgil intersected with the romance tradition. Wolfram represented Clinschor as the poet's nephew, and some of Virgil's magical inventions (especially a mirror that reflects events from all over the Roman Empire) are adapted and included in the story of Clinschor. In the compilation *Dolopathos* Virgil teaches the hero's son astrology, and in *Escanor* he even tutors a fairy in the magic arts.

An entirely distinct body of material, which also became subject matter for romances, pertained to Alexander the Great and those in his service, such as Aristotle. Stories of Alexander are replete with gems that counteract the enchantments used in combat, wondrously fashioned animals with mechanical birds on their antlers, and other magic. When certain of Alexander's "barons" are transporting gems, demons assault them physically, and invisible hands hurl sticks and stones about their camp; the precious stones turn out to be owned by the demons, who jealously guard them for their occult powers. When Alexander establishes possession of them they prove their magical power by protecting him from wild beasts and demons.

With the stories of Alexander, however, we enter a new area of

Fig. 12a. Combat of Wigalois with Roaz the Enchanter, from a fourteenth-
century manuscript

Fig. 12b. Virgil breaking a bottle containing demons, from a fourteenth-century manuscript

inquiry. These legends had been preserved in various traditions: Greek, Latin, Arabic, Armenian, and so forth. While much of the Alexander tradition was known in earlier medieval Europe, it was supplemented in the later Middle Ages by new lore, which entered into the West as part of a large body of material ascribed to Alexander's tutor Aristotle. If these tales are relevant to the study of courtly romance, they are also part of a different topic: the infusion of Arabic learning that significantly altered Western notions of philosophy, science, and magic.[16]

[16] George Cary, *The Medieval Alexander*, ed. D. J. A. Ross (Cambridge. Cambridge University Press, 1956).

6

ARABIC LEARNING AND THE OCCULT SCIENCES

——— • ———

As we have seen, the common tradition of magic was by no means uniform, but varied its themes from time to time and from place to place. We have also seen how the rise of the courts as cultural centers around the twelfth century brought something new, which existed alongside the older forms of magic. A far more basic change was introduced in the twelfth century, however, with the rise of a new kind of learning that included scientific astrology and alchemy. The common tradition itself had incorporated elements of classical lore: remedies from Pliny or from Marcellus Empiricus, for example, were included in medieval leechbooks. But the new learning claimed to be more deeply rooted in ancient philosophy and science, and presented itself in a more rigorous and sophisticated guise. Like most forms of scholarship it lent itself to popularization, and thus the boundaries between the common tradition and the new magical learning did not remain rigid. Yet the fact remains that in the twelfth century something new was introduced, however complex its relationship with the older tradition became.

One qualification must be made at once. The people who studied astrology and alchemy in the twelfth and following centuries would not usually have thought of themselves as magicians. Their *enemies* might so brand them: those conservatives who harked back to Isidore of Seville included astrology, if not alchemy, under the heading of magic. It was only in later centuries, especially at the end of the Middle Ages, that practitioners began to see themselves as engaged in natural magic. In the meantime, however, both conceptual and practical links were forged between the new learning and the common tradition which make it impossible to study the one in isolation from the other.

THE TRANSFORMATIONS OF EUROPEAN INTELLECTUAL LIFE

In very broad terms there were two major factors that deeply affected the intellectual life of Europe in the later Middle Ages: first, the rise of universities out of earlier cathedral schools; and second, the importation of Arabic learning, including the transmission of Aristotelian philosophy and science from Arabic culture.

The major centers for learning in the early Middle Ages had been for the most part monastic. There were places one could go for medical study, and people with learning were sometimes attached to courts, but the only places that provided systematic education in a variety of subjects were monasteries. From the eleventh century, however, it was schools attached to the cathedrals that fostered most advancement in learning. Located in the towns, these cathedral schools provided education for some of the diocesan clergy, and also for people who, without intending to become priests, wanted preparation in the liberal arts so they could proceed to legal careers or service to rulers. If a cathedral school had a particularly eminent teacher it might draw students from all across Europe; Latin was the language of instruction in any event, so linguistic boundaries posed no difficulty. In the second half of the twelfth century a major further development occurred, the rise of universities. By the late fourteenth century there were universities throughout Europe, which continued to teach the liberal arts but also had faculties for theology, medicine, and law.

If magic had any place in the university curriculum it was only indirectly. Astronomy was one of the liberal arts, and could be taught in such a way as to include astrology, which traditionally was included among the branches of magic. Indeed, the borders between "astrology" and "astronomy" were fluid in medieval parlance, and the distinction between the two fields was drawn in various ways. Raymond of Marseilles equated the two terms, for example, while the *Mirror of Astronomy* ascribed (probably rightly) to Albert the Great distinguished the disciplines and dealt with both of them. What is most important for the history of magic is that the universities produced educated individuals who could go on to study learned forms of magic or "occult sciences" even if these were not subjects for formal study.

The cathedral schools and universities fostered a commitment to intellectual inquiry which led many scholars beyond an interest in the traditional texts. What this meant in most cases is that they wanted more knowledge about classical learning, which they could obtain from scholars in the Islamic world. Doing so was difficult: relations between Christendom and Islam had never been cordial, and the Crusades had aggravated the mutual antipathy. Yet there were border territories, particularly Spain and southern Italy, where historical circumstance had brought Christians and Muslims together, and cultural contact was possible in these places.

Among the subjects which Islam had inherited from late Greek antiquity were astrology and alchemy. These sciences had, to be sure, undergone much change. Having been imported into Persia and India, Greek astrology had been developed and modified there, and Arabic astrologers learned and incorporated many of these adaptations. They had also had to respond to challenges within their own culture: Muslims had raised many of the same objections to astrology that Christian writers had posed and would soon revive, and writers such as al-Kindi (d. ca. 873) and Abu Ma'shar (787–86) had to confront this opposition in establishing astrology on a scientific basis and giving it an established place among the branches of learning. Alchemy too was developed among the Muslims, particularly by Jabir ibn Hayyan (ca. 721–ca. 815), known in the West as Geber (and not to be confused with an influential European alchemist of the later Middle Ages who adopted the same name).

During the eleventh century, when Christians of Western Europe were fighting for the reconquest of Spain from the Muslims, they had only slight access to this Arabic learning, but in the twelfth century the floodgates opened. In the twelfth century well over a hundred works were translated from Arabic into Latin, or else written in Latin specifically as paraphrases of Arabic learning. The earliest known translator of the period was Adelard of Bath (ca. 1080–ca. 1155), who translated works on astrology and astral magic as well as an important set of astronomical tables. The most prolific was Gerard of Cremona, with sixty-eight known titles to his credit, including a handful of astrological writings. Abu Ma'shar's *Greater Introduction* to astrology became available in 1133, and Ptolemy's *Tetrabiblos* was translated in 1138. One of the most popular astrological works, a series of a hundred aphorisms falsely ascribed to Ptolemy under the title *Centiloquium*, was translated into Latin at least four times by the middle of the century. Often the translators worked in collaboration with Arabic-speaking aides, perhaps either Christians or Jews, who sometimes did the initial translation into Spanish or another vernacular tongue, leaving it to be put into Latin. Christians engaged in such labor might do so with uneasy conscience: one translator concluded his effort with the tag, "finished, with praise to God for his help and a curse on Mahomet and his followers."[1]

---

[1] Quotation translated by S. J. Tester, *A History of Western Astrology* (Woodbridge: Boydell, 1987), 53. For general information on the transmission of Arabic culture see Charles S. F. Burnett, "Some comments on the translating of works from Arabic into Latin in the mid-twelfth century", *Miscellanea Mediaevalia*, 17 (1985), 161–71; Marie-

It would be misleading to suggest a sudden revolution in medieval thought. While there were many in the twelfth century who absorbed the fruits of Arabic science, there were many more who rejected or ignored these developments. John of Salisbury, for example, rejected astrology but for his knowledge of it drew mainly on Augustine, Macrobius, and Martianus Capella rather than the recently translated Arabic writers. Like most historical changes, the transformation of medieval learning took time for its full impact. By the thirteenth century no one could ignore the flood of Arabic texts that had poured into Western Europe, but even then there were many who opposed it or rejected certain of its implications.

Although European scholars showed particular fervor in absorbing Muslim scholarship, in the process of doing so they absorbed Jewish influences as well. Jewish scholarship had long flourished within the Muslim world; as we have seen, Jews seem to have helped in transmission of Arabic texts to the West. In addition, some Western scholars working in the occult sciences obtained access to specifically Jewish texts. One astrological work, for example, gives Hebrew names for the planets and for the signs of the zodiac, and other data, and its prescriptions for divination require transliterating the letters of a person's name into the Hebrew alphabet for their numerical values.[2] Nor did Western scholars, preoccupied with these new discoveries, neglect earlier Latin materials: works such as Julius Firmicus Maternus's writing on astrology were now rediscovered.

The main beneficiaries of this new learning were men who had been trained in the cathedral schools and in the newly emerging universities. To be sure, the occult sciences did not remain their monopoly. Even in the twelfth and thirteenth centuries, clerical advisers to princes could convey to them the essence of this learning. To some extent in the thirteenth century, and far more in following centuries, Arabic writings and derivative compilations were translated into the vernacular languages for the benefit of laypeople. Throughout the later Middle Ages, however, these new forms of learning would have been primarily the preserve of those with formal education, the clergy and the physicians in particular.

Thérèse d'Alverny, "Translations and translators", in Robert L. Benson and Giles Constable, eds., *Renaissance and Renewal in the Twelfth Century* (Cambridge, Mass.: Harvard University Press, 1982), 421–62; Dorothee Metlitzki, *The Matter of Araby in Medieval England* (New Haven: Yale University Press, 1977); and Tester, *History of Western Astrology*, 147–53.

2 Charles Burnett, "Adelard, Ergaphalau and the science of the stars", in Charles Burnett, ed., *Adelard of Bath: An English Scientist and Arabist of the Early Twelfth Century* (London: Warburg Institute, 1987), 133–46.

Fig. 13a. Twelfth-century Muslim horoscope

THE PRACTICE OF ASTROLOGY

The most basic use of astrology was in making horoscopes, which would indicate the influence that the stars and planets had on a person at birth or at any other juncture in life. Some of the complications of a medieval horoscope can be shown from two twelfth-century examples, one Arabic and one Latin. The Arabic horoscope was done in Egypt, in 1146, for an eight-year-old boy (Fig. 13a). It has a central rectangle, surrounded by twelve rectangular or triangular segments (for the twelve astrological "houses"). Most of the information given in these segments pertains to the positions of the planets on the eighth anniversary of the child's birth: Jupiter, for example, is at a specific location in the constellation Aries. In the margins the astrologer gives the positions of the planets eight years earlier, at the time of the child's birth. Some of the information, however, pertains not to the child himself but to his father; as Ptolemy had recognized, a horoscope for a child can be used as a guide to the future of the child's parent.[3]

---

[3] Bernard R. Goldstein and David Pingree, "Horoscopes from the Cairo Geniza", *Journal of Near Eastern Studies*, 36 (1977), 123–29.

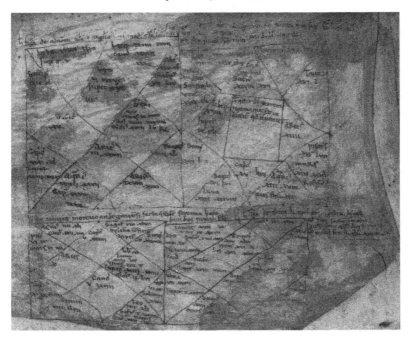

Fig. 13b. Twelfth-century Western horoscopes

The Western manuscript in question actually gives a series of four horoscopes (Fig. 13b). One of them is labeled a "figure for the arrival of a certain person in England." The second has the caption inside a central square: "The question concerning the army of Normandy; and the conclusion is that it will not come." The third pertains to a deceased count of Anjou, and the fourth is a "figure for the commerce between two persons."[4] The astrological information given for these horoscopes points to 1151 as the year to which they refer. They all have political bearing, though their precise intent is obscure. The first one, for example, could be intended as a guide to what will happen if the unnamed person arrives in England, but more likely the question is *whether* he will do so. The question might have been whether Henry of Anjou (1133–89) would invade England with his Norman troops, in which case the horoscope might have been made by a friend of Henry (such as Adelard of Bath) or an enemy.

These horoscopes indicate some of the purposes that astrology served.

[4] J. D. North, *Horoscopes and History* (London: Warburg Institute, 1986), 96–107; cf. idem, "Some Norman horoscopes", in Burnett, ed., *Adelard of Bath*, 147–62.

First, knowing where the stars and planets were located at birth (or on the anniversary of a birth) could show how the heavenly bodies affected a person's character and general destiny. Marriages, career decisions, and other plans might be made accordingly. Secondly, astrology might be used for "interrogations": given a particular time for a trip, a marriage, a battle, or some other vital action, what outcome would this undertaking have? Thirdly, it might be used for "inceptions": given a specific undertaking, what would be the most auspicious moment to undertake it? In the second and third cases the crucial factor would not be the configuration of stars and planets at birth, but rather their location at the present time or the near future.

Astrology had implications for medicine. A surgeon or barber-surgeon was supposed to know which signs of the zodiac governed which parts of the body, because it was dangerous to operate or bleed a patient when the wrong constellation was dominant. Physicians too would need to know such things, and for that reason astrology was studied perhaps more systematically in medical schools than in other branches of medieval universities. The University of Bologna, eminent for its medical studies, had a professor to teach fledgling physicians how to gauge the influence of the stars on human bodies.

Astrological science was also deemed useful for rulers. Various forms of fortune-telling seem to have been popular at court, but none more than astrology. Even in ninth-century Gaul, we are told, all the great lords had their own astrologers, and a chaplain to William the Conqueror (reg. 1066–87) was so dedicated to astrology that it was said he would spend his nights gazing at stars rather than sleeping. After the infusion of Arabic science astrology gained further prominence. Readers of the pseudo-Aristotelian *Secret of Secrets* would have learned from it how Aristotle was supposed to have advised Alexander the Great never to embark on war, indeed not even to eat or drink, sit down or rise up without consulting an astrologer. (The same book also mentions a stone which will secure victory in battle, and a Dominican who translated the work into French pondered why Alexander had to fight so hard when he had such power at his disposal.)

To what extent did rulers actually allow their decisions to be guided by astrology? We know a great deal about their interest in matters astrological, but relatively little about their actual application of this interest in their political affairs. It has been suggested that, while there were astrologers aplenty in late medieval England, the kings seem to have paid them little heed.[5] Elsewhere they seem to have had more influence, though it is not

---

[5] Hilary M. Carey, "Astrology at the English court in the later Middle Ages", in Patrick Curry, ed., *Astrology, Science and Society: Historical Essays* (Woodbridge: Boydell, 1987), 41–56.

always easy to tell whether their alleged influence was merely legendary. One wonders, for example, whether Guido of Montefeltro (d. 1298) really waited for his astrologer (standing atop a belltower) to signal the proper configuration of the stars before he galloped off into battle. Less dramatically, Charles V of France, who founded a college for astrology and astrological medicine at Paris, and who had astrological writings translated into the vernacular, obtained an astrological reading on his bride before marrying her.

According to the chronicler Matthew Paris, the emperor Frederick II (reg. 1215–50) used astrologers to cast his children's horoscopes and to determine whether his plans were destined for success; he did not even consummate his marriage to the empress Isabella until the astrologers had announced the most propitious time for doing so. Michael Scot (ca. 1175– ca. 1235), whose early career had been devoted mainly to natural science, turned more to astrology when he came into Frederick's service. He advised the emperor regarding which phases of the moon were best for seeking counsel, and told Frederick not to have his blood let when the moon was in Gemini, for fear that he would be punctured twice rather than once. Scot himself tells us that the emperor deliberately went to a barber-surgeon at the proscribed time, to test this warning. The barber dismissed the advice and proceeded to let the emperor's blood, but then accidentally dropped his lancet on Frederick's foot and caused a serious wound.[6]

As S. J. Tester has observed, the astrologers' function at court seems to have been ascertaining "when" rather than "what" or "whether."[7] They were charged with finding the most appropriate moment for any crucial act. One historian has surveyed more than two hundred key events in the reigns of the Habsburg dynasty, such as coronations, treaties, marriages, and battles, and has taken the positions of the stars (by medieval reckoning) for each of these events. Marriages turn out to have taken place at astrologically propitious times more often than other occurrences. This is scarcely surprising; it would be difficult to control the timing of battles and other affairs of state, but marriages could easily be postponed to await appropriate conjunctions of the stars.

The emperor Rudolph I seems to have been especially attentive to astrological concerns. Even his birth, while presumably not arranged by deliberate choice, portended an auspicious reign: he was born on 1 May 1218, when Mars and the sun were in close and powerful conjunction, Mars being the planet of war and the sun being a dominant influence for

[6] Charles Homer Haskins, *Studies in the History of Mediaeval Science* (Cambridge, Mass.: Harvard University Press, 1924), 272–98.
[7] *History of Western Astrology*, 196.

monarchs. He was crowned as emperor on 24 October 1273, when the same heavenly bodies were in conjunction. When he fought the most decisive battle of his career, again these bodies were in the most favorable conjunction possible, and he was married under a conjunction of Venus and Mercury. (A conjunction of Venus and the sun might have been still more propitious, but such events occur only about every forty-three weeks, while Venus and Mercury are conjoined roughly twice as often.) Whether Rudolph had an official court astrologer is unknown, but these decisions may have been influenced by Henry of Isny, one of his closest confidants, who could have learned astronomy and astrology during his student years at Paris, and who was present when Rudolph was married. Several chronicles allege that Henry practiced sorcery and had dealings with demons, which may hint at an interest in astrology. In any case, it seems likely that someone with astrological knowledge guided Rudolph in timing key events. Among the Habsburg successors who seem to have continued this practice was the emperor Frederick III (reg. 1440–93), whose complex wedding arrangements may have become so by the need to accommodate both diplomacy and astrology.[8]

What we know for sure is that rulers did not appreciate having astrologers forecast the time and manner of their demise. As in the Roman Empire, so too in medieval Europe predicting the death of a ruler was a hazardous business, at least bordering on treason. One of the men implicated along with Margery Jourdemayne in 1441 was an astrologer who in his written work had explained how to predict a person's death. When he helped show that Henry VI was teetering on the edge of the grave, the king needed an alternative horoscope to recover his composure.[9]

When unaccustomed sights appeared in the sky, galvanizing public attention, the astrologers were the obvious experts to consult for guidance. Thus, in 1368 a comet appeared over much of Europe and provoked much speculation. A German or Polish astrologer, evidently writing in the service of some monarch or prince, saw the comet as a portent of misfortune for Scandinavia and other lands to the North. The fact that it appeared in the house of Taurus was a generally bad sign, portending widespread disease, warfare, death of cattle, conflagrations, frost that would ruin the harvest, and other calamities. Other characteristics of the comet gave warning of violent thunderstorms and of hot winds that would destroy crops. A French astrologer, perhaps also working in the service of a court, interpreted the comet as foretelling misfortune for

---

[8] Helmuth Grössing and Franz Stulhofer, "Versuch einer Deutung der Rolle der Astrologie in den persönlichen und politischen Entscheidungen einiger Habsburger des Spätmittelalters", *Österreichische Akademie der Wissenschaften, Philosophisch-historische Klasse: Anzeiger*, 117 (1980), 267–83.

[9] Carey, "Astrology at the English court", 50–3.

England, since Parisians first saw it in the part of the sky more or less corresponding to the direction of England, and because it was first seen in the house of Taurus. This interpreter also pointed out that the planet dominant at the time the comet appeared was not England's planet Saturn but France's planet Jupiter. In short, ill fortune for the enemy meant good fortune for one's own land, which was news that a monarch would be pleased to hear.[10]

PRINCIPLES OF ASTROLOGY

Astrology presupposed a certain view of astronomy, or the way the cosmos was structured. Certain facts would have seemed obvious to any medieval European: during the course of the day the sun travels in an arch across the southern sky, from east to west; at night the moon proceeds in a similar though not identical path. Both of these heavenly bodies would have been known as "planets." With some astronomical education an observer could learn to distinguish five other planets also moving across the sky in essentially the same way, though at different speeds: Mercury, Venus, Mars, Jupiter, and Saturn. Further from Earth but still traveling along roughly the same path in the sky were twelve constellations that made up the "zodiac": Aries, Taurus, Gemini, and the rest. Whereas the planets moved at various rates of speed, the constellations of the zodiac traveled in a regular progression. The entire series of constellations would travel across the southern sky, then loop around beneath the Earth, while the planets were traversing their own more complex routes along the same basic path.

This much would have been accepted as noncontroversial in medieval educated company. Because everyone recognized that the planets and stars of the zodiac circled the Earth in regular progression, the zodiac itself became a symbol for the passage of time, and was represented as such in various artistic contexts. Signs of the zodiac might occur, for example, in books of hours or prayerbooks for the laity. Their use did not commit an artist or author to any theory about the *influence* that the stars and planets exerted.[11] The zodiac by itself was, in modern terms, astronomical rather than specifically astrological.

Yet most Europeans would also have recognized that these planets and stars, and to a lesser extent other stars outside the zodiac, did influence human affairs in various ways. Precisely what influence they held was intensely controversial. The sun had obvious effects: it illuminated things,

---

[10] Hubert Pruckner, *Studien zu den astrologischen Schriften des Heinrichs von Langenstein* (Leipzig and Berlin: Teubner, 1933), 73–85.

[11] Tester, *History of Western Astrology*, esp. 129.

heated them, and dried them out. But astrologers held that the sun, which is far more noble than earthly fire, could do many other things as well, and could work in subtle and occult ways. So too could the other heavenly bodies. All the planets and stars (and astrologers sometimes referred merely to "the stars" as shorthand for all the heavenly bodies) had some measure of power over earthly affairs, although it might be difficult to determine the nature and degree of a heavenly body's influence. The degree of power exerted by one of these bodies depended partly on its position in the sky. If it was just rising at the eastern horizon it was "in the ascendant," which was an especially powerful position. Directly over-head, too, it would exert strong influence.

If one knew the identity and position of each plant and star one could in large measure gauge the *degree* of its impact. The *nature* of that influence, on the other hand, was inherent in each star and planet, not something relative to its position in the sky. Each planet had its own nature, effects, and areas of influence. The moon was feminine, watery (and thus cold and moist), powerful especially during a person's infancy, and associated with madness (hence "lunacy") and chastity. Venus was feminine, airy (thus hot and moist), powerful in adolescence, and linked with sensuality. So too, each of the other planets had its special characteristics.

The path along which these heavenly bodies traveled was divided into twelve "houses" of unequal size, six of which were in the visible sky and the other six below the horizon. Thus, as a planet moved through the sky it would pass through all twelve houses in succession. The area of life that the planets influenced would depend in part on what house they were in at a given time. A planet in the first house would have general influence on personality, while in the second house it would affect material fortunes, and in the third it would help determine the character of one's family. In other houses, a planet would influence relations with parents or spouse, sexuality and children, health, and so forth. Thus, if Mars happened to be in the tenth house at a crucial time it could mean that one was destined to become a soldier, since Mars was warlike in nature and the planets in the tenth house influenced a person's career. The same planet in the eighth house would have very different meaning: that being the house governing death, it could portend death in battle.

The planets and stars exerted special influence at certain times, particu-larly birth. An infant just coming from the womb was still soft and malleable and thus especially susceptible to the influence of the heavenly bodies. Having Jupiter in the ascendant at birth would be a generally good sign. If Mars were in the seventh house one might expect a stormy marriage. Because the Wife of Bath in Chaucer's *Canterbury Tales* was born with Venus in the ascendant, however, she was fated to a lifetime of sexual passion. Apart from these influences at birth, any critical juncture in life would be an appropriate time to consult the positions of the planets. One would not want to enter battle when Mars was in a weak position, but one might wish to arrange a marriage for a time when Venus was dominant, or perhaps when Venus was close to (or "in conjunction with") the sun, which would strengthen her influence.

The constellations of the zodiac traveled slightly faster than the sun, so that as these bodies revolved around Earth the sun would be traveling with Aries one month, Taurus the next, and so forth. To speak of certain people as "Sagittarians," for example, is to say that they were born at a time of year when the sun was traveling in conjunction with Sagittarius. Modern popular lore has made this factor the very essence of astrology, but in astrological science it was merely one of numerous factors to be weighed in making any prediction. Among the many further complications is the association of planets with constellations: the sun is most powerful when in the same house as Leo, for example, and Saturn is strengthened by Capricorn during the day and by Aquarius at night.

These were the basic principles on which astrology rested.[12] But whether its principles were correct or not was a controversial question, and many would have challenged them. One of the most influential discussions of the matter was in Augustine's *On the City of God*, which admitted that stars might *predict* future events but denied that their motions could *produce* future events. Augustine and later writers rejected the notion that the stars exert a determinist force that would constrain human will. Even the predictive force of astrology was at best tentative and imperfect: otherwise how could one explain the cases of twins who, born under essentially the same astrological influences, nonetheless led very different lives? In following centuries, arguments against astrology came to be routine and derivative. Isidore of Seville acknowledged its role in predicting the weather, and allowed that the heavenly bodies influenced the growth of crops and even human health, but could not believe that the stars regulate human souls or that a person's fate could be read at birth in the stars. Other writers, such as Gregory the Great, borrowed his distinctions or expressed themselves in similar terms. The sheer weight of Augustine's and Isidore's authority was enough to render astrology suspect.

In later medieval Europe certain basic applications of astrology were noncontroversial: its influence on the human body and on climate was generally accepted, and thus there was little objection to its use in healing

---

[12] For a more detailed presentation see Wayne Shumaker, *The Occult Sciences in the Renaissance: A Study in Intellectual Patterns* (Berkeley: University of California Press, 1972).

or in predicting the weather. Far more problematic was its use in predicting human behavior. Helinand of Froidmont, a late twelfth-century
Cistercian monk, argued that for the planets to have the kind of influence
ascribed to them they must have intelligent souls, and thus be either angels
or demons, and if they are angels how can they sometimes do evil? The
most serious objection to astrology in the later Middle Ages was the
danger of determinism: if the stars governed human affairs, did they not
infringe human free will and divine omnipotence? Gerard of Feltre in the
thirteenth century posed the problem sharply in his *Summa on the Stars*: "If
the stars make a man a murderer or a thief, then all the more it is the first
cause, God, who does this, which it is shameful to suggest."[13]

Even as a means for predicting human behavior, however, astrology
had its defenders. The argument was essentially threefold: first the astrologers and their advocates delimited carefully the claims that astrology
could make; secondly they provided examples suggesting that it actually
worked; and thirdly they provided philosophical and scientific support
for its assumptions.

Those who defended astrology typically insisted on certain major
qualifications. First, they insisted that while astrologers of antiquity
actually worshiped the stars those of their own age subjected the stars to
scientific examination. This was in large part a tactic for undercutting the
opposition of Augustine and other early Christian writers; they may have
been right in opposing the idolatrous astrologers of their own era, but
their arguments do not apply to later astrologers. Yet there were more
difficult challenges, such as the problem of determinism which seemed
inherent in all astrology. Drawing on a distinction made even in antiquity,
the defenders of astrology argued that the stars were not causes but merely
signs of future events. This did not altogether solve the problem of
determinism, since even if the stars did not cause events their efficacy as
signs might presuppose some determining cause. Thus, three further
qualifications were vital: astrology could predict general trends but not
particular chance events; it could not predict with certainty; and the free
human will could override the influence of the stars. Freedom of the will
was the most important concern. Perhaps few people availed themselves
of their freedom, yet in principle everyone had the power to overcome
astral influences. Both Albert the Great (ca. 1200–80) and Thomas Aquinas agreed that the stars can influence the body, and that the body in turn
can influence the soul. Thomas in particular argued that most people are
ruled by their bodily passions or appetites; very few have the strength of
intellect and will be needed to overcome their bodily impulses. For the

bulk of humankind, therefore, the influence of the stars upon the body will go unopposed. Yet the will remains free in principle, and those who exert themselves may counter the effects of the stars. The argument was usually supported with a maxim ascribed to Ptolemy: "The wise man rules the stars."[14]

Certain others in the thirteenth and following centuries were more enthusiastic and less critical about astrology. Guido Bonatti denied precisely such qualifications as Thomas maintained. For him astrology held the key to all knowledge:

All things are known to the astrologer. All that has taken place in the past, all that will happen in the future – everything is revealed to him, since he knows the effects of the heavenly motions which have been, those which are, and those which will be, and since he knows at what time they will act, and what effects they ought to produce.[15]

Yet this extreme view was very much a minority opinion. Among philosophers and theologians from the late thirteenth century onward the more common conclusion was that the stars and planets exert a strong yet resistible influence on human affairs. Even this much was sometimes denied: Nicholas Oresme (ca. 1325–82), for example, maintained that the stars influence earthly objects only by shedding heat and light.

Further support for astrology came from appeal to what we would call case histories. One writer from the late twelfth century, for example, told how he had been at Jaffa when a new ship was about to sail. Being known as an astrologer, he was asked to determine what fate the stars held for this vessel. He calculated the position of the heavenly bodies, and began trembling as he realized the ship was destined to founder. He himself escaped disaster by not boarding it, but the crew decided to set sail despite his warning, and soon after they left harbor the vessel was in fact shipwrecked. Another story, set in India, involved two boys, one a prince whose horoscope suggested he should be a craftsman, and the other a weaver's son whose horoscope indicated he should be a great dignitary. The outcome, of course, was that the two boys grew up as the stars decreed, not as their families expected. On the other hand, what about people born under the same stars but in fact destined to very different lives? In response to this challenge the astrologers could cite a tale from Julius Firmicus Maternus about a king and a peasant who were born at the same time. The king ruled over his kingdom; the peasant, while deprived of the same kind of power, nonetheless was a dominant figure who ended

---

[14] The usual forms were *Homo sapiens dominatur astris* or *Sapiens dominabitur astris*; *homo* would usually be read here, as often in medieval Latin, to exclude *femina*.

[15] Theodore Otto Wedel, *The Mediaeval Attitude Toward Astrology, Particularly in England* (New Haven: Yale University Press, 1920), 79 (with quotations translated).

up ruling in his own figurative realm. The logical extension of these stories was the claim that astrology actually rested on empirical study of numerous case histories. One writing of pseudo-Aristotle thus claims to report the results of a survey, in which horoscopes cast for twelve thousand men provided a proper data base for astrology.

More than anything else, however, it was the philosophical and scientific grounding of astrology that gave it a respected position in the European intellectual world. Arabic astrologers such as Abu Ma'shar had refined the philosophical underpinnings for astrology, using eclectic but loosely Aristotelian arguments to show in systematic detail how the more perfect quintessence of the heavenly bodies could exert power over the lesser bodies on Earth. It was the backing of this philosophical cosmology that did most to ensure that astrology would gain credence in the universities of western Europe.

Astrologers might also gain a hearing in Neoplatonist circles. To be sure, there were Neoplatonists whose focus on the "intelligible" world of the spirit drew their attention away from the physical world, but there were also Neoplatonists influenced more by the cosmology of Plato's *Timaeus* and by the work of Macrobius. Those of the latter sort inclined to see the cosmos as an integrated totality, within which even divine influence is mediated through the stars rather than intervening directly upon earth.[16] Even so, however, the Neoplatonist tradition disposed its adherents to see the cosmos as a *living* system with complex and unpredictable influences, not as a system of mechanical and regular influences on which a science of prediction might be based. It is one thing to say in the abstract that the macrocosm of the universe will exert constant impact on the microcosm of the individual human being. It is something quite different to isolate and analyze specific influences, and that was a tendency more to be expected from the Arabic synthesis of learning, with its grounding in Aristotelian cosmology.

While astrology could be useful in ascertaining the influence of the stars and predicting things that would happen, its underlying principles could also be helpful in explaining certain occult or mysterious phenomena within nature. This is a topic that arises in various philosophical writings of the thirteenth and following centuries, and one of the fullest treatments is to be found in Thomas Aquinas's treatise *On the Occult Works of Nature*.[17] The examples Thomas gives are phenomena we would not

[16] Tullio Gregory, "La nouvelle idée de nature et de savoir scientifique au XIIᵉ siècle", in John Emery Murdoch and Edith Dudley Sylla, eds., *The Cultural Context of Medieval Learning* (Dordrecht: Reidel, 1975), 193–218.

[17] Joseph Bernard McAllister, *The Letter of Saint Thomas Aquinas De Occultis Operibus Naturae Ad Quemdam Militem Ultramontanum* (Washington, DC: Catholic University of America Press, 1939).

usually recognize as magical, and indeed he does not apply that term to them: he is trying to explain such things as the power of a magnet to attract iron and the power of rhubarb to act as a medicinal purgative. While his examples are thus quite ordinary, he nonetheless speaks of "occult" powers – those which cannot be ascribed to the physical makeup (or "elements") of the objects in question – and his reasoning would apply to other occult processes that would more often be called magical.

Thomas says at the outset that a higher agent can work through a lower one in either of two ways. The higher agent may impress some kind of "form" upon the lower agent, as when the sun illuminates the moon and causes it to become luminous. Or else it may simply use the lower agent as a tool, the way a carpenter uses a saw. When the lower agent consistently has the same effect every time it is applied, we must assume that the higher agent has impressed a form upon it; such powers are part of the essence of these lower agents. This is the case with the powers inherent in magnets and rhubarb. Where do these forms come from? Thomas, like Aristotle, sees the stars and planets as responsible for the generation and decay of all corruptible bodies: when a mineral is formed in the ground, or a plant grows in the soil, these processes can be traced to the influence of the heavenly bodies, which affect all things on earth by their passing through the sky. It is the stars and planets, then, which by their motion impress those forms on magnets, rhubarbs, and all other things, endowing them with both ordinary and occult powers.

In writing this treatise Thomas was not doing astrology, nor was he even addressing the question whether the stars can foretell human conduct. What he had in common with the astrologers was simply the belief, which both he and they found already worked out in Aristotelian cosmology, that the stars have influence on earthly persons and objects in ways that are not manifest (and are thus "occult"). It is sometimes argued that magic is not in fact a branch of science but rather of technology; it would be more in keeping with medieval usage to say that it is a practical rather than theoretical science. Yet it lent itself to theoretical explanation, and what Thomas was articulating was a theory of the cosmos that could suffice to account for a wide range of occult phenomena.

ASTRAL MAGIC

In the same treatise Thomas explicitly distinguished natural channels of astral influence (such as magnets and rhubarb) from those artificial astrological images sometimes used in magic: images bearing signs of the constellations or planets, through which the power of these heavenly bodies is drawn down and concentrated so that it can be used in magic.

The latter, he says, can work only as tools of some extrinsic agent, by which he means a demon. Others would have disagreed, and argued that such images can have effect naturally, without demonic intervention, though this position is not easy to find in formal philosophical literature. Because this magic sought to change rather than merely learn one's destiny, its effect was entirely distinct from that of astrology proper, and for that reason it has been proposed that it be called "astral" rather than "astrological" magic.[18] Treatises on such magic made their way from the Arabic world to the West: works ascribed sometimes to known historical writers and sometimes to the mythical Hermes Trismegistus.

How this magic worked can be seen, for example, in the instructions that Thabit ibn Qurra (ca. 836–901) gives for ridding a place of scorpions. The first step is to make an image of a scorpion out of copper, tin, lead, silver, or gold, while the constellation Scorpio is in the ascendant. One must write the name of this constellation and various other astrological information on the image, then bury it in the place that is to become free of scorpions. While burying it one should say, "This is the burial of it and of its species, that it may not come to that one and to that place." It is still better to make four such images and bury them in the four corners of the place in question.[19]

This procedure may seem innocent enough, but Thabit and others recommended similar techniques for many purposes, not all so blameless. Astral images could help in recovering a husband's affections, gaining the favor of a king, regaining stolen property, destroying a town or any other place, inflicting illness, preventing a person from performing some action, bringing concord to enemies or enmity to friends. John Gerson (1363–1429) wrote against a physician who had tried to heal kidney disease by using a medal with an image of a lion and certain characters inscribed on it. Sometimes the instructions called for writing the name of the victim on the image. Often they listed spices or herbs to be used in fumigating it. Incantations might also be recited over it: some treatises give names of spirits to be invoked as an aid in this magic. Once duly prepared, the image might be worn over one's heart or otherwise carried on one's person, though most often it was to be buried. The Latin preface to the translation of one such treatise recognized that such magic might give offense, but argued that God had given it to his servants as a tool for the good and for vengeance against malefactors. Granted, it might at times be misused; but should the axe be blamed if it is used sometimes for killing people rather than cutting down trees?

[18] Frances A. Yates, *Giordano Bruno and the Hermetic Tradition* (London: Routledge, 1964), 60.
[19] Lynn Thorndike, "Traditional medieval tracts concerning engraved astrological images", in *Mélanges Auguste Pelzer* (Louvain: Bibliothèque de l'Université, 1947), 217–73.

The best known work of astral magic was an Arabic text known in the West as *Picatrix*.[20] This was translated from Arabic into Spanish at the behest of Alfonso the Wise, and then found its way into Latin. The author (or rather compiler, since the work is an unwieldy collection of related materials) professes a dualistic view of the world, in which spirit stands exalted above matter, yet the basic point of the work is to show how spirit itself, dwelling at its purest in the stars, can be brought down to earth and work upon matter. Occasional statements of grand principle are interspersed in a great mass of specific instructions. Inscribe a set of markings or talismanic signs on a piece of linen under the proper astrological conditions, add the name of a person, and set fire to the cloth, and the person named will be compelled to go wherever you want. Write other signs on a lead tablet and hide it in any habitation, and you will draw down the power of Saturn in such a way that the place will become depopulated. Elsewhere the reader is told to bury such images for the desired effects. Alternately, the power of the heavenly bodies can be channeled through "prayers." One chapter tells in detail how to pray to the planets, first listing the situations appropriate for petitioning each of them, then giving the properties of each and proposing formulas for prayer (which might well have served as models for the astral prayer in Chaucer's *Franklin's Tale*). As smoke rises from one's censer, one is to invoke the planets by their names in various languages, praising them for their powers, and "conjuring" them to aid one's designs. The book also lists magical substances with wondrous properties: mandrake, laurel, the brain of a hoopoe, the blood of a bat, and so forth. Sometimes these suffice by themselves as potions, but elsewhere they are to be burned as "fumigations" and their smoke acts as a kind of incense to enhance the power of an image or a prayer. On occasion the work speaks of constraining demons to perform one's will, but this theme is seldom explicit.

We find ourselves here on the fringes of the occult sciences, in an area that shed disreputability upon the movement as a whole and enhanced critics' suspicions of astrologers generally.

ALCHEMY

Like astrology, alchemy was a form of occult knowledge that required extensive learning. Also like astrology, it arose in antiquity, lived on in the Byzantine and Muslim worlds, but survived in the West only in fragmentary form until Arabic materials were translated in the twelfth century. In 1144 Robert of Chester translated into Latin the first alchemical treatise

[20] Pingree, ed., *Picatrix*.

ever accessible to Europeans. Soon he and other translators of the era made Westerners familiar with Arabic terms basic to chemistry and alchemy alike: "alkali," "naphtha," "alcohol," "elixir," and the word "alchemy" itself.

The essential point of alchemy is to discover the elixir or "philosopher's stone," which can transmute lead or other base metals into gold and silver. In their search for this elixir alchemists would spend years working over increasingly complex furnaces and laboratories, attempting to refine, sublimate, fuse, and otherwise transform their various chemicals. In the process they produced much improvement in the tools of experimentation; their furnaces and stills, for example, contributed to the techniques of later chemical experimentation.

Alchemists assumed an intricate system of affinities between chemicals and other forms of being. Like the astrologers they assumed a consonance between microcosm and macrocosm. For their purposes this link was suggested most fundamentally by the association between metals and planets: between gold and the sun, silver and the moon, iron and Mars, quicksilver and Mercury, and so forth. They thought that observation of the heavens could show the most favorable times for working with these metals and other chemicals. When alchemists work under a waxing moon, for example, they obtain purer metals.

Like astrology, alchemy rested upon philosophical principles most clearly and authoritatively stated by Aristotle and developed by Scholastic philosophers. Of particular importance was the notion that all matter is reducible to four elements (earth, air, fire, and water), which are further reducible to "prime matter." If all metals are composed of these same basic elements in various proportions, then should it not be possible to recombine the elements to obtain other, higher forms of matter? This was the alchemists' dream.

The writings of the alchemists are often obscure and veiled in symbolism. Their opacity can be seen in one classic text that the alchemists claimed as their own: the *Emerald Table*, a series of cryptic sayings allegedly written on an emerald slab and discovered in the tomb of Hermes Trismegistus:

As all things were by the contemplation of one, so all things arose from this one thing by a single act of adaptation. The father thereof is the Sun, the mother the Moon. The Wind carried it in its womb, the Earth is the nurse thereof. It is the father of all works of wonder throughout the whole world. The power thereof is perfect.[21]

And so on. Alchemists explained that the "one thing" is the elixir, whose father is gold and whose mother is silver. Other sayings in the text were

[21] Translated in E. J. Holmyard, *Alchemy* (Harmondsworth: Penguin, 1957), 97–8.

interpreted as referring to various procedures carried out in the alchemical laboratory.

Far more straightforward was a popular manual of alchemy from later medieval Europe, the treatise *On Alchemy* ascribed to Albert the Great. The greater part of this work was a practical, point-by-point introduction to the various tools and procedures of the trade: the kinds of furnaces used, the vessels, the chemicals, and the stages in preparation of chemicals. The author explains that "calcination" is a process of reducing a substance to powder by exposing it to fire, to remove the moisture that unites its component parts. "Distillation" is purification of a liquid by allowing its vapors to rise and be separated from the dregs. Among the most important chemicals are sulphur and mercury; before the philosopher's stone can be prepared, sulphur must be dissolved, whitened, and fixated as follows:

First, boil sulphur in strong acid for a whole day. Let it first be well ground, and remove the superabundant scum. Afterwards allow it to dry, grind it, and add as much of the prepared alum as I have taught, and put it into the vessel for sublimation for mercury, knowing that less fire is to be applied than for mercury. Turn down the fire and slowly sublime it for a whole day. Take it out in the morning and you will find it sublimed and black. Sublime it a second time and it will be white. Sublime it a third time, with salt added, and it will be very white. Again sublime it a third time, with salt added, and it will be very white. Again sublime it a third time and a fourth time up to the fixation point, and set it aside.[22]

This treatise also contains advice for the aspiring alchemist. It is important, the author insists, to have a house in a secluded place for alchemical work. He warns against starting to work without sufficient funds. And he admonishes the pupil to avoid all dealings with princes, who will harass the alchemist whether he is successful or unsuccessful, though for different reasons in the two cases. Many would-be alchemists, he says, fail through misunderstanding, debauchery and folly, careless-ness, lack of funds, or irresolution.

A particularly engaging introduction to medieval alchemy is the writing of Thomas Norton, an alchemist in fifteenth-century Bristol who claimed that he had learned by age twenty-eight how to confect the elixir of gold. In his *Ordinal of Alchemy* he tells how he traveled over a hundred miles to find his master in this art, and in forty days he learned from him all of its secrets, but when he set about preparing the elixir back at home his product was stolen from him twice.[23]

Even more than Albert the Great, Norton devotes himself to render-ing wise counsel. He warns against trusting in superstitions, in false

[22] *Libellus de alchimia, ascribed to Albertus Magnus*, trans. Sr. Virginia Heines (Berkeley: University of California Press, 1958), ch. 38 (translation adapted).
[23] *The Ordinall of Alchimy by Thomas Norton of Bristoll, Being a facsimile reproduction from Theatrum chemicum britannicum* (London: Arnold, 1928).

astrologers, and in necromancy, "for it is a property of the Devil to lie." For the work to proceed correctly everything must be in proper concord. The alchemist's mind must be in accord with the work itself, properly stable and comprehending. The workmen must be in accord with the craft, working in orderly shifts. The instruments must be in accord with the work, all the vessels having the proper shapes and materials. The place too must be in accord with the work, without drafts or other disturbances. Places "where lechery is used" are inappropriate. And the work must be in accord with the heavenly spheres: it must be done under proper astrological conditions. Norton's insistent refrain is that people without the proper training in metaphysics and physics should leave alchemy alone, since they are doomed to failure. He laments that "every estate" has its hand in this art: everyone from popes and cardinals down to glaziers and tinkers. We need not take this claim entirely at face value; most other sources suggest that the practitioners were mainly clerics and physicians (in the late thirteenth and early fourteenth century, for example, the Franciscan and Dominican orders felt obliged several times to forbid their members to practice alchemy), yet Norton had perhaps met or heard of people of varied status who at least dabbled in the art.

He tells numerous stories of people who have met with hardship, even disaster, in their quest for alchemical gold. A priest near London, reputed to be "half a leech" because of his medical skill, determined that with the proceeds from his alchemy he would perform an act of service: he would build a bridge across the Thames. After long deliberation he decided that he would light his bridge with luminous carbuncles. But after still more deliberation he went nearly mad worrying about where he would find enough carbuncles for his purpose. After a year he had made little progress in his search for gold; he did not even have brass for his efforts. In another case, the king of England heard of a monk who had made 1,000 pounds of gold in less than half a day. When the monk was dragged from his monastery and asked about his gold, he told a sad tale. He had accumulated enough gold to send 20,000 men to the Holy Land, and kept it for a long time, hoping to find a king who might go on crusade, but because of the trouble it had cost him he eventually cast it all into a lake. The king soon dismissed the monk, but others from the court, perhaps more credulous than their monarch, apprehended and detained him for several years, hoping to benefit from his art.

After several such cautionary tales Norton proceeds to discuss the elements of alchemy. First there is the "gross work," the heavy labor of mining and working with minerals. The alchemist should not expend his efforts on such work but should leave it to servants. The "subtle work," on the other hand, falls to the alchemist himself, who must be trained in

Fig. 14. Alchemist's laboratory, from Norton's *Ordinal*

metaphysics and physics so that he will understand this work. The gross work must not be done by clerics (meaning here educated men); the subtle work can only be done by a cleric. The respective roles of the educated master and uneducated servants is suggested by the depictions given in an early manuscript of Norton's work (Fig. 14): the servants get their hands dirty while the master sits and gives directions. The alchemist himself must understand the effects of hot and cold, dry and wet. He must know, for example, that heat causes dry things to become white, as in the case of burnt bones or lime, while cold engenders whiteness in wet things, such as ice and frost. He must learn to recognize the states of things by color, odor, taste, and fluidity. Physicians distinguish nineteen different colors of urine, but alchemists have a hundred more colors they must recognize in their chemicals. Taste would be an excellent way to analyze substances except that it can be dangerous. Norton tells of two foolish men who imbibed a bit of the "white stone" in hopes of relief from their sickness, but because they had taken it before it was fully prepared they became paralyzed until the alchemical master came with an antidote. Alchemists must also learn to distinguish various degrees of heat. One who has become a true master of the art will ultimately be able to produce not only the while stone (needed for production of silver) but the red as well (required for alchemists' gold). What he will discover is that the red stone is hidden within the white one and may be released by fire. "Then is the fair White Woman married to the Ruddy Man."

With curious frequency, medieval sources speak of alchemy as useful for health as well as wealth. The elixir has medicinal properties ascribed to it, as do other alchemical concoctions. Thus, in 1456 twelve men petitioned Henry VI of England for permission to practice alchemy: among them were two of the king's own physicians and another physician who was a friend of the duke of Gloucester. In granting permission for three of these petitioners to engage in alchemical work, the king recalled that the elixir was a medicine that would easily cure all illnesses, prolong human life in undiminished strength, cure wounds, and serve as antidote to all poisons. Only as an afterthought did the king add that transmutation of metals into "true gold and very fine silver" could help enrich his kingdom.[24] One key to this conception of alchemy is provided by the treatise *On Consideration of the Fifth Essence* by John of Rupescissa. What seems at first odd about this work is that it applies the notion of the fifth essence to alcohol. It gives various means for distilling the alcohol found in wine, and he tells how to "fix the sun in our sky" by treating the alcohol with heated gold to enchance its already marvelous medical powers. Rupescissa may have been the first to use alchemical technology and vocabulary in this way.[25] One might suppose that his work is not really on alchemy at all, but what is more to the point is that many people seem to have been using alchemical techniques, equipment, and language for purposes other than simply trying to confect gold and silver. Clearly Rupescissa (d. ca. 1365)

[24] D. Geoghegan, "A licence of Henry VI to practise alchemy", *Ambix*, 6 (1957), 10–17 (with translation and quotation).
[25] Robert P. Multhauf, "John of Rupescissa and the origin of medical chemistry", *Isis*, 45 (1954), 359–67.

was not unique in proposing that alchemy could produce new kinds of drugs from chemical rather than biological sources. In that respect alchemy provided a breakthrough in pharmacology, however great or small the immediate payoff from this breakthrough may have been.

Alchemists were notorious for making fake gold and silver, which turned to dross when tested. Echoing a Psalm verse, Albert the Great lamented that this fraudulent gold "does not gladden the heart" like true gold. Chaucer conveyed a widespread view of alchemists in *The Canon's Yeoman's Tale*, which presents the alchemists as rogues who spend so much time around noxious chemicals that they smell like goats, and who rob people of their money by persuading them they can produce gold or silver. They can take silver pieces and insert them into a piece of charcoal, from which, not surprisingly, they then produce silver. Or they pretend to obtain it by stirring a crucible, but the stick they use is hollow and has silver filling inside it. They feign conversion of copper into silver, but they accomplish this feat only by having silver up their sleeves. Evidently there were in fact alchemists who tried to pass off false gold or silver as the real item. To curb this practice Pope John XXII stipulated that anyone who made or circulated such counterfeit gold or silver should pay a fine in real gold or silver equal in weight to the false metal. The pontiff provided special penalties for clerics caught in these practices.

Even Chaucer's story-teller, however, does not see all alchemists as scoundrels; some of them are merely fools. This attitude too was widely shared. Johannes Trithemius speaks with verisimilitude when he tells of several people who were ruined by alchemy. He speaks of a man who squandered a fortune in his alchemical pursuits, then disappeared and left wife and children behind. He knows of an abbot who left his abbey in debt because of his alchemical research, and a Carthusian prior who wasted five or six years on these pursuits. Trithemius concludes:

Alchemy is a chaste whore who has many lovers but deludes them all and never falls into the embrace of any. She turns the foolish into madmen, the wealthy into paupers, philosophers into simpletons, and those she has deceived into talkative deceivers, for while they know nothing they profess to know all.[26]

Why, then, did many intelligent people take alchemy seriously? Partly, no doubt, because hope sprang eternal. Partly because other research was being done under the name of alchemy. But also because the allure of secret knowledge was in itself strong, and even stories of wretched failure could not deter those romantic intellects who craved the fascination of deep and mysterious learning.

[26] J. R. Partington, "Trithemius and alchemy", *Ambix*, 2 (1938), 53–9.

THE CULT OF SECRECY AND BOOKS OF SECRETS

The European writings on astrology and alchemy may have reached a fairly broad audience by the fifteenth century, but they were seldom intended for the masses. Quite the contrary: the authors of these works often exerted themselves to restrict their own audience. This was especially true of alchemists, but astrologers too sometimes donned the cloak of secrecy. Albert the Great's astrological work, *The Mirror of Astronomy*, contains a solemn warning that its teaching should be kept secret, and for obvious reasons *Picatrix* is obsessed with this concern. The theme is common in works on magic generally. In his treatise on gems Marbode of Rennes argued that if the common people learned of their mysterious powers the value of the mysteries would be diminished. Roger Bacon quoted this text and others against the breaking of secrets, then suggested a series of ways to preserve the occult character of nature's own knowledge. A person writing about such things should use enigmatic phrases, invent secret words and alphabets, mix together different languages, abbreviate heavily, and so forth. The secrecy of magic was also the stuff of legends: Alexander Neckham (1157–1217), for example, told how Aristotle had certain of his subtler works buried along with him in a sepulcher so well concealed that no one has found it, though when Antichrist comes he may be able to read these books.

When medieval writers used the term "occult," they used it in reference the hidden powers of nature, but they did not typically use the term with reference to special branches of knowledge, or the "occult sciences." The latter term is nonetheless useful, first of all as a kind of shorthand for "sciences dealing with occult powers," but secondly as a characterization of the learning itself, which was something reserved for the few and concealed from the many. Those who studied these things studied hidden powers, and sometimes (not always) kept their knowledge about those powers hidden.

Alchemical writers warn constantly that their works must not fall into the wrong hands. The treatise *On Alchemy* ascribed to Albert warns against revealing the secrets of the art to anyone, but particularly "the foolish," who will fail in their efforts and in their frustration will envy those who succeed. Thomas Norton is even more insistent on this point. The art of alchemy is so holy that it must be taught orally, with the seal of "a most sacred, dreadful oath," and its deepest secrets must never be committed to writing. At one point Norton fears that he may be telling too much, and he adds, "But my heart quaketh, my hand is trembling, when I write of this most secret thing." When the alchemist grows old he may entrust his knowledge to a single suitable pupil, but no more than one. Otherwise evil people will gain the knowledge and use it to disrupt the peace and overthrow rightful princes.

The writers of magical manuscripts, alchemical and otherwise, did at times use cipher. Usually this involves nothing more than replacing each vowel with the consonant that follows it in the alphabet.[27] Thomas Betson, in what appears to be a relatively earnest mood, after discussing the interchangeability of astrological and alchemical terms, recommends using such techniques to keep the occult sciences from falling into the wrong hands, though he does not make it entirely clear which hands are the right ones. Another writer uses such cipher in a prescription for seeing hidden things:

So that you may see what others cannot see, mix the bile of a male cat [*de cbttp mbscxlp = de catto masculo*] with the fat of an entirely white hen [*gblllnf = galline*] and anoint your eyes with it, and you will see what others cannot see.[28]

Still another manuscript goes to the trouble of transliterating key words into runes, although the manuscript itself comes from southern Germany, and how the author or scribe acquired his rather sophisticated command of the runic script is unclear.[29]

Why this emphasis on secrecy? Two reasons occur repeatedly in the literature: the subjective need to maintain an aura of mystery, and the alleged objective need to keep the secrets out of the hands of bunglers who will give magic a bad name by their very failure. In the case of alchemy there is also a social motive, the fear that an indefinite supply of gold will only lead to misuse and laziness.[30] The factor one might expect to be cited is conspicuously absent: the magicians do not typically concede in private that their magic is a sham and that their tricks must be kept hidden so people will accord them greater power than they in fact have. This argument might indeed have applied to performative magic, which plays a relatively minor role in medieval magic generally. For the most part, however, the magicians at least claim to be convinced that their magic

[27] Thf rfsvlt js spmfthjng ljkf thjs.
[28] St. John's College, Cambridge, MS E.6., fol. 7ʳ–8ᵛ (the writer's alphabet does not include J, K, V, or W); Bodleian Library, MS Ashm. 1398, fol. 144ᵛ. Cf. Bodleian MS e Mus. 219, fol. 186ʳ⁻ᵛ. For general information on medieval cryptography see Bernhard Bischoff, "Übersicht über die nichtdiplomatischen Geheimschriften des Mittelalters", *Mitteilungen des Instituts für österreichische Geschichtsforschung*, 62 (1957), 1–27, esp. 4. For use of cipher in recipes for contraceptives, see Percival Horton-Smith Hartley, *Johannes de Mirfeld*, 44.
[29] Hartmut Beckers, "Eine spätmittelalterliche deutsche Anleitung zur Teufelsbeschwörung mit Runenschriftverwendung", *Zeitschrift für deutsches Altertum und deutsche Literatur*, 113 (1984), 136–45. It is not only the material for explicitly demonic magic that is here disguised. For very different uses of runes see Charles S. F. Burnett, "Scandinavian runes in a Latin magical treatise", *Speculum*, 58 (1983), 419–29.
[30] Gerhard Eis, "Von der Rede und dem Schweigen der Alchemisten", *Deutsche Vierteljahrsschrift für Literaturwissenschaft und Geistesgeschichte*, 25 (1951), 415–35.

actually does work. What needs to be guarded is not their means for deception, but the sources of their actual power. Even when they give instructions for harmful magic, the writers do not say that they are afraid of being caught and brought to justice. Rather, they say that their "experiments" must be kept secret because of their "great power."

This cult of secrecy can be explained in large part as an outgrowth of the cultural setting for magic. What we have called the common tradition was widely available in medieval society, but the new occult sciences were originally the possession of certain clerics. Doubtless there was much pressure to lower this barrier and share this extraordinary learning, particularly if it could be put into simpler form for popular consumption. The emphasis on secrecy came partly, no doubt, as a reaction to this demand for popularization. The scholars who held jealously to their occult learning were in effect declaring that they would not allow it to become debased through assimilation to the broader, common tradition; rather, they would preserve it in its purity and retain its power for themselves.

The insistence on secrecy highlights a dimension of the occult arts that might otherwise be less clear: their value simply as a form of knowledge. From the viewpoint of these writers, knowledge might *bring* power but it also *was* power. Knowing mysterious things was in itself valuable, even if the knowledge was never put to effect in action. In the extreme cases magic was intended for the sole aim of gaining knowledge: to learn all that happens on earth, the secrets of everyone's mind, and even heavenly things, one manuscript recommends beheading a hoopoe at sunrise, under a new moon, and swallowing its heart while it is still palpitating.[31] The point is not so much to gain control over the world, though magic might also accomplish that. More basically, it is cherished simply because it brings hidden things to light, or at least to the dim visibility of the shadows.

In keeping with this cult of the occult, works on magic were sometimes referred to as "books of secrets," even if they had only tenuous connection with this new learning, and indeed even if there was no real secret about their contents. In the later Middle Ages a *Book of Secrets* ascribed to Albert the Great circulated quite widely. It contained various kinds of magic, none of it as sophisticated as technical astrology or alchemy; it was essentially a work of popularization, but with added glamor derived from the pretense of secrecy. By far the most influential work in this genre was

---

[31] British Library, MS Sloane 3132, fol. 56ᵛ. Bodleian Library, MS e Mus. 219, fol. 186ᵛ, gives instructions for more limited knowledge: to learn the language of the birds, take the heart of a hoopoe or the tongue of a kite and put it in honey for three days and nights, then place it under your tongue.

the pseudo-Aristotelian *Secret of Secrets*, which one author with pardonable exaggeration has called the most popular book in medieval Europe.[32] Widely accepted as an authentic work by Aristotle, this book was well known in its Latin version, was translated into nearly every vernacular language of Europe, and was even put into poetic paraphrase. It purports to contain Aristotle's instructions to his pupil Alexander the Great. In fact, it is a motley compilation of material, put together in several different Arabic versions during the early Middle Ages long before its translation into Latin. Much of it is devoted to principles of statecraft and personal health, but natural magic also appears in its pages. Medicine, the powers of gems, astrology, and related topics are all included. The show of secrecy is carried beyond the title: much of the work, claiming to represent Aristotle's esoteric learning, is concealed in riddles and other cryptic formulas, and Aristotle exhorts Alexander not to violate the divine mysteries by letting the book fall into the wrong hands. One could hardly find a better example, however, of a further reason for this display of secrecy: the semblance of mystery is itself a splendid advertisement, and a way to ensure wide distribution of a work.

A further result of all this show of secrecy was the rise of legends about people who engaged in magic or were thought to do so. They claimed to have wondrous powers; very well, said the legend-mongers in effect, let us see their wondrous deeds! Men who had unexpectedly won favor at court, perhaps as advisers to monarchs, were subjects for legend formation. Equally vulnerable were scholars whose dazzling intellects aroused more envy than popularity, particularly if they had studied in Muslim lands or dabbled in scientific experiments. In chronicles especially, but also in treatises, correspondence, and other writings the legends evolved.

Gerbert of Aurillac (ca. 940–1003) provides an early example of this process. As a student of philosophy and other disciplines he had traveled to Spain (though not in fact Toledo, as legend always had it), where he studied logic. After returning to central Europe he was close to the court of the German emperors, and with their patronage he rose in dignity and power within the Church, eventually becoming Pope Sylvester II. By the late eleventh century a cardinal named Benno was explaining Gerbert's rise to power in conspiratorial terms: not only he but other popes had risen to their office by magic, and indeed throughout the century they had perpetuated a school of magic in Rome. Cardinal Benno told how Satan had promised Pope Sylvester he would not die until he celebrated mass in Jerusalem. The pope thought this meant he was safe, but one day he said

---

[32] M. Gaster, cited in Lynn Thorndike, "The Latin pseudo-Aristotle and medieval occult science", *Journal of English and Germanic Philology*, 21 (1922), 248–9.

mass in the Jerusalem church at Rome and was called to death during the liturgy, and in desperation he cut off his tongue and one hand to atone for his sins of necromancy.

Similar legends grew up around Michael Scot, Albert the Great, Roger Bacon, and many others.[33] Legends told about any of these figures might be transferred to others. The process was long familiar in hagiography, or legends of the saints, and stories of the necromancers constituted a sort of inverse hagiography. Thus, twelfth-century legend told how a public statue at Rome had an outstretched finger and bore the inscription "Strike here." Many people tried striking the finger itself, but Gerbert noted where the *shadow* of the finger fell at noon, returned to that spot at night, and dug an opening to a marvelous golden palace lighted with a magic carbuncle. Essentially the same tale was told of Virgil. More than one of these legendary wizards is supposed to have manufactured a head that would talk to him. Albert the Great was supposed to have made a bronze head which was so talkative that Thomas Aquinas had to smash it with a hammer to keep it from distracting him in his studies; the same invention is ascribed to Roger Bacon. Certain themes in these legends, such as distortion of time so that a few minutes seem like twenty years, are borrowed from (or by) the romances.

Of special importance in many of these legends is the magician's book of magic. Gerbert was said to have abducted two things from his teacher: his daughter and his book. In the legend of Virgil – which furnished material both for the romances and for these tales about scholarly magicians – we read that the poet's book of magic was buried along with him, and its discovery and exhumation is a story unto itself. The power of the book, and specifically the aura of mystery surrounding a book of magic, here finds eloquent expression.

THE RENAISSANCE MAGUS

Occult learning feeds perennially on antiquity, and when occultists cannot find ancient sources to suit their purposes they will invent them. Arabic writers served the cause of occult knowledge in the West by making available the sciences of ancient Greece, much reworked over the centuries, and this infusion of ancient learning kept Western occultists busy for several generations. By the late fifteenth century, however, the Humanist movement led some occultists to dig deeper into the ground of classical antiquity, where they found further and (they thought) more authentic materials for their study.

---

[33] William Godwin, *Lives of the Necromancers: or, an Account of the Most Eminent Persons in Successive Ages, Who Have Claimed for Themselves, or to Whom has been Imputed by Others, the Exercise of Magical Power* (London: Mason, 1834).

Fig. 15. Hermes Mercurius Trismegistus, in the pavement of Siena cathedral.

The mythic figure taken as a kind of patron saint for this movement was Hermes Trismegistus, whose image appears on a mosaic pavement laid at the cathedral of Siena in the 1480s (Fig. 15). Standing beside the Sibyls, Hermes is depicted here not as a magician but as a supposed prophet of Christianity, though his connections with magic, astrology, and alchemy could hardly be put out of mind or distinguished altogether from his prophetic powers.

The Humanists of the fourteenth through sixteenth centuries were heirs to earlier students of antiquity, and while they conceived themselves as witnessing a renaissance (or "rebirth") of classical knowledge they were in fact continuing a much earlier fascination with ancient Greece and

Rome. Some of them had studied Greek; by the later fifteenth century Byzantine scholars were readily available in Italy. To that extent these Humanists had better access to the Greek texts of antiquity than had their twelfth-century forebears. They also had a great many more manuscripts of classical materials, and were able to read Greek or Roman works that earlier readers did not know. One finds among them, more than among their predecessors, an interest in classical learning inspired by secular as well as religious concerns. This last factor, however, had little relevance to their interest in magic: for them magic was a religious phenomenon, related in complex and often problematic ways to traditional Christianity.

Humanist scholars of the late fifteenth and early sixteenth centuries include some of the most vigorous devotees of magic. Marsilio Ficino combined his Platonic philosophy with a serious interest in medicine, and produced a treatise on astrological medicine grounded in Neoplatonic philosophy. Jacques Lefèvre d'Etaples (ca. 1450–1536) combined magic and astrology with a Pythagorean interest in the power of numbers. Johannes Reuchlin (1455–1522), a noted Hebrew scholar, exalted the occult powers of names and other words. Johannes Trithemius, while disclaiming the title of magician, proposed a system of secret writing, argued the possibility of a sort of telepathic communication, and claimed to have revealed knowledge of many wondrous things.

It is Ficino who most fully represents the tradition of the Renaissance magus in the second half of the fifteenth century. When he was still a young man, Cosimo de' Medici commissioned him to translate from Greek the *Hermetic Corpus* ascribed to Hermes Trismegistus. Cosimo had already asked him to translate the works of Plato, but when a monk appeared in Florence with the Hermetic manuscript in hand Plato had to wait: Hermes was considered (falsely) the more ancient authority and thus the more important.[34] Years later, Ficino wrote his work *On Life* as a medical treatise based on astrological principles; the third and final section of this work in particular tells how to benefit as fully as possible from the positive influences of the stars. He recommends "solar" objects above all for their beneficial influence: gold, chrysolite, amber, honey, saffron, the lion, and other repositories of the sun's beneficent influence. Even people with golden hair are worth associating with because they transmit solar effects. Jupiter, too, radiated fine, life-supporting virtues, and the other planets' power could also be put to salutary use.

While Ficino also saw astral images as means for channeling the power of the stars and planets, he looked askance at such artificial techniques. He explained how inscribing figures on material things – thus making talismans of them – could help by disposing them to receive astral

[34] Yates, *Giordano Bruno*, 1–19.

influences. He described how learned men of antiquity had put astral images on rings, and how one philosopher had lived 120 years by using such devices. In principle, however, he insisted that he was only describing such practices, not recommending them. Astral medicines, he said, were more potent than astral images for three reasons: the powders, liquids, unguents, and other such stuff used by astral medicine absorb the influences of the stars more easily than the hard matter used for images; being taken internally, medicines penetrate the body more effectively; and being concocted of many different ingredients, they capture more of the stars' or planets' essence than an image made from a single material.

Ficino was drawing on various sources for his astral magic.[35] He was one of the first Westerners since late antiquity to know the work of Plotinus at first hand, and he claimed explicitly to be providing a commentary on the work of this founder of Neoplatonic philosophy. Plotinus had seen all of nature as pervaded with magical influences, and Ficino captured the spirit of this notion with his maxim that "Nature is everywhere a magician." Yet he, unlike his predecessors in the West, also knew the later Neoplatonists such as Porphyry and Iamblichus and drew heavily from their thought. The most important notion for him was that of a world soul or cosmic spirit, a concept found among Neoplatonists but traceable further back to the Stoics. This spirit is like the human spirit, but is found throughout the cosmos. Powers from this cosmic spirit are beamed toward Earth from the stars and planets, and the task of the magician is to discern and channel these powers. Of the various means for so doing, some are more material (especially stones and metals), while others are more spiritual (words, songs, and so forth), and as a good Neoplatonist, Ficino ranks these means in a hierarchy with the more obviously material ones at the bottom and the spiritual ones at the top.

The kind of music Ficino had in mind as a means for channeling these cosmic influences is largely a matter for conjecture. We know from other writings of his that he used "Orphic" hymns, named after the magical song of Orpheus, the musician of Greek myth. Ficino speaks also of accompanying his own song on an Orphic lyre, though the words seem to have been more important to him than the melody or accompaniment, since it was words that bore meaning.

Other Renaissance mages, perhaps inspired by the same Neoplatonist preference for spiritual over material means for magic, shared Ficino's interest in exploiting the powers of music. Giovanni Pico della Mirandola (1463–94) spoke of Orphic hymns as a uniquely efficacious form of magic, and their contemporary Lodovico Lazarelli wrote a Hermetic dialogue in

[35] D. P. Walker, *Spiritual and Demonic Magic, from Ficino to Campanella* (London: Warburg Institute, 1958), used here extensively.

which Lazarelli himself is represented as leading the king of Aragon into ecstasy with his hymns. One of these compositions, a paean celebrating the power of human creativity as analogous to God's own creative power, begins: "Ah, my mind, ponder now these great mysteries. Who made all things from nothing? The word of the Father, alone. May he be blessed, this Word of the Begetter!" Having heard this hymn, the king exclaims that he is inflamed with love and stunned with awe, much as a person is stunned when touching a torpedo-fish! The same reverence for the magical power of music can be seen also in Reuchlin's work. While emphasizing the difficulties and hazards of magical hymnody, Reuchlin depicts an initiation into mystical knowledge through liturgical ceremony that involves preparatory hymns. We have few words for such magical song, and no melodies; indeed, the magicians may simply have improvised their music. What we know is not the precise nature of their singing but the theoretical place it held in their thought.

Ficino and his fellows needed to defend these fascinations of theirs. Christ himself, Ficino argued, healed the sick and taught "his priests" to do so with words, herbs, and stones. Should it be scandalous, then, if Ficino (himself a priest) did likewise? Indeed, the magi of the gospels were wise men and priests, and were held in high esteem. As for the underlying conception of magic, Ficino links his theories to a Neoplatonic conception of a living cosmos, and he professes only disdain for those who see the lowliest plants and animals as having life but deny that the cosmos itself is alive.

While most of these writers needed to defend themselves from attackers, Pico actually courted controversy. In 1486 he went to Rome and there set forth nine hundred theses for public debate. In these propositions Pico upheld the value of natural magic, by which the forces inherent in nature are brought together and made efficacious, but he claimed also to have found a source of magical power far higher than those in nature. A young man of astonishingly broad erudition, Pico had become intensely interested in the Hebrew tradition of magic and mysticism known as the Kabbalah. In keeping with this fascination he asserted that words can have magical power – but only words in Hebrew, which were taught to Adam and Eve by God himself, and which derive their power from having been spoken by God's own voice. Mastery of the Kabbalah can give a person unimagined magical skill, though a dabbler who uses the Kabbalah carelessly can be destroyed by demons. (When Pico spoke of "demons" he used the word in two senses: following the Neoplatonist philosopher Porphyry, he proposed that in addition to the demons normally so called there are powers within matter than can also be called "demons.") At his most enthusiastic, Pico insisted that magic grounded in the Kabbalah is the only effective magic.

Later in his brief life Pico modified his tone and published a strong condemnation of the astrologers' errors. But even then he did not deny that there was such a thing as legitimate astrology or valid magic, and this later work can be read as primarily a defense of astral magic such as Ficino's, which Pico seeks to distinguish from the fatalistic astrology he is attacking.

Among those who hastened into the controversy with Pico was Pedro Garcia (d. 1505), who took up the opposite extreme by repudiating all magic as illegitimate. He doubted that there were such things as occult powers hidden in nature and manipulable by magicians. Or if there were such powers the only way to learn about them was from the instruction of demons. And if these powers did exist they were highly unstable, unpredictable, and thus unserviceable for practical purposes. As for the Kabbalah, Garcia denied that it was an ancient tradition traceable to Moses; it was, he asserted, an offshoot of heretical Judaism springing from the Talmud.[36]

Pico's interest in the Kabbalah was shared by others, such as Lefèvre d'Etaples and Reuchlin.[37] In his dialogue of 1494, *On the Wonder-Working Word*, Reuchlin reminds the reader of the magic that sorceresses in classical literature worked by the power of their words, but then argues that the most potent magic is not to be found in Greek or Egyptian words but rather in Hebrew. So too, real power was not to be found in those charlatans of Reuchlin's own day who ascribed their writings to Solomon and other worthies but in fact practiced demonic magic. There is indeed power in natural magic: God has implanted occult properties in coral, for example, which give it value as an amulet. The focus of the dialogue, however, is the wonder-working power of names for God. In Exodus 3:14, God gave Moses the classic Tetragrammaton or four-letter divine name ("YHWH") which, like other Hebrew words, is spelled without vowels. Reuchlin uses the form "IHUH" for this divine name, to which he assigns a wealth of numerological symbolism and miracle-working power. The ultimate wonder-working word, however, is an expansion of this, "IHSUH", a variation on "Jesus". Like certain writers from early Christian centuries, Reuchlin exalts this name of Christ as having power to work multiple wonders. It can change rivers into wine, it protected Paul against serpents on the island of Malta, it gave other

---

[36] Lynn Thorndike, *The History of Magic and Experimental Science*, vol. 4, 529–43.
[37] Charles Zika, "Reuchlin's *De verbo mirifico* and the magic debate of the late fifteenth century", *Journal of the Warburg and Courtauld Institutes*, 39 (1976), 104–38.

disciples power against dragons, and so forth. It must be used together with the cross; word and gesture combine to accomplish the highest of all forms of magic. Like Pico and other Humanist mages, Reuchlin shows himself here thoroughly orthodox, but more than Pico he stresses his eagerness to wed his occult learning to the Christian tradition.

The magic of these Renaissance mages might invoke supernatural as well as natural powers, and to that extent it transcends the categories we have been using. Once again magic becomes linked to religion, but out of sophistication rather than naïveté. On the other hand, however, the mages had to defend themselves against the charge of demonic magic. We have already seen that this argument arose in the debate over Pico, and the question arose in subtler form in the writings of Ficino.

Repeatedly Ficino insisted that he was advocating only natural magic.[38] His songs were not incantations addressed to demons. If images of any kind held magical power, it was not because demons inhabited them; in any case, he did not advocate worshiping demons, even if they were present in images. From various writings of his we know that he did have a theory about demons and their place in the universe. Both the New Testament (e.g. Ephesians 6:12) and the Neoplatonist tradition conceived of spirits as present in the heavens, and Thomas Aquinas had thought of the heavenly bodies as guided by angels. In Ficino's view the planets had good and bad spirits associated with them. He recognized other kinds of demons as well: some dwelling above the heavens, and others present on Earth. The planetary demons have bodies made of air or ether, and are involved in transmitting astral influences to Earth. Thus, while in his work *On Life* Ficino sees magic as a channeling of cosmic powers, he suggests elsewhere that astral influences are subject to demonic intervention, though he nowhere puts the two theories together and concludes that magic can and should involve relations with these planetary demons. On at least two occasions he used astral magic to *expel* demons associated with Saturn, and thus he dabbled in a kind of astrological exorcism. He did not advocate *using* the powers of such demons. But the wary reader might well suspect that he was doing so in secret, and the suspicion would be all the more plausible since others in his day were in fact engaged in explicitly demonic magic. If Ficino, Reuchlin, and other Renaissance magicians took pains to distinguish their magic from the demonic sort, it was because both kinds of magic were very real – and the similarities between them, if not real, nonetheless appeared so to many onlookers.

---

[38] Walker, *Spiritual and Demonic Magic*, 45–53.

7

NECROMANCY IN THE CLERICAL
UNDERWORLD

.

John of Salisbury in his *Policraticus* tells an experience from his own youth. He was studying Latin from a priest, using the Psalms as the texts for study. As it happened, however, his teacher was an adept in the divinatory art of crystal-gazing, and abused his trust by making John and a somewhat older pupil participate in these activities. The idea was to anoint the boys' fingernails with some sacred chrism so that images would appear reflected in the nails and would impart information. Alternatively, a polished basin might be used as the reflecting surface. After certain "preliminary magical rites" and the requisite anointing, the priest uttered names "which by the horror they inspired, seemed to me, child though I was, to belong to demons." The other pupil declared that he saw "certain misty figures," but John himself saw nothing of the sort and was thus ruled unqualified for this art. John goes on to say that almost all the people he knew who engaged in such practices were punished later in life with blindness and other afflictions. He knew only two exceptions, including the priest who had taught him Latin; both of these men repented and entered into religious life as monks or canons, and even they were punished somewhat for their offenses.[1]

What should we make of John's recollection that the priest had recited the names of demons? Was this the fruit of childish imagination or faulty memory? One might think so, except that the Munich handbook (discussed in Chapter 1) contains detailed instructions for conjuring demons in precisely the way that John recounts, and for the same purpose. The magic of the Munich manual is explicitly demonic, and there is no reason

[1] *Frivolities of Courtiers and Footprints of Philosophers*, ii.28, trans. Joseph B. Pike (London: Oxford University Press, 1938), 146–7.

to doubt that the rites of John's Latin teacher were equally so.[2] Evidently what we have here is an example of the necromancy that seems to have flourished within the clerical underworld of the later Middle Ages.

This story is not the first indication in the West that such practices were known. A century earlier, Anselm of Besate had put together a series of accusations against his cousin Rotiland. The charges were intended as a rhetorical exercise, and we need not take them seriously as charges against Rotiland in particular, but on the other hand we cannot rule out the possibility that Anselm intended his portrayal to have verisimilitude, and in later centuries similar accusations were being made very much in earnest. Rotiland is supposed to have gone out of town one night with a boy, buried the lad up to his waist, and tortured him with some kind of acrid fumes. As the boy underwent this abuse, Rotiland supposedly recited a formula that began, "As this youth is held captive in this place, so may girls be captive to my love." Part of his incantation was in "Hebrew, or rather diabolical, words," though the characters given in the account are actually garbled Greek letters. To avenge his mistreatment, the boy later stole Rotiland's "notebook of necromancy," and Rotiland conjured up a dead man "by diabolical art" to recover the book. This necromancer is supposed to have committed a second offense in the company of a Saracen or Muslim physician; this time he is charged with using the hand of a dead person to break into a house, and with murder as well.[3] This account proves little, but raises the question whether necromancy was being used even in the eleventh century, and whether we have here a fanciful elaboration of actual experience.

Both John of Salisbury and Anselm of Besate were speaking of necromancy, in the sense of that term that was most common in the later Middle Ages. Originally the word had meant divination (*mantia*) by conjuring the spirits of the dead (*nekroi*). Circe was the classic necromancer of Graeco-Roman tradition, and the witch of Endor was the archetypal necromancer of the Bible. When medieval writers interpreted such stories, however, they assumed that the dead could not in fact be brought to life but that demons took on the appearance of deceased persons and pretended to be those persons. By extension, then, the conjuring of demons came to be known as necromancy; this was the ordinary meaning of the term in later medieval Europe. Necromancy was *explicitly* demonic magic. Other forms of magic might be taken as *implicitly* demonic, and even a person who wore an amulet or recited a charm might be suspected of implicitly demonic magic. The necromancer, however, actually in-

---

[2] For the Munich manuscript, see above, Chapter 1, n. 3.

[3] Karl Manitius, "Magie und Rhetorik bei Anselm von Besate", *Deutsches Archiv für Erforschung des Mittelalters*, 12 (1956), 52–72.

voked demons or the Devil, and often did so by invoking their names, whether familiar or unfamiliar.

THE MAKING OF A CLERICAL UNDERWORLD

Who were the necromancers? Both in legend and before the law it was clerics above all others who stood accused of necromancy. To speak of the necromancers as clerics, however, is to speak with inevitable imprecision, since the term "cleric" could have many meanings. This was true of the Latin *clericus*, and equally of the English translations "cleric" and "clerk." Most broadly the term could refer to anyone, even a boy still in adolescence, who had been tonsured as a mark of pious intent to be ordained. A bit more narrowly, it meant a person who had been ordained at least to lower orders: someone who had been ordained, for example, as a doorkeeper, a lector, or an acolyte. These offices had originally been connected with specific tasks, but in later medieval Europe they were merely steps that one took up the ladder toward the priesthood – steps that were available even for those who did not intend to climb all the way to the top of that ladder. One of the minor orders to which a cleric would be ordained was that of exorcist, and in the ordination ceremony he would receive a book of exorcisms as a symbol of his theoretical function. He might never perform a real exorcism in his life, but if he went astray he might indeed have occasion to command demons. Students in medieval universities would be ordained to lower orders as a matter of course; anyone who went to a university would obtain ordination and thus qualify as a cleric. In other contexts "clerk" referred to someone who had *not* been ordained at all but helped the priest in various liturgical and practical functions.

Apart from this multiplicity of meanings, the identification of clerics was complicated by the informality of clerical training and the laxness of control over ordination. Aspirants to the priesthood in medieval Europe did not go to seminaries, where they might have gotten theological education linked with spiritual guidance. Seminaries were virtually unknown. Those who could afford to go to universities might do so, and from the thirteenth century onward bishops generally encouraged such a course of studies, but this would have been the exception, not the rule. The less affluent and less ambitious would still have been trained in a kind of apprenticeship. They would serve under a parish priest in a town or village, learn from him how to perform the rituals, and then present themselves to the bishop for ordination. They were expected to have at least a rudimentary knowledge of Latin, ritual, and doctrine, but the examinations were not uniformly strict, and reformers often protested the

154 Necromancy in the clerical underworld

numbers of unqualified candidates who slipped through. A visitation of the clergy in early fifteenth-century Bologna turned up clerics who could not read their breviaries, and the bishop who made this visitation felt obliged to repeat his predecessor's mandate that only an ordained priest could celebrate the mass.[4]

Many were ordained to lower orders and continued to claim the privileges of clergy although they had no clerical employment; they might indeed be employed as merchants or artisans while still claiming to be clerics. Others, it seems, claimed falsely to be clerics to obtain the benefits of clergy, particularly immunity from secular jurisdiction when they got into trouble. In some places these rogues came often before the law, on a variety of charges. In 1385, for example, a murderer and robber in Paris claimed to be a cleric, but during the trial he confessed that he had never gone to school and had merely had a barber shave his head to avoid the rigor of the law. In any case, these pseudoclerics differed little from those real ones who no longer functioned as such and had forgotten their learning and their prayers.[5]

Even a man who had been ordained as a priest might or might not have a regular position as curate or assistant in a parish. In the late Middle Ages, pious people often endowed positions for "chantry priests" to say mass for their souls after death and thus secure their speedy release from purgatory, and many clerics were in effect semi-employed in such positions. A chantry priest was expected to say the divine office each day as a minimum by way of private prayer, and was expected to say mass each morning according to the terms of the endowment. Once these duties were fulfilled he would usually be free for the rest of the day. Having time on his hands, he might readily get into trouble. Necromancy was merely one of the forms this trouble might take: not the most common form, perhaps, but not the least interesting. Some of these priests might be assigned to teach Latin grammar to young boys of the parish, but anyone who thought such employment would keep clerics out of trouble might have done well to read John of Salisbury.

Monks could also enter into this clerical underworld. Since the early Middle Ages, most monks in the West had also been priests. In a monastery where discipline was strict and surveillance careful, monks could be kept to their prayer and honest labor, but in a monastery that

---

[4] Peter Heath, *The English Parish Clergy on the Eve of the Reformation* (London: Routledge, 1969); A. Hamilton Thompson, *The English Clergy and Their Organization in the Later Middle Ages* (Oxford: Clarendon, 1947); Denys Hay, *The Church in Italy in the Fifteenth Century* (Cambridge: Cambridge University Press, 1977); Paul Adam, *La vie paroissiale en France* (Paris: Sirey, 1964).

[5] Bronisław Geremek, *The Margins of Society in Late Medieval Paris*, trans. Jean Birrell (Cambridge: Cambridge University Press, 1987), 135–66.

needed reform the monks might pursue less holy pastimes. One monk at Florence, named John of Vallombrosa (fourteenth century), was keenly interested in books during his early years in the monastery and spent day and night absorbed in them. Unfortunately he developed an attachment to the wrong kind of books, learned the art of necromancy from them, and began to practice it in secret. Eventually the other monks learned of his preoccupation; he denied it at first, but eventually was forced to admit his guilt. Several years in a dungeon left him broken in body and barely able to walk about, yet penitent and given to solitude as a spiritual discipline.[6]

If monks could engage in necromancy, so too might friars. Alleged necromancers at the court of the antipope Benedict XIII (reg. 1394–1423) were supposedly in contact with an entire group of Franciscan magicians in southern France. One Franciscan theologian, Gilles Vanalatte, was charged with obtaining a book of magic from the Muslims. Benedict himself was accused of taking instruction in necromancy and using a notorious book of magic called *The Death of the Soul*, and a book of necromancy was ostensibly once found tucked away in his bed. Other figures in this alleged conspiracy include the prior general from an order of military monks and a young Benedictine monk.[7] There is little hard evidence against any of these people, and it is tempting to assume the charges were concocted, but there is nothing unlikely about people in these positions dabbling in magic of various kinds, including necromancy.

Doubtless there were some nonclerical practitioners of necromancy as well. Necromantic conjurations sometimes appear in books otherwise devoted to medical material, which could indicate that they were used by clerics with an interest in medicine or by nonclerical physicians. For the most part, however, these magicians seem to have been clerics in one or another sense.

What do all these groups – diocesan priests, men and boys in minor orders, monks, and friars – have in common? What is most important for our purposes is that they all would have had at least a little learning, and for them this learning was a dangerous thing. Basic knowledge of the rites of exorcism, and perhaps an acquaintance with astrological images and other kinds of magic, might well lead them to experiment with conjuration. If they had access to the infamous books of necromancy, and if they were curious enough to try them out, that was all they needed for membership in this clerical underworld. The members of this company were no doubt

6 *Acta sanctorum*, March, vol. 2 (Paris and Rome: Palmé, 1866), 49–50.
7 Margaret Harvey, "Papal witchcraft: the charges against Benedict XIII", in Derek Baker, ed., *Sanctity and Secularity: The Church and the World*, Studies in Church History, 10 (Oxford: Blackwell, 1973), 109–16.

linked by similar purpose more than by any formal or lasting bonds, and certainly there is no evidence that they were organized as a group. The moral literature often represents necromancy as a fascination of youth, which the practitioners outgrow and renounce as they become older, but which leaves its mark on their later lives. The Dominican reformer Johannes Nider (d. 1438) tells about a certain Benedict, whose life can be glimpsed from other sources as well as from Nider.[8] In his youth he was a notorious necromancer, minstrel, and mime, a man "of gigantic height and frightful appearance," who lived a dissolute life and followed his "demonic books of necromancy." Through the prayers of his sister, however, he was snatched from the demons' jaws. Penitent, he went about to various rigorous monasteries seeking admittance, but his appearance and notoriety gained him little sympathy. Finally a monastery in Vienna took him in, and he gained fame for his holiness and preaching, but even so he found himself molested by demons through life. Whatever kernel of historical fact may underlie this story, in Nider's hands it becomes a kind of moral example with a dual thrust: it affirms the possibility that even a necromancer can find salvation, yet it warns of the lingering perils from a youth devoted to this iniquity.

It is impossible to say in a particular case whether the legends and the legal records are grounded in fact. We do not know for sure that John of Vallombrosa was practicing necromancy; his abbot may have put a bad face on study of more innocent astrology or some other occult knowledge. Benedict's necromancy, which Nider recounts with horror, may have amounted to little more than the tricks of performative magic. But instructions for authentic necromancy do survive, and marginal comments in them make it clear that *someone* was engaged in these practices. Given the nature of these instructions, which presuppose a command of Latin and of ritual forms, the finger of suspicion points toward the clergy. The legends and the judicial accusations had verisimilitude, if not accuracy: they had the right sort of person in mind, if not the guilty individuals.

FORMULAS AND RITUALS FOR CONJURING SPIRITS

The Dominican inquisitor Nicholas Eymericus (1320–99) evidently had ample contact with necromancers. He reported in his *Directory for Inquisitors* that he had confiscated books such as the *Table of Solomon* and

---

[8] Richard Perger, "Schwarzkünstler und Ordensmann: Aus dem Leben des Schottenpriors und Seitenstettner Abtes Benedikt (+ 1441)", *Wiener Geschichtsblätter*, 32 (1977), 167–76; Georgine Ververka, "Der merkwürdige Fall 'Benedikt': Biographie oder Predigtmärlein?", ibid., 177–80.

Honorius the Necromancer's *Treasury of Necromancy* from the magicians themselves, and after reading these books he had them burned in public. His knowledge of their contents was expanded by confessions the necromancers made to him and other inquisitors. Their books recommended numerous forms of forbidden magic: baptizing images, fumigating the head of a dead person, adjuring one demon by the name of a higher demon, inscribing characters and signs, invoking unfamiliar names, mixing the names of demons with those of angels and saints to form perversions of prayer, fumigating with incense or aloes or other aromatics, burning the bodies of birds and animals, casting salt into fire, and much more. If some of these practices entailed implicit worship of the demons, others were more explicit: the necromancers genuflect and make prostrations in the demons' honor, promise them obedience and devote themselves to their service, sing chants in their honor, and offer not only animals but their own blood as a kind of sacrifice. They practice a kind of asceticism as well in their exercise of demonic magic. They fast, macerate themselves, and observe chastity with the perverse motive of honoring demons. Likewise out of reverence for the demons, they dress themselves in black or in white garments.

We cannot assume that Eymericus was simply inventing these charges. When he says he has read the necromancers' books we have no reason to suspect he is lying. Other orthodox writers such as John Gerson, who seems also to have been familiar with the genre, corroborate much of what he had to say, and a writer like Cecco d'Ascoli (burned for his errors in 1327) gives extensive information on necromancy even when professing to condemn it. For better or for worse, some of this material survives. The Munich handbook is a prime example of the sort of document Eymericus dealt with. It contains a wealth of magical operations, which, following standard usage of the era, it refers to as "experiments." Similar or identical material can be found in other manuscripts as well, at least in fragmentary form. Eymericus confiscated such materials in Spain, and there is evidence for parallels at least in Italy, German, France, and England. William of Auvergne claimed that when he was a student at Paris in the early thirteenth century he saw books apparently of this sort. An inquisitor in Italy had a book with "diabolical figures" reduced to ashes "so that from it another copy can never be made."[9] In 1277 the archbishop of Paris condemned "books, rolls, or booklets containing necromancy or experiments of sorcery, invocations of demons, or conjurations hazardous for souls."

[9] Gene A. Brucker, "Sorcery in early Renaissance Florence", *Studies in the Renaissance*, 10 (1963), 18–19 (with translation of quotation).

The uses of necromancy were legion. One conjuration in the Munich handbook, for example, is intended to summon a demon who will impart unsurpassed mastery of all the arts and sciences without any effort on the part of the necromancer. Evidently the author was an ambitious but not particularly diligent scholar. In general, however, the aims of this magic fall into three main categories. First, it is used to affect other people's minds and wills: to drive them mad, to inflame them to love or hatred, to gain their favor, or to constrain them to do or not do some deed. It is not only human beings who can be thus constrained, but spirits and animals as well. While necromancy is not often used to work bodily harm, it can lead to discomfort that is physical as well as mental. A twelfth-century manuscript in Reims, for example, has a conjuration calling upon the demons to afflict some victim so that he cannot sleep, eat, drink, or do anything else.[10] In all likelihood, however, the ultimate goal here as in similar cases is to afflict the victim as a means toward some further goal: to keep him from sleeping, eating, and so forth, until he fulfills the necromancer's will.

Secondly, the necromancer can create illusions. He can create the illusion of a boat or a horse which will take him wherever he wishes to go. He can conjure forth an extravagant feast with banqueting and entertainment. (When writers of fiction said that such illusions might be accomplished "by craft or by necromancy," they were not necessarily joking.) Equally illusory is the use of necromancy to raise the dead: a consecrated ring, placed on the hand or foot of a corpse, will suffice to summon six demons in turn, each of whom will animate the body for one day so that it can rise up and speak. The same ring, put on the finger of a living person, will make him appear dead until it is removed.

The third main purpose of necromancy is to discern secret things, whether past, present, or future. The Munich handbook gives detailed instructions for divinatory necromancy, corresponding closely to the account given by John of Salisbury. There are formulas for finding stolen goods, for identifying a thief or a murderer, for discerning whether a friend is sick or well, on the road or elsewhere, and in general for obtaining knowledge of anything that is uncertain. The desired information is to be provided by spirits, who will appear to a virgin boy (or, exceptionally, a girl) in a crystal, on a mirror, on the blade of a sword, on the greased shoulder blade of a ram, or on the boy's fingernail. Alternatively, if the purpose is to identify thieves, the thieves themselves may appear in the reflecting surface. In one procedure there are guidelines for what the boy should say when a spirit in the form of a king appears in his fingernail: he

---

[10] Robert-Léon Wagner, *"Sorcier" et "magicien": Contribution à l'histoire du vocabulaire de la magie* (Paris: Droz, 1939), 49 n. 2.

should invite the spirit to dismount from his horse and bring a throne to sit on; he should ask if the spirit is hungry, and if so he should suggest sending for a ram to eat; when the king has dined, the boy should have him remove his crown, put his right hand on his head, and swear to tell the truth. A medieval reader would perhaps have found nothing comic in the notion of a young boy holding such discourse with a shadowy image in his fingernail. The prospect might instead arouse horror, fascination, or both. In another case a conjuration is intended to obtain visions of "angels" in sleep, so they may impart knowledge of past, present, and future things.

While the techniques for necromancy can become complex, they reduce to a few main elements: magic circles, conjurations, and sacrifices are the most striking elements in this magic.

Magic circles may be traced on the ground with a sword or a knife, or else inscribed on a piece of parchment or cloth. Sometimes they are simple geometrical forms with perhaps a few words or characters inscribed about the circumference. More often, however, they are complex, with inscriptions and symbols of various kinds inside, positions for various magical objects, and a designated place for "the master," meaning the necromancer. Both the material to write on and the fluid to use as ink may be specified. The Munich manual has the necromancer writing an inscription with the blood of a "mouser" on a piece of linen, which is then to be buried near the house of one's victim. Another inscription is to be written with the blood of a hoopoe. Yet another is to be written "in the Hebrew manner," presumably meaning from right to left, with the blood of a bat. John Gerson speaks of virgin parchment and the skin of a lion as used for invoking demons, apparently as materials for magic circles.

One particularly interesting circle from a fifteenth-century magical miscellany has the basic form of a single band with a triangular band inscribed within it (Fig. 16). In the center various objects are depicted: a sword, a ring, a vessel for oil, a sceptre, and a square tablet with the Tetragrammaton and four crosses on it. Inscriptions within the triangular band give various holy names separated by crosses. In and near the circular band are magical characters, crosses, and words, such as the common magical word "AGLA" (which has been deciphered as standing for *Ata Gibor Leolam Adonai*, Hebrew for "Thou art mighty for ever, O Lord"). One inscription outside the triangular bands says that this "figure of friendship" should be made at the hour of Venus, while another such inscription says that it is a "figure for the making of bridges and [discovery of] treasures." This is, then, a multi-purpose circle, with purposes that vary and with alternative inscriptions (given at the bottom of the page) to be used accordingly.

The term "circle" should not be construed as referring primarily to the

Fig. 16. Magic circle, from a fifteenth-century manuscript

actual circular border or band, which seems to have been less important to the necromancers than the signs and inscriptions with which it was filled. While there is ample evidence in medieval Europe for the importance of circles as foci of magical power, the necromancers evidently conceived them mainly as enclosures within which various signs and objects might be contained. The circular bands served as places to put inscriptions, which usually consisted of names for God or snippets from Christian liturgy. One magical circle has fully five concentric bands with formulas such as

Salue crux digna ("Hail, O noble cross"), and a complex of crosses, stars, and other signs in its center.[11] Nor is there much evidence that the borders had a protective function. As we will see, legends about the necromancers interpreted these circles as protected devices within which the magicians were safe from demons, but there is little reason to think that necromancers themselves viewed them in this way. One experiment in the Munich handbook expressly says that the demons will come, when invoked, *inside* the circle. In another case, however, the periphery does have special significance: one experiment for love magic involves a circle within which the lovers can rendezvous, and the instruction says it is best if it has a wide circumference to allow them ample space.

If the circles given are inscribed on cloth or parchment they may have powers other than conjuring demons. Thus, a circle intended primarily to summon a demon in the form of a horse may be used to protect its bearer from hostile horses, and if it is accompanied by the blood and tooth of a horse it will cause death to any horse that beholds it. A circle designed as part of a ceremony to resuscitate a dead person can be used for love magic, or for ascertaining whether a sick person will die, or for keeping dogs from barking. If they are traced on the ground, however, the circles are, so to speak, disposable. The Munich handbook is usually careful to instruct the necromancer when he should erase the circle, presumably so as to leave no evidence of his magic, though possibly also to prevent others from using it.

If the circle (taken as including both border and contents) is the main visual element in the necromancer's techniques, the conjuration is the key oral component. The conjuration usually revolves about one or another imperative verb for "command": the necromancer addresses the spirits with the order, "I adjure you" or "I conjure you" to appear and carry out some deed. Beyond this, the formula may be embellished in numerous ways. Standard Christian prayers are often mingled with conjurations to enchance their power: the Psalms, portions of the litany of the saints, and so forth. One experiment requires kneeling with folded hands, turning toward heaven, and confidently saying a "prayer" to "the most high and benign King of the East." The instructions sometimes say to repeat a conjuration three times, or seven times, or once in each of the four compass directions, or even four times in each of these directions.

Conjurations in the Munich handbook repeatedly instruct the spirits to appear in a pleasant, nonthreatening form. The accompanying text tells that when they do come it will be in the form of a king, a staff of servants, a

---

[11] British Library, MS Sloane 3556, fol. 1ᵛ.

band of sailors, a black man, or above all a knight. One fifteenth-century German manuscript now at Prague says that the Devil will come in the form of a black dog and will answer all questions.[12]

Apart from the visual and oral elements in necromancy there were operative components: deeds that the magician performed, particularly sacrifices and sympathetic rituals. The Munich manual has the necromancer invoking the spirits at a crossroads with "the sacrifice of a white cock," which he beseeches them to accept. Another experiment requires taking a captive hoopoe along to the place of conjuration; at one stage in the proceedings the demons will ask for this bird, and when they have sworn to obey the necromancer he will give it to them. (Indeed, the Munich handbook says explicitly that the hoopoe "has great power for necromancers and invokers of demons" and is thus often used of their purposes. Albert the Great corroborates this testimony, reporting that the brain, tongue, and heart of the hoopoe are especially valuable for enchanters.) An early thirteenth-century conjuration in a manuscript now at Paris gives cryptic instructions which have been decoded and translated as, "Take a bat and sacrifice it with [your] right hand; with [your] left hand draw blood from [its] head."[13] It was widely believed that demons (like the ghosts of classical literature) can be enticed by blood, especially by human blood; thus, according to Michael Scot, necromancers often use water mixed with blood, or wine that resembles blood, "and they sacrifice with flesh or a living human being, such as a bit of their own flesh or of a corpse . . . knowing that the consecration of a spirit in a ring or a bottle cannot be achieved except by the performance of many sacrifices."[14]

The sacrifice was thus usually of an animal, but sometimes other substances were offered to demons. The necromancer might be required to scatter milk and honey in the air, or to place ashes, flour, salt, and other items in jars which would be placed within the magic circle. The Prague manuscript tells the magician to offer coal, bread, cheese, three shoeing-nails, barley, and salt as "presents" for the demons.

When necromancy entails image magic it is usually sympathetic: the action carried out on the image is transferred to the person represented. Thus, love magic may involve writing the names of demons on an image of the intended person, so that these demons will afflict her until she submits to the necromancer's will. The demons symbolically represented

[12] Hartmut   Beckers,   "Eine   spätmittelalterliche   deutsche   Anleitung   zur Teufelsbeschwörung mit Runenschriftverwendung", *Zeitschrift für deutsches Altertum und deutsche Literatur*, 113 (1984), 136–45.

[13] Marie-Thérèse d'Alverny, "Survivance de la magie antique", in Paul Wilpert, ed., *Antike und Orient im Mittelalter* (Berlin: de Gruyter, 1962), 159, 173.

[14] Lynn Thorndike, "Some medieval conceptions of magic", *The Monist*, 25 (1915), 123 (with translations of quotations).

on the image are to be really present in the woman. To gain favor from some dignitary the magician carves an image of that person, bearing a crown if he is a king, or other symbols of power as the case demands. Then he makes a second image to represent himself, and writes on these images the names of the persons represented. He binds a small iron chain to the neck of the potentate's image, places the other end of the chain in the hand of his own image, makes the image of the potentate bow before his own image, and so forth.

Often these sympathetic operations are accompanied by incantations explicating the gestures. If the necromancer is trying to arouse hatred between two friends he may heat two stones (representing the victims) over a fire, then cast them into frigid water, then strike them together. While so doing he will say, "I do not strike these stones, but I strike N. and N. whose names are written here." An experiment for love magic involves the formula, "as a hart longs for the fountain, so may N. long for my love, and as the raven longs for cadavers, so may she desire me, and as this wax melts before the fire, so may she desire my love."

Secrecy is vital to all these operations. The Munich handbook warns the necromancer at various points to keep the experiments secret because they have "great" or "ineffable power." Equally important is carrying out the experiments in a secret place, and guarding carefully the book "in which all power is contained." The *Book of Consecrations*, a text incorporated in the Munich handbook and found elsewhere as well, instructs its user to keep it carefully concealed so it does not fall into the hands of "the foolish."

If the necromancer wants to repeat an experiment he may need to go through the original ceremony each time. In some cases, however, he may be able to make the demons swear the first time they appear that in the future they will come whenever called. He may have the demons "consecrate" some object, which will allow him to call them on subsequent occasions. A magic circle may itself be thus consecrated, or a bridle may be consecrated and then used to recall a spirit in the form of a horse.

The necromancer may also wish to undo the harm he has done, and this is easy enough if the original magic was accomplished through sympathetic operations that can be reversed. If stones have been buried to arouse hatred, friendship may be restored by digging up the stones, heating and crushing them, then casting the fragments into a river while saying, "May all enmity be removed . . . by the mercy of the beneficent God, who does not respect the malice of sinners, amen." If a cloth with an inscription on it has been buried near a victim's house, the bewitchment may be undone by digging it up and burning it, then casting the ashes into a flowing stream. The effect may be guaranteed by reciting the formula, "Just as this fire consumes this cloth, so may all this work which I have done against N. be wholly consumed." The demons who have caused the damage may be released from this service, with words such as, "I, N., absolve you to go as you will."

One might well wonder what in fact happened when the necromancers followed all these complicated instructions. Did the power of suggestion work upon their minds? Did demons appear? Did they try one or two experiments in vain and then give up? John of Salisbury's experience suggests a combination of results. Sometimes the magic would not work, in which case the necromancer or his assistant would simply abandon the effort, perhaps blaming the results on personal disqualification. At other times the results would be persuasive enough to convince the believer that his belief was well grounded. Most of the goals sought by this particular form of magic were in some way psychological and intangible, which would make it hard to prove that an experiment had utterly failed. If the magician tried to kill a person by magic and that person survived, the failure would be clear, but if the object was favor at court or enmity between friends one could often point to apparent success, even if it was not dramatic.

The author of the Munich manual admits little possibility of failure, and provides testimonials to the efficacy of his magic. He tells how an experiment for love magic was used by Solomon, who obtained any woman he desired by using it. After telling the various uses for a particular magic circle, he says that he has personally experienced all the effects he is describing, and he is leaving aside those he has not experienced. At another juncture he addresses a courtly reader, whether real or hypothetical: "You have often seen me carry out this work at your court." Stretching plausibility to the breaking-point, he tells how he once played a trick on the emperor and his nobles while they were out hunting. Summoning a band of demons, he had them attack the emperor as if they were human rebels, then erect an illusory castle in which the emperor could take refuge. The demons were in the process of besieging the castle when the time limit for this experiment ran out, whereupon rebels and castle all suddenly vanished, leaving the emperor and his men standing, perplexed, in a marsh.

In reading the necromancers' formulas one may find oneself growing sympathetic toward the inquisitors who condemned all these works and pomps. The blasphemous use of ritual, the invocation of spirits for amoral or straightforwardly destructive purposes, and the sheer megalomania of the necromancers can appear repulsive to modern as well as medieval eyes. These writings do, however, reveal certain things about the society that spawned them. The necromancers and the inquisitors alike believed in the awesome power of ritual. More specifically, they believed that by fulfill-ing certain outward and objective standards ritual could have automatic power. Inward disposition of the heart was not decisive; what counted most was the correct observance of outward forms. The host was effec-tively consecrated at mass, even if the priest was personally irreverent. So too, the necromancers believed, God could be effectively mocked and his power used for evil ends if the rituals of necromancy were correctly performed. Necromancy thus parodied the basic late medieval under-standing of ritual.

THE SOURCES FOR NECROMANCY

Necromancy is a blend of various practices, all incorporated into the framework of explicitly demonic magic. The sympathetic operations for sorcery, found in the common magical tradition without any overt appeal to demons, are here recast. Animals which appear elsewhere in magical lore, such as cats and hoopoes, here became sacrificial offerings to the demons. Divination using reflective surfaces (catoptromancy) becomes a means for conjuring evil spirits. Essentially, however, necromancy is a merger of astral magic and exorcism. The former is a foreign import, derived from Islamic culture; the latter is essentially a domestic product, long established within Christendom, though there is reason to suspect the influence of Jewish tradition in the development of this component. Even in early Christianity, forms for exorcism seem to have been molded according to Jewish practice; later Jewish influence shows especially in the reliance on holy names as forces to use against the demons.

The influence of astral magic shows quite clearly in the Munich handbook. The author comments after one experiment that all the Spanish, Arabic, Hebrew, Chaldean, Greek, and Latin "necromancers and astrologers" are agreed on its efficacy, and he cites books, evidently dealing with astral magic, from which it is taken. Experiments recom-mended in this manual are to be performed at fixed times: on a Saturday before sunrise and under a waning moon, on a Thursday under a waxing moon, at the first hour of a Wednesday under a waxing moon, under a new moon, and so forth. Most importantly, the boundary between astral and elemental spirits on the one hand and fallen angels on the other becomes confused, and necromancers appeal at times to one sort of spirit, at times to another. Michael Scot says that astrological images can serve to conjure not only the powers that rule the planetary orbits and demons associated with the moon, but also the damned spirits present in the wind. There is much justice, therefore, to John Gerson's complaint that astrol-ogy, a handmaid of theology and "a noble and wonderful science, revealed to Adam", has been "disfigured by vain observances, impious errors, sacrilegious superstitions."

The practice of fumigation, common in astral magic, was taken over into necromancy. The ceremonies often require fumigating an image with the fumes of myrrh and saffron, fumigating a circle with the marrow of a dead man, fumigating a circle with frankincense and myrrh, or fumigating a divinatory mirror with aloes, ambergris, myrrh, and frankincense. One list of fumigations in the Munich handbook gives a special formula for each day of the week, correlated with some particular purpose. On Thursday, for example, one burns frankincense or saffron to bring concord between enemies. Also perhaps borrowed from the tradition of astral magic is the practice of burying images. An experiment to gain favor with a potentate calls for carrying his image secretly throughout town, and if possible going into his very presence with the image secretly on one's person; then one should bury the image, "and you will see wonders." The details of this operation parallel closely those found, for example, in *Picatrix*.[15] So too, one can find precedent in astral magic even for animal sacrifices to spirits.

It would be wrong to conclude, however, that necromancy is simply an extension of astral magic, with the demonic element in this magic made overt rather than merely implicit. Equally important is the other side of necromancy, its link with exorcism. We saw in Chapter 4 that the adjurations of the common magical tradition are difficult to distinguish from exorcisms. Ordinarily, however, the healer or exorcist is trying to dispel the demons or the diseases they cause. The healer or exorcist conquers the demons, calling upon all the supernatural aid he can muster, and reminding the evil spirits that God's power is greater than theirs and is now being used against them. Necromancers use the same formulas with very different intent. Orthodox exorcists and necromancers both use the terms "exorcise," "conjure," and "adjure" interchangeably. The Munich handbook, for example, regularly uses the formulas, "I exorcise and conjure you," or "I invoke and conjure and exorcise and constrain you." The *Book of Consecrations* explicitly speaks of the necromancer as an exorcist. The difference, of course, is that while the orthodox exorcist is struggling to dispel demons, the necromancer is trying to allure and use them for his ends. One lengthy conjuration contained in the Munich handbook is clearly adapted from an exorcism; this provenance shows, for example, in the following passage:

I command you, O most wicked dragon, by the power of the Lord, [and] I adjure you in the name of the Lamb without blemish who walks on the asp and the

---

[15] *Picatrix* even refers to its magic several times as "necromancy," though most of it falls more clearly into the closely related area of astral magic; the distinction may work better for Latin than for Arabic texts.

basilisk, and who has trampled the lion and the dragon; may you carry out quickly whatever I command. Tremble and fear when the name of God is invoked, the God whom hell fears and to whom the virtues of heaven, the powers, dominations, and other virtues are subject and whom they fear and adore, and whom cherubim and seraphim praise with untiring voices. The Word made flesh commands you. He who was born of a virgin commands you. Jesus of Nazareth, who created you, commands you, to fulfill at once all that I ask of you, or all that I wish to have or to know. For the longer you delay in doing what I command or order, the more your punishment will increase from day to day. I exorcise you, O accursed and lying spirit, by the words of truth.

The vocabulary of exorcism is all familiar, though the formula is obviously altered: instead of commanding the evil spirit to depart, the necromancer calls on him to serve.

Like the exorcist, the necromancer routinely commands the demons by the power of holy persons, names, events, and objects. The early thirteenth-century conjuration mentioned above includes the formula. "I conjure you by the Father and the Son and the Holy Spirit, by Mary the mother of the Lord, by Mary Magdalene, and Mary [the mother] of James, and Salome" (cf. Mark 16:1). Elsewhere the demons are adjured by the Trinity (perhaps the most common source of power), by God in his capacity as creator, by Christ as the Word by whom God created, or by Christ in his function as judge on the last day. The power of the saints in heaven and the Church militant of Earth can be called into service. Even the hierarchy of demonic spirits in hell can be called upon to constrain the demons whose presence is desired. "Tetragrammaton," a term for the unspoken name of God, appears routinely as if it were itself one of his names. The formulas may cite the ineffable names of the creator "at which all things in heaven, on earth, and beneath the earth tremble." Various names of Christ are used, including Ely, Sother, Adonay, Sabaoth, Alpha and Omega. And names of spirits may be used to constrain other spirits: one conjuration lists thirty-three names of "angels who are powerful in the air." Events of the Old and New Testaments are often included; one conjuration gives a précis of the Old Testament that runs to one and a half folios. Demons are made to quake by being reminded of the coming of Christ and the sentence they will hear at the Last Judgment. Among the objects whose power gets coopted are the sun and moon; the heavens and Earth; all animals, creeping things, and flying things, whether bipeds, tripeds (!), or quadrupeds; the wounds of Christ and the crown of thorns; all the characters of Solomon and the magical experiments of Virgil (!). In short, the demons are told that they have marshaled against them "all things which have power to terrify and constrain you." In all of this the conjurations are following the spirit – and often the letter – of orthodox exorcism.

The stance of the conjurer, like that of the exorcist, is at the same time both coercive and petitionary: he commands the demons, but only by such power as is granted to him by God. The necromancers clearly did see themselves as constraining the demons by their commands. This claim provoked writers such as Arnold of Villanova and John of Frankfurt to retort that demons could not be coerced, and that if they came at all when summoned they came voluntarily, though they might persuade the necromancers that they were constrained so as to ensnare them more effectively. What these writers could not accept was the notion that God would aid the necromancers in this process. The necromancers' own stance vis-à-vis God was, in any case, different from their stance toward demons. This is quite clear in the *Book of Consecrations*, where the "exorcist" presents himself as a humble and unworthy supplicant before God, beseeching divine aid to attain power over demons. The same mentality is at least implied elsewhere, since the conjurer constantly uses orthodox prayers, both on the magic circles and in the conjurations themselves, in an effort to coopt the divine power for his own ends.

Why God should consent to this use of his power is obscure. One possibility is that the necromancers held an amoral conception of God, as a being who could be influenced (if not coerced) by prayer to bestow his aid in all sorts of dubious enterprises. Alternatively the necromancers may have persuaded themselves that their causes were in fact holy: that if they were destroying their enemies they were righteous in so doing, that if they sought hidden treasures they would use them only for noble purposes, and that if they won the love of married women God would at least wink at their misconduct, even if he did not smile.

Like manuals of orthodox exorcism, the books of necromancy insist on ascetic preparation and ritual purity (if not moral integrity) as prerequisites for commanding the demons. The experiments call upon the necromancer to fast, to be bathed and shaven, to be dressed in white, and so forth. The conjurer is sometimes instructed to abstain from sexual contact for a certain number of days before performing an experiment; although orthodox exorcists were supposed to be celibate clerics, committed to permanent rather than temporary chastity, late medieval books of exorcism sometimes impose precisely the same restriction.[16] These ascetic procedures may be intended not simply to entice demons but also, and perhaps more importantly, to protect the necromancer from the demons. Cecco d'Ascoli remarks that these conjurations require prayer and fasting precisely because of their "great peril." It would be naive, of course, to expect orthodox writers to approve of these practices. According to Gerson, the practitioners of these arts only compound their guilt by

---

[16] Adolph Franz, *Die kirchlichen Benediktionen im Mittelalter*, vol. 2 (Freiburg i. B.: Herder, 1909), 567 n. 4.

performing actions that are in themselves holy: their deeds are all the worse because they thus debase these observances.

More often than not the necromancers were quite unambiguous about the kind of spirits they were invoking. The Reims conjuration says explicitly, "I conjure you, O devils who fell from heaven . . . I conjure you, who in hell adore Beelzebut as your worthy prince." The Munich handbook and the Paris manuscript, too, invoke Satan, Beelzebub, and Lucifer, and other spirits of unmistakable identity such as the demon Berich. The Prague manuscript gives a relatively simple formula: the necromancer should go out into the fields at night and cry out, "Diabolo diaboliczo, Satana sathaniczo, come here to me, I wish to speak to you, and take the presents that I have brought you."[17] And the Munich manual speaks of constraining "malign spirits," "airy powers and infernal princes," or simply "demons."

If necromancy is essentially a blend of astral magic and exorcism, however, it is not surprising to find occasional ambiguity about the spirits who get invoked. Some sources speak of neutral spirits, whether astral (associated with the heavenly bodies) or elemental (connected with natural powers on Earth). The Munich handbook says at one point that the spirits who come as sailors and transport the necromancer in an illusory boat are "between good and evil, neither in hell nor in paradise." Cecco d'Ascoli gives Oriens, Amaymon, Paymon, and Egim as the names of spirits who rule over the four compass directions and have legions of subordinate spirits at their service. One passage in the Munich manual suggests that good spirits should be invoked for good purposes, and evil spirits for wicked ones, but things are not always so simple: both kinds of spirit get invoked for purposes that are moral, immoral, or simply amoral.

Did genuinely benign spirits appear, or were they evil demons posing as angels of light? One orthodox test for the status of an angel was whether its name was traditional. The only good angels with names officially recognized are Gabriel, Michael, and Raphael. As early as the eighth century, when a priest supplicated the angels Uriel, Raguel, Tubuel, Adin, Tubuas, Sabaok, and Simiel, the bishops of his region condemned his prayer because the names were unfamiliar, which suggested to them as to even earlier authorities that these angels were in fact fallen.[18]

Attitudes toward even explicitly evil spirits might vary. The Munich manual tells the necromancer at one point that when the demons come he should greet them with a pious wish: "May the Lord in his mercy restore

[17] The use of ordinary names for the Devil, along with the general simplicity of the instructions, has prompted the editor of this text to suggest that it reflects folklore rather than learned tradition. Even when it is more clearly learned and clerical, however, necromancy often incorporates elements of common folklore.

[18] Aron Gurevich, *Medieval Popular Culture: Problems of Belief and Perception*, trans. János M. Bak and Paul A. Hollingsworth (Cambridge: Cambridge University Press, 1988), 66–7.

you to your former state," presumably meaning their condition as unfallen angels. Even a writer on the border of orthodoxy, however, would normally be cautious. Cecco d'Ascoli tells that Floron was from among the cherubim, that he knew numerous secrets of nature, that he had been captivated within a mirror but had deceived many by his ambiguous oracles. "So beware of these demons, because their ultimate intention is to deceive Christians to the discredit of our Lord Jesus Christ."[19]

Among the writings of the necromancers are catalogues of spirits with their forms, powers, and attributes. One fifteenth-century French manuscript, for example, lists Bulfas, a great prince whose function is to arouse discord and battles; Gemer, a great king who teaches people the virtues of herbs and all sciences, and both heals and inflicts diseases; Machin, who teaches the virtues of herbs and of gems, and transports the "master" from one region to another; and other spirits.[20] In the light of this material it is not surprising that critics of magic should see even herbal lore as something taught by demons: the necromancers themselves held this view.

The mentality of the necromancers is in any case difficult to penetrate, but certain of their writings are utterly baffling. A classic instance is the *Sworn Book* ascribed to a certain "Honorius Son of Euclid" of Thebes.[21] The clearly fictional premise of this work is that under the pressure of persecution from the pope and his cardinals eighty-nine magicians from Naples, Athens, and Toledo have assembled to ensure the survival of their art. They have entrusted to Honorius the task of compiling a grand summary that will contain all of its essentials. Fearful that this sacred work will come into alien hands, however, they have agreed that there will never be more than three copies of it, that a master who has a copy will entrust it only to a proven disciple, and that if he has no such heir he will bury it in a secret place before he dies. The text itself consists mainly of "prayers," some in Latin and others in what appears to be pseudo-Hebrew. Fumigations are also prescribed, and names of angels given. Kabbalistic influence shows most clearly in the complex instructions for constructing a magic pentangle. Most of the work, however, deals with invocation of spirits. The spirits addressed are neither straightforwardly demonic nor conventionally angelic; they correspond more to the spirits of astral magic, though there is little other astrological influence in the work.

The prayers given in this book can be used for various purposes,

[19] Thorndike, "Some medieval conceptions", 125.
[20] Trinity College, Cambridge, MS o.8.29, fol. 179^v–182^v.
[21] British Library, MS Royal 17.A.XLII; cf. Thorndike, *A History of Magic and Experimental Science*, vol. 2, 283–9.

though the goal highlighted throughout is a vision of God.[22] At one juncture the author says that the magician must go to mass and perform other holy works, and warns that if all this is done to any evil end it will redound to the magician's condemnation. Yet the list of purposes envisaged for this magic includes a wide variety of goals, not all of them noble. The magician can use this magic for learning the powers of herbs and for gaining knowledge of all secrets. He can also use it to open locked doors, inflict sickness and death, destroy kingdoms and empires, and perform other works that few would consider holy. The author may sincerely have believed that this magic was not demonic, but no inquisitor would have indulged this plea.

Further wrinkles in the complex mentality of the necromancers are suggested by a fifteenth-century manuscript that gives instructions for love magic. The heading reads, "Experiments which King Solomon devised for the love and courting of a certain noble queen, and they are experiments of nature." What follows is a list of magic tricks; presumably Solomon is supposed to have used these to entertain his beloved. He tells how to make a hollow ring leap and run through the house, how to carry fire in your shirt or hands, how to cause a person to strip, how to make a great flame explode in the face of a companion, and so forth. All these tricks are presumably meant as ways to a woman's heart. At the very end, however, the "experiments" abruptly change their tone and character; if up to this point they have been "experiments of nature," the last of them hardly qualifies for this description. It tells how to make a lead ring on the day and at the hour when Venus is dominant. After making the ring one should fast through the day, then go out at night and offer sacrifice with the blood of a dove. Writing with this blood on the skin of a hare, one should inscribe the name and sign of the "angel" Abamixtra. After this ceremony has been carried out, one should approach the desired woman with ring in hand, and she will obey one's every wish. Certain key words in the instruction are given in cipher, but not enough to obscure the sense.[23]

The most perplexing feature of this text is its mixture of apparently playful tricks and seemingly serious necromancy. Was the author in fact a serious proponent of demonic magic trying to disguise his mischief under a cloak of levity? Or was he rather a mere prankster using a necromantic formula as the mysterious climax to an essentially playful collection? The

---

[22] The theologians of Paris in 1398, perhaps with this book in mind, condemned the belief that magic could attain that goal.

[23] British Library, MS Sloane 121, fols. 90ᵛ–93ᵛ. The words in cipher are *mxlkerem* and *xolkntbtem*, for *mulierem* and *volintatem (sic)*. The name of the angel may be "Abanuxtra," but "Abamixtra" seems the more likely reading.

most plausible answer, perhaps, is a combination of the two: the same man could have different moods, and his magic could have different modes. It is not unlikely that people attracted to one form of magic would at least dabble in others as well.

NECROMANCY IN THE *EXEMPLA*

The Pilgrimage of the Life of Man, an allegorical poem by Guillaume de Deguilleville (d. after 1358) translated into Middle English by John Lydgate (ca. 1370–1449), contains an episode in which the Pilgrim encounters a messenger of Necromancy. The messenger tells how his mistress, Necromancy, runs a school for scholars such as himself. Only those sent by Covetousness enter that school. What the scholars learn is how to invoke spirits and make them answer questions and obey commands. This power comes ultimately from the great King, namely God. The messenger demonstrates by tracing a circle on the ground, with characters and figures (Fig. 17). Previous scholars in this academy, he says, include many luminaries: Solomon, Virgil, Cyprian, and Abelard. The Pilgrim protests: surely Solomon and Cyprian repented before death! And surely these arts are diabolical and damnable. The messenger, however, remains unpersuaded, and the Pilgrim is lucky to escape without being destroyed by Necromancy herself.

The identity of the messenger in this story is unclear. While he is not explicitly spoken of in the text as a cleric, he is essentially a scholar, and what he gains from his mistress is a kind of learning. Necromancy herself, as a schoolmistress, carries a book entitled *The Death of the Soul*; this is not simply an allegorical motif, but the actual title of a medieval book of necromancy. Yet the image of the messenger probably comes rather from the tradition of sermon *exempla* than from any other source.

Preachers struggling to dissuade their congregations from sin often made their argument by telling edifying *exempla* or anecdotes, and among these stories are certain influential legends about magicians. The prototype of these tales is the legend of Theophilus, who is supposed to have learned from a Jewish sorcerer how to make a pact with the Devil by renouncing Christ and giving a written document to the Evil One. Later he regretted this deed but was unable to recover his pact until he prayed to the Virgin and secured her intercession. The original version of this legend comes from sixth-century Asia Minor, and in Latin it got retold in numerous variations, which served much later as a basis for the story of Faust.

Caesarius of Heisterbach (ca. 1180–1240), a Cistercian monk, gave several pertinent *exempla* in his *Dialogue on Miracles*. In one of these a

Fig. 17. The Pilgrim encountering a student of Necromancy, from Lydgàte, *Pilgrimage of the Life of Man*

knight who does not believe in demons nonetheless challenges a cleric "famous for his skill in necromancy" to conjure some fiends and thus overcome his disbelief. After some protestation the cleric takes the knight to a crossroads, traces a circle in the dirt, and warns that to protect himself from the demons the knight must stand inside the circle. When the demons come they try to terrify the knight with howling wind, grunting swine, and other means. Finally the Devil himself comes as a terrifying phantom, towering over the trees, cloaked in a dark robe. The Fiend represents himself as a useful servant of his friends, including the cleric who has summoned him. He accurately recounts the knight's sins, thus proving that no evil is hidden from him. Repeatedly he makes requests, all of which the knight refuses. Finally he stretches out his arm as if to snatch the knight and haul him away. Terrified, the knight cries out, and the cleric comes rushing to his aid, whereupon the Devil vanishes. For the rest of his life the knight has a deathly pale complexion and is scrupulously moral.[24]

This tale contains three motifs that are common in these necromantic *exempla*. First, the circle is clearly seen as a protective enclosure. Caesarius elsewhere tells of a priest who steps outside the circle and is attacked so viciously by the Devil that he soon dies, and in yet another *exemplum* a necromancer's client rushes from the circle in pursuit of a beautiful woman, only to have his neck wrung like that of a hen being slaughtered.[25] This recurrent motif, which does not seem grounded in the rituals of the necromancers themselves, may be a way of dramatizing the precarious situation of those who dabble in necromancy: a way of saying, in effect, that one step in any wrong direction will lead to imminent perdition.

Secondly, the Fiend himself is shown as a lying and untrustworthy servant. This theme is nicely reflected in an *exemplum* told by John of Frankfurt about a bishop who gave himself over to a demon in exchange for honors but who made many enemies. One day these foes were attacking his castle and he consulted his demon to see if he should flee. The demon told him, "Don't! Stay put! Your enemies will come forth meekly and will be subject to you." Inspired to false confidence, the bishop stayed, his castle was captured, and he was burned for his offenses. Before he expired, however, the demon explained that his Latin could be differently construed as, "Don't stay put! Your enemies will come thrice in strength and will set fire beneath you."[26] Could the demon help it if the bishop had misunderstood? The moral could apply to necromancers and ordinary folk alike: he who trusts a demon deserves the consequences.

The third theme is the possibility of repentance. All good preachers know the principle of first arousing fear and then proffering hope. In

---

24 Caesarius of Heisterbach, *The Dialogue on Miracles*, trans. H. von E. Scott and C. C. Swinton Bland, vol. 1 (London: Routledge, 1929), 315–17; cf. ibid., 317–20.
25 D. L. d'Avray, *The Preaching of the Friars: Sermons Diffused from Paris before 1300* (Oxford: Clarendon, 1985), 198–202.
26 The first version is *Non, sta secure, venient inimici tui suaviter et subdentur tibi*; the second is *Non sta secure, venient inimici tui sua vi ter, et subdent ur tibi*. Hansen, *Quellen und Untersuchungen*, 79.

another of his *exempla* Caesarius tells of a student who does homage to the Devil merely by holding on to a stone that the Fiend gave him, in return for academic eminence. Fearing for his soul, however, the student throws away the stone and loses all his ill-gotten knowledge, but does save his soul. In yet another case, set in Toledo, a necromancer's pupil even gets dragged down into hell, and the master has to retrieve him through subtle negotiation with the Devil. Restored to life, the pupil leaves Toledo, and atones for his sins as a Cistercian monk.

These tales must have been effective propaganda, and must have done much to arouse fear of necromancy in the preachers' congregations. But the question must surely have occurred, "What does all this have to do with us?" Most of the evidence suggests that the legends were right in showing the necromancers as clerics: few laypeople would have had the command of Latin and of ritual necessary to work the "experiments" contained in the Munich handbook and other such sources. When they heard and repeated these stories, however, laypeople must have wondered whether other magicians as well were engaged in explicitly demonic magic. If even clerics could be guilty of such transgression, what of the old woman or the village leech who used odd herbal remedies and superstitious charms? Perhaps they too were practicing necromancy? The historian may venture a cautious negative answer to this question, but contemporaries were not always so generous.

8

PROHIBITION, CONDEMNATION, AND PROSECUTION

There were many reasons for opposing magic. Those who practiced it were in danger of physical and spiritual assault from the wily demons they sought to master. Even in its apparently innocent and entertaining forms it was at best frivolous and vain. It could involve presumptuous encroachment on the mysteries and creative powers of God. It involved erroneous assumptions about the demons, their power, and their dignity. All these arguments occur in medieval discussion of magic. In legislation the central concern was fairly simple: magic can do grievous harm to other people. In moral and theological condemnations there were two further grounds for opposing magic: it may rely on demons even when it seems to use natural forces, and it makes sacrilegious use of holy objects or blasphemously mingles holy with unholy words. These anxieties may seem difficult to share in an age that widely professes disbelief in both religion and magic, but simply to understand the historical record we must be able to grasp what a threat magic represented in an age when its power was almost universally taken for granted.

It is perhaps misleading to distinguish between moral and theological condemnation on the one hand and legal prosecution on the other. When moralists condemned magic they often cited legal enactments to show that it was immoral, and legislation always presupposed a moral stance. This interpenetration of the moral and the legal is effectively suggested by a German woodcut of 1487 warning against sorcery (Fig. 18). A witch in the center has demons around her and a bottle, presumably filled with a potion, in her hand. In separate circles are various authorities who had condemned magic, or whose words or experience served to warn against it: King Saul, the apostle Paul, Isaiah, Pope John XXII, an emperor, Saint

Augustine, and the theologians of Paris; the circle on the bottom has a picture of the Devil himself, with an open book. The text below gives pertinent quotations from or about each of these figures.[1] Legal prohibitions and moral condemnations are mixed at random in this effort to show that all authorities are united against sorcery.

While the two approaches thus go hand in hand, it may be useful to deal first with the legal prohibitions, which were developed early and then endlessly repeated, and which were relatively simple and straightforward in their contents. Then we can turn to the more elaborate statements of moral condemnation, for which more of our evidence comes from the later Middle Ages.

LEGAL PROHIBITION

In principle there were two kinds of legislation against magic: that of the secular authorities, such as emperors, kings, and town governments; and that of the Church, which continued through the Middle Ages to enact canons binding on clergy and laity.[2] Secular law could prescribe any of various penalties, including execution, for the crime of magic, but it was usually more concerned with the harm worked by magic than with the magical ceremonies themselves. The Church could require penance for the sin of magic or could excommunicate the offender, and was usually concerned with the offense against God as much as with any harm done to human victims. Yet this distinction, helpful as an index to general trends, breaks down at various points. Many secular rulers in the Middle Ages were under the influence of churchmen and issued laws clearly reflecting clerical concerns. Indeed, there were times when ecclesiastical legislation got taken over into secular codes. The distinction is thus real but not absolute.

Early medieval law codes of the various Germanic peoples typically included strictures against harmful magic. A sixth-century code of the Visigoths, for example, refers to sorcerers who travel about and get paid by peasants for putting curses on their enemies' crops and animals. The same law code refers to sorcerers who arouse destructive tempests. It seems to have made little difference whether the harm was done by magic or by

---

[1] See Paul Kristeller, ed., *Holzschnitte im Königl. Kupferstichkabinett zu Berlin*, ser. 2 (Berlin: Cassirer, 1915), 36–7. The quotations are from 1 Chronicles 10:13, 1 Corinthians 10:20, Isaiah 47:11–12, John XXII's *Super illius specula*, an imperial statute, the writings of Augustine, the condemnation of magic issued in 1398 by the theologians at the University of Paris, and Ecclesiasticus 13.

[2] For this and following sections Joseph Hansen, *Zauberwahn, Inquisition und Hexenprozess im Mittelalter, und die Entstehung der grossen Hexenverfolgung* (Munich: Oldenbourg, 1900), is still useful.

Fig. 18. Fifteenth-century woodcut: warning against sorcery

purely natural means; some of the codes deal with poisoning and harmful magic in close association with each other, as if there were little difference. Lawgivers under clerical influence sometimes showed religious concerns: the Ostrogothic king Theodoric (reg. 493–526), for instance, threatened death for conjurers because they were dealing with pagan gods, and the sixth-century Visigothic code proclaimed that sorcery could not bring about a person's death if it did not involve idolatry. In effect, the authors of these codes were (like many churchmen) assimilating natural magic to demonic magic.

Some of the strongest secular legislation against magic in early medieval Europe was that of Charles the Great, or Charlemagne. In a capitulary for the newly conquered Saxons he declared that all those found guilty of sorcery or divination should be turned over to the Church as slaves, while those who sacrificed to the Devil (i.e. to Germanic gods) should be killed. In his *General Admonition* for his kingdom in 789, Charles included provisions against enchanters and other magicians; these measures were taken over from the early church canons sent to him for his enforcement by Pope Hadrian. Here Charles appealed explicitly to the strict prohibition of Moses against sorcery.

Later rulers could build on these early prohibitions, but seldom did much to develop them. King Roger II of Sicily (reg. 1112–54) prescribed execution for anyone using poisons, presumably whether natural or magical, and indicated in vague terms that love magic should be punished even if no one was hurt: an indication that magic was evil in itself, apart from its potential harm to others. More often, however, the concern of secular rulers was with the actual damage rather than with the means for inflicting it.

Within the ecclesiastical tradition it is difficult to distinguish sharply between legal and penitential practice. The penitentials, which we have already discussed, were handbooks for priests to use in confession. The penances prescribed might be harsh: one such manual requires three years of fasting on bread and water, then four years of lighter penance, for using magic to kill a person or to raise storms. In principle the system was voluntary. The penitent submitted to the priest and willingly accepted the penance. Yet some penitentials include synodal canons amid their guidelines, which suggests that there was no rigid distinction between legislation and penitential norms.

Specific procedures would vary from one jurisdiction to another, but the general outlines of ecclesiastical hearings are clear from instructions issued in 800 at a synod in Freising. This document specifies that when people have been charged with incantation, divination, weather magic, or other sorcery and have been captured, the archpriest of the diocese should subject them to thorough examination in the hope of eliciting a confession. If necessary they should be tortured, though not to the point of jeopardizing their lives; they should be kept in prison until they resolve to do penance for their sins. By no means should they be released merely after paying compensation, without a formal inquiry.

It might have occurred to churchmen and secular authorities alike that all their legislation was doing little to curb the exercise of magic. One senses more than slight frustration in the complaint of the bishops at a synod of Pavia in 850 that the magical arts still flourished, that sorcerers were still arousing passionate love and hatred by magical means, and that they even killed people by magic. These evildoers were subject to the strictest penance and should be readmitted to the Church only on their deathbeds. The exasperation can only have increased as centuries passed and there was no perceptible change in popular practice.

Apart from legislation proper, in high and late medieval Europe there were legal commentaries and consultations that further developed the concepts of magic. The legal profession gained new sophistication when universities began teaching law in the high Middle Ages, and one result was detailed reflection on the principles underlying prosecution for magic. Thus, when a woman from the diocese of Novara was accused of witchcraft around the 1330s, the court sought advice from Bartolo of Sassoferrato, one of the most prominent lawyers of the day. In response, he first considered the woman's religious crime of idolatry. By her use of magic she had renounced Christ and baptism, and for that reason she deserved death according to the "law of the gospel," which is higher than any other law.[3] Furthermore, Bartolo found grounds in Roman and canon law for executing a woman who has committed offenses against God. But what is she has repented of these crimes? If she has done so, and if the judge deems her repentance sincere, he should spare her life. Bartolo thus left the matter to the judge's discretion. Secondly he considered the woman's crimes against humankind. She was accused of killing children by merely touching them. Is this in fact possible? The children's mothers testified that she had bewitched them, and that the children did in fact die. Bartolo had heard certain theologians suggest that sorcerers can harm and even kill others with their touch or with the evil eye. Yet he is not a theologian, and this question he leaves to the theologians and to "holy mother Church." The significance of his work for our purposes is that it shows a new-found sense of caution about legal norms and about the grounds for legal action. As trials for magic increased in the later Middle Ages, there was little real change in the laws against magic but a great deal of development in these guidelines for prosecution.

³ His gospel text (of dubious relevance) was John 15:6.

MORAL AND THEOLOGICAL CONDEMNATION

Preachers and other moralists had condemned magic in late antiquity, and they still found it necessary to do so even in the late Middle Ages. The problem was perennial, and so was the campaign against it. When Franciscan and Dominican friars emerged as popular preachers in the thirteenth century, condemnation of magic was one of the staple topics in their sermons. The Franciscan preacher Bernardino of Siena (d. 1444) found a moral wasteland all around him: people used incantations to cure disease and divination to explore the future, they deceived their fellow mortals with magical illusions, and in short they devoted themselves more to superstitious than to pious observance. In their campaign against such things Bernardino and other preachers were perhaps no more and no less successful than in their war against drunkenness, adultery, and gambling.

While preachers would usually restrict themselves to preaching, they might on occasion take direct action. Bernardino's biographer tells how he gathered and burned a great heap of magical paraphernalia, including medicaments over which magical incantations had been sung, and writings with signs and characters evidently referring to demons. On another occasion Bernardino attacked yet another form of popular "idolatry." He discovered that people in one location were taking their children out to a spring for purification, "like a new kind of baptism," and with these and other rites they paid veneration to the Devil. He aroused his congregation's fury over this custom, and they joined him, with crosses in hand, as he marched out to this place and destroyed a shelter that had been erected there.

Preachers and authors like Bernardino seldom made fine distinctions; they were more inclined to conflate subjects that we might consider quite distinct. An author might begin by condemning astrology and divination, then proceed to the folly of those women who believed they rode about at night with Diana, then attack the practice of singing the requiem mass to cause someone to die faster, then move on to a general diatribe against the Egyptian days and other superstitious observances, charms and inscriptions to enhance the power of herbs, and so forth, all in a discussion of "constellations."[4] So too, in *The Pilgrimage of the Life of Man*, the allegorical figure Sorcery carries magical writings and images, herbs gathered under specific constellations, ointments, a hand (representing chiromancy), and assorted other appurtenances. All such things were patently the Devil's work.

The central underlying concern of the moralists was, in any case, the

---

[4] Jacobus, *Omne bonum*, British Library, MS Royal 6.E.VI, fols. 396^v–397^v; cf. MS Harley 275, fols. 149^r–153^r.

possibility that magic might be demonic even when it seemed innocent. It was easy enough for most Christians to agree that demonic magic was immoral; the difficulty was in telling whether a particular practice did or did not involve appeal to demons. One of the most common tests was whether it contained unintelligible words that might in fact be invocations of demons in some unknown tongue, or strange names that might be names for demons. The *Malleus maleficarum* conveys this widely shared fear when it warns that charms must not contain explicit or implicit invocation of demons, such as reference to "unknown names."

Later medieval writers with any theological savvy tried to puzzle out precisely which forms of magic *could* be natural, and which *must* be demonic. They endeavored to work out the boundaries between natural and demonic magic. What is remarkable is how much power they were willing to concede to the occult powers in nature, without positing demonic intervention. Certain thirteenth-century and later writers recognized that the evil eye (or "fascination") might work in natural ways. Some, relying on Arabic sources, explained this phenomenon by arguing that the human soul can in many ways affect other persons: the soul is superior to the body, and has power over its own body and other people's as well. Indeed, some held that the soul even has power to change inanimate matter, to cause fire, and so forth. Roger Bacon, appealing to the authority of ancient Greek writers, told how "a menstruous woman looking in a mirror infects it and causes a cloud of blood to appear in it," and how certain women with double pupils can kill men with a glance. So too, individuals with infirm bodies and souls corrupted with sin can cause evil by their mere thought, if they have a vehement desire to harm others. Bacon even speculated that "infectious emanations" might be projected mechanically, as when Alexander the Great, instructed by Aristotle, managed to catapult the infection of a basilisk over the walls of a city he was besieging.

One of the most puzzling questions was how incantations could have effect. William of Auvergne systematically ruled out various possibilities, but did not exclude the possibility of some natural cause behind their effect. Nicholas Oresme suggested that the imagination of the hearer is affected by certain physical properties in the words themselves, rather than the signification of the words. Disturbance of the imagination in turns affects the body.[5] Some authors had fairly sophisticated understanding of how autosuggestion works. In his discussion of divination and superstitions, Ralph Higden suggested why these might at times seem valid:

---

[5] Bert Hansen, *Nicole Oresme and the Marvels of Nature* (Toronto: Pontifical Institute, 1985).

when good things are expected to happen, then minds are much strengthened and so, by their more strenuous action, labours are improved: when, on the contrary, evil is suspected, the mind weakens and acts sluggishly so that, through lack of spirit, evils are not restricted, but allowed free rein.[6]

Furthermore, as we have seen, philosophers and theologians were willing to concede numerous wondrous effects worked through the power of the stars.

Powerful, awesome, and mysterious as nature might be, however, the theologians and philosophers were not willing to see all magic as natural. Even in granting the possibilities of natural effect they often tended (like Augustine) to suspect that demons were somehow involved. Thomas Aquinas dealt with these matters at some length in his *Summa Against the Gentiles.* He did not deny that some magic works through the powers of heavenly bodies, but denied that all of it works thus. Magicians may note the positions of the stars, and may prepare their herbs to receive astral influences, thus giving the impression that they rely on these alone. But some of the things they do involve consultation of rational beings, such as ascertaining the presence of stolen property. Magicians sometimes even summon apparitions and speak with them, and these figures divulge information surpassing normal knowledge. The heavenly bodies cannot do these things. Nor can they unlock doors, make people invisible, or cause inanimate things to move or speak. When magicians use invocations and adjurations, and write characters and figures, they are clearly address-ing intelligent beings. Since the magicians often use these arts for evil purposes, one can scarcely believe that these beings are anything but demons.[7]

From the early centuries of Christianity, churchmen warned about the dangers of deliberately or inadvertently invoking demons. Toward the end of the Middle Ages, when fear of magic grew all the more intense, the warnings multiplied. Women who place magical objects beneath the threshold of a house to work their bewitchment, or who utter some curse over an apple, are making offerings and paying homage to the demons who carry out mischief on their behalf. Women and men who perform rituals at wells or over ponds to produce hailstorms are in fact conjuring demons whether they know it or not. Even women who administer healing herbs are not beyond suspicion. Demons are most likely to know the medicinal uses of herbs, and they may teach these uses to their friends.

[6] G. R. Owst, "*Sortilegium* in English homiletic literature of the fourteenth century", in J. Conway Davies, ed., *Studies Presented to Sir Hilary Jenkinson* (London: Oxford University Press, 1957), 289 (with translations of quotations).

[7] Thomas Aquinas, *Summa contra gentiles,* iii. 104–7.

Much ink was spilled in discussing whether demons – and thus, by extension, magicians – can in fact do the things ascribed to them. The challenge was to find a balance between conceding them too much power and acknowledging too little. If they had too much power they would infringe the prerogatives of God; thus, for example, it would be blasphemous to the creator to suggest that demons can create new creatures or change existing ones from one substance to another. If demons seem to change people into asses or other animals, the effect is only an illusion. Some writers made much the same argument about changes in the weather, but by the thirteenth century theologians were arguing that demons could arouse destructive storms, as Exodus 9 and Job 1 seemed to attest. Could they cause sexual impotence? Yes, Thomas Aquinas and other authorities concluded. As a lawyer in the late fifteenth century, Ulrich Molitoris encountered many cases in which women charged their husbands with impotence, but physicians testified that there was no natural cause, and thus they must be bewitched. Could demons foretell the future? Following Augustine, most authors argued that they could do so only through subtle conjecture, not through genuine foreknowledge, which God alone has. Even if magic worked wholesome ends, and even if divination sometimes proved true, this was only because demons sometimes do people favors to win more followers. To that end the demons might even be able to take on bodies, which they fashioned out of physical elements gathered from the air, but serious doubt remained about whether these humanoid demons could perform genuine bodily functions such as digestion and sexual intercourse. The central concern of the theologians, in any case, was to explain how magic might be demonic, and this question required as much ingenuity as explaining how it might be natural.

The results of all this mental effort were two main conclusions: first, that many types of magic might be natural; but secondly, that virtually all types might be demonic. Even if magic involved some feat beyond the power of demons, it could still be carried out through demonic cunning and illusion. To some extent the second conclusion canceled out the first. It made little difference that much magic could be explained in natural terms if the suspicion of demonic intervention remained. Like moralists generally, late medieval moralists tended to fear the worst, and it was all too easy to find confirmation that demons were at work.

The danger of demonic magic was not, however, the theologians' and moralists' only concern. Even if popular customs did not entail demonic magic, they might involve false claims about the power of words, objects, and gestures, and this is the essence of what later medieval writers meant by "superstition," a charge closely related to that of magic.[8] The term "superstition" had earlier applied to remnants of pagan tradition, and the word never lost this meaning altogether. In the later Middle Ages, however, when paganism as an integral system of beliefs and practices was a distant memory in most parts of Europe, the term often referred to misuse of religion: use of holy things for power beyond what they in fact held, imputation of power to unauthorized observances, and use of authorized observances without the proper intention. If a moralist presumed to judge a person's intention defective, he was more likely to charge that person with superstition than with magic. By either definition superstition might overlap with magic, but they were not in principle the same thing.

It was essentially as superstition that many writers condemned charms. The authors of the *Malleus maleficarum* protested that some of these formulas contain falsification of the Bible, by which they presumably meant apocryphal stories. When passages from the Bible are written out, the authors insist that no vain hope be placed in the manner of their inscription or any other external factor, which would imply that power resides in the words themselves; all attention must be directed to the meaning of the texts rather than the manner of their inscription, and the results must be entrusted to God's will. Other authors, such as John of Frankfurt, were even more cautious about charms, and argued that they have no inherent power (unlike herbs and gems) and are not established by God (unlike the sacraments). They are not found in the Bible, and do not have the sanction of the saints or of the Church, and thus must be either demonic or merely human. The sheer diversity of these formulas makes them suspect: different people use different words, each thinking that the precise formulas have special power. John Bromyard (fourteenth century) raised similar concerns about a popular charm that ran, "Holy Mary enchanted her Son from the bite of elves and the bite of men, and joined mouth to mouth, blood to blood and joint to joint, and so the child recovered." Bromyard asked, with evident exasperation:

> What Christian would not call those words false and contrary to the Catholic faith! For never did such infidelity occur to the Mother of God. How could they have power to save man or beast?[9]

If prayers have efficacy, he insisted, it is only because of the moral value of the person who prays them. Linking prayers with apocryphal stories and magical formulas debases them and adds nothing to their power.

---

[8] Dieter Harmening, *Superstitio: Überlieferungs- und theoriegeschichtliche Untersuchungen zur kirchlich-theologischen Aberglaubensliteratur des Mittelalters* (Berlin: Schmidt, 1979).

[9] Owst, "*Sortilegium*", 294–5.

Even if superstition does not involve appeal to demons, it may of course still be inspired by them. All sin is in that sense demonic: it is the result of the demons' temptation. This is presumably what John of Frankfurt has in mind in refuting an argument sometimes made for superstitious charms: people claim they are using holy words, and thus their practice is not diabolical, but this claim itself is a diabolical fraud.

The muddle that could ensue from this complex of conceptions and definitions is well illustrated by the trial of Werner of Friedberg in 1405.[10] Werner was tried not for magic but for holding certain beliefs about magic and related subjects: that blessings are licit; that if they were not, the Church would not bless ashes, palms, and so forth; that the names of the magi may be used to prevent epileptic seizures; and that the Latin for "The Word was made flesh" may be carried to avert diabolical deception. Someone told the authorities that Werner had preached such notions, and an episcopal judge summoned him for interrogation. The judge asked at one point if he knew any *superstitious* blessings, and he said he did know just one: "Christ was born, Christ was lost, Christ was found again; may he bless these wounds, in the name of the Father and of the Son and of the Holy Spirit." Indeed, he had used this blessing himself, and found that it worked. The interrogator went on to ask what he told people in confession when he heard they had used blessings. He said he permitted them unless they contained invocation of evil spirits.

Werner evidently shared one concern with others of his age: there were numerous blessings that contained apparently meaningless words, and these might well be names of demons. While articulating that concern, however, he seems to have missed his judge's further concern about superstitious observances. When asked if he knew any superstitious blessings he gave an example that did not really qualify – and then admitted using it himself! When asked about his counsel in confession he again showed himself inattentive to the whole question of superstition. If he could not instruct his flock properly about these matters he was failing in his duties.

Werner's judge, like Bernardino, was essentially a reformer. Many in the later Middle Ages were eager to reform the Church "in head and members," from the papacy on down. By attacking superstitious beliefs and practices, and by holding popular devotion to higher standards than had usually been maintained or demanded, they were doing their part to reform Christendom. They might be heavy-handed in doing so. They

---

[10] I am indebted to Robert E. Lerner for information on this case. For the document and a somewhat different interpretation, see his article, "Werner di Friedberg intrappolato dalla legge", in *La parola all' accusato* (Palermo: Sellerio, 1991), 268–81.

might have little understanding, let alone sympathy, for the popular customs they sought to uproot. Yet they were moved by a zeal to purge Christian society of false beliefs and observances. Many of their contemporaries were addressing the same problems by preaching, by instruction in the confessional, and by writing manuals for priests so as to raise the standards of clerical learning. This program of reform overlapped with that of the sixteenth-century Reformers, though Luther and Calvin had very different notions about how and where to aim the reforming axe. We miss the historical significance of these activities unless we see them as part of a broad effort at reform.

The program of reform might be not only heavy-handed but also misogynist. Moralists often saw women especially as prone to magic and superstition because of their supposed moral and intellectual weakness. Ulrich Molitoris, after writing at length on the powers of demons, closed his treatise with an apparently gratuitous warning specifically to women, urging them in particular to be on guard against the Devil's wiles. Reforming passion linked to this sort of bias was enormously dangerous, and, as we will see, it led to extreme fanaticism. Even if the zeal of the reformers went astray, however, it was grounded in an urge that sober Christians of the late Middle Ages would have taken as good and holy.

PATTERNS OF PROSECUTION

Most of the known trials for magic in the early Middle Ages, and a surprising proportion even from later centuries, involved important political figures as defendants, accusers, or victims. The reasons, however, are not hard to find. These sensational, high-society trials were the ones most likely to be recorded by chroniclers and other writers, and thus we are more likely to know about them than about trials involving ordinary townspeople and villagers. Gregory of Tours (ca. 540–94) told in his *History of the Franks* about accusations of magic at the royal court of sixth-century Gaul. Queen Fredegund, for example, widely suspect of sorcery, was accused of poisoning and bewitching the swords that killed an enemy king. So too in 899, when the emperor Arnulf died of a stroke two people were executed for having bewitched him. The story was similar when William of Aquitaine fell mortally ill in 1028 and clay images were brought forth as evidence of a woman's sorcery. We have already discussed cases from the ninth and twelfth centuries involving royal marriage impeded by magic. The heyday of these sensational trials came in the early fourteenth century, when several people were charged with using magic against Pope John XXII and against the king of France. The trial of the Templars in 1307–14 was a classic instance of prosecution for complex political and religious reasons and surely did much to enhance concern about magic. In the course of the trial, which was orchestrated by the royal court of France, the members of this military religious order were charged with venerating a magic head and a cat, among many other offenses. King Philip IV (reg. 1285–1314) was eager to dissolve the Templars and confiscate their property. Pope Clement V (reg. 1305– 1314) – the first of a series of fourteenth-century popes who came from France, resided at Avignon, and had to struggle against domination by the French monarch – was unable to resist Philip and protect the order. Some of the Templars were thus sentenced to life imprisonment, while others were burned; a fifteenth-century representation depicting the execution of one group of Templars shows the king of France and the pope as both present for the event (Fig. 19), which is historically inaccurate but a fitting symbol for the involvement of both these authorities in the complex event.[11] While the graph of such politically charged cases would show peaks and troughs, however, the phenomenon seems to have been a more or less constant factor in the history of medieval magic.

We know much less about prosecution at lower levels in the social scale, but we get some glimpses from cases of vigilante action. Thus, the citizens of Cologne in 1075 hurled a woman from the town walls because she had supposedly been bewitching men with her magical arts. In 1128 the people of Ghent eviscerated an "enchantress" and paraded her stomach about town. The role of popular outrage is especially clear in a case at Vötting from 1090, at a time when local political rivalries left the area without effective government. Three women fell suspect as sorceresses and spoilers of people's crops. They underwent the ordeal by water as a test of their innocence, and though they were successful the populace remained unconvinced. They were whipped to make them confess, but they refused to do so. Nonetheless, the people burned them alive.

Feudal courts in the villages and municipal courts in the towns might in the end inflict the same punishment, but their proceedings were usually less arbitrary. We know little about the involvement of feudal courts in these matters. In the late tenth century an English widow and her son were convicted for driving iron stakes into a man's image, whereupon the woman was drowned and her son, who fled, was outlawed, but this information comes from a record of ensuing land exchange, and we do not even know what court was involved.[12]

---

[11] Malcolm Barber, *The Trial of the Templars* (Cambridge: Cambridge University Press, 1978); Peter Partner, *Murdered Magicians: The Templars and Their Myth* (Oxford: Oxford University Press, 1982).
[12] Jane Crawford, "Evidences for witchcraft in Anglo-Saxon England", *Medium Aevum*, 32 (1963), 113.

Fig. 19. Burning of the Templars

It is difficult to know for sure when municipal governments became involved in prosecution for sorcery, but the gradual growth of towns in the twelfth and following centuries led to autonomy in government, including criminal justice, and it is likely that sorcery was from the outset among the crimes that could be heard in city courts. Caesarius of Heisterbach tells of a young cleric in the German town Soest around 1200 who had refused a woman's amorous advances. When she then accused him of having bewitched her, it was the municipal court that burned him as a sorcerer. Until the late Middle Ages, however, municipal courts retained what is known as "accusatory" procedure: a trial would begin only when an aggrieved party pressed charges in court and took responsibility for proving them; if the accusers did not prove the allegations, they would typically be liable to the same punishment that the accused would otherwise have suffered. In other words, if a man took a woman neighbor to court and accused her of bewitching his cattle, she might be executed if he could prove the allegation, but if he could not do so *he* would be executed. This was clearly an effective way to discourage prosecution, especially for a crime such as sorcery, for which tangible evidence was rare.

In the high and late Middle Ages, prosecution of magicians increasingly fell to inquisitors. In the early thirteenth century Pope Gregory IX (reg. 1227–41) began the practice of appointing inquisitors to search out heretics. This task had previously been left to local bishops, but as the threat of heresy grew more intense the pope found it necessary to supplement (not replace) the episcopal courts with the aid of these special itinerant judges. Their procedure was "inquisitorial" rather than accusatory, which is to say that they undertook prosecution on their own initiative, without waiting for an aggrieved party to lodge an accusation and take responsibility for proving the charges. The judge could use intimidation, and torture if necessary, to secure a confession. (These methods were adopted by secular courts as well in the late Middle Ages, largely in imitation of ecclesiastical procedure.) The possibilities for securing conviction were greatly enhanced, to say the least. Theoretically there were various legal safeguards to ensure that the use of torture would not result in condemnation of the innocent, but in the late Middle Ages these restrictions were widely disregarded. Thus equipped with considerable power, Franciscan and Dominican friars serving as inquisitors went through towns and villages scrutinizing popular religious life more carefully and systematically than it had ever before been examined.

A thirteenth-century guide to inquisitorial interrogation lists numerous forms of magic that the inquisitors might raise in questioning suspects: experiments with reflecting surfaces, invocation of demons, use of magic circles, sacrifices to obtain responses from demons, use of human heads or other bodily parts to obtain love or hatred, observation of the allegedly inauspicious "Egyptian days" and other superstitions, use of charms over herbs, baptism of images, use of the eucharist or chrism or baptismal water for any magical experiment, and so forth.[13] This interrogatory suggests how suspicion on one count might lead to suspicion on others as well: once the inquisitor got started it would be only natural for him to continue down the list and see just how many crimes the suspect had committed.

Not long after inquisitors were first appointed, they encountered occasional reports of sorcery. An inquisitor at Le Mas Saintes-Puelles had a woman brought before him in 1245 as a "diviner." Her neighbors had

[13] C. Douais, "Les hérétiques du Midi au treizième siècle: cinq pièces inédites", *Annales du Midi*, 3 (1891), 377–9.

paid her to put magical charms on their clothes, perhaps as a form of love magic, and she had used magic to work cures as well. Yet she managed to persuade the inquisitor that she was not heretical; in the course of the trial she confessed that she did not even believe her own magic had any effect.

Cases of this sort, however, could easily have absorbed the inquisitors' energies and distracted them from other business. Thus, in 1258 and 1260 Pope Alexander IV declared that they should not dissipate their efforts by prosecuting people for magic unless their magic savored of heresy. Nonheretical magic should be left to the purview of local authorities. Inquisitors who wanted to deal with such cases thus had to argue that all magic implies heresy, and the usual way to make this point was to reduce natural magic to demonic magic, then to show that alliance with demons in itself entails false belief about these evil spirits. It was easy enough for Nicholas Eymericus and others to show that *necromancy* involved a false belief that demons were worthy of veneration, but magic of the common tradition as well could be represented as demonic and heretical. Apart from formally articulated theoretical heresy, there was such a thing as practical heresy implicit in a person's actions. Such reasoning led John XXII, following counsel from several theologians, to direct the papal inquisitors against necromancers and other magicians.[14]

Some of the trials in the later Middle Ages seem to have been directed against genuine necromancers. A case before an ecclasiastical court south of Paris in 1323 involved a group of monks, canons, and laymen, who were plotting to invoke the demon Berich from inside a circle made from strips of cat skin. An inquisitor in Florence condemned one Niccolò Consigli to the stake in 1384 for various kinds of magic, including conjurations, exorcisms, and a frustrated attempt at murder by sympathetic magic and invocation of Lucifer, Satan, and Beelzebub. Consigli possessed books of necromancy, which the inquisitor, following standard procedure, had burned.[15] There is no reason to doubt that the defendants in these cases were in fact necromancers. Indeed, a great many of the trials in the late Middle Ages, especially in the fourteenth century, seem to have been directed against clerics engaged in necromancy.

Yet matters were not always so simple. Inquisitors and other judges, aware that necromancy was a problem in certain quarters, sometimes confused even natural magic with this much more serious offense. An episcopal court at Sleaford in 1417 tried a man named John Smith for "the

[14] Anneliese Maier, "Eine Verfügung Johanns XXII. über die Zuständigkeit der Inquisition für Zaubereiprozesse", *Archivum Fratrum Praedicatorum*, 22 (1952), 226–46.

[15] G. G. Coulton, trans., *Life in the Middle Ages*, 1 (Cambridge: Cambridge University Press, 1928), 160–3. Gene A. Brucker, ed., *The Society of Renaissance Florence* (New York: Harper & Row, 1971), 361–6.

art of necromancy and sorcery and illicit and prohibited conjurations and invocation of malign spirits," which sounds very much as if he had been using something like the Munich handbook. In fact, however, he had merely been using divination with bread to detect a thief who had broken into the local church. He had used this procedure only once, but defended it as legitimate, and even claimed that Peter and Paul had engaged in such practice, though it is not clear what basis he had for this notion.[16] An inquisitor at Florence in the 1340s found that various people were saying charms over plants to use them for cures and other innocent magic. Several people – a widow, a monk, the rector of a church, and others – had to pay fines for engaging in these practices. When the inquisitor charged that a physician had bought a book of herbal remedies containing elements of "necromancy," however, the physician did not submit meekly, but insisted that the book contained nothing of the sort.[17] Since the terminology for magic was ill-defined and highly connotative, its more reckless opponents would naturally incline to use the strongest language possible.

Even if a person was practicing illicit magic, however, it might be possible to do so with impunity until someone decided to make an issue of the matter. The factors that could precipitate such a development would be altogether unpredictable. The safest generalization is that fingers would point most quickly at someone who had established a reputation for being a bad, disagreeable neighbor. Dorothea Hindremstein, tried by a municipal court at Lucerne in 1454, is a perfect example.[18] Some time earlier her mother had been burned for sorcery in Uri, and if Dorothea had not fled she would have been burned as well; in the meantime she had been made to swear that she would not return to Uri. Her neighbors and even her husband at Lucerne eventually concluded that she had inherited her mother's power to lay curses on people. One neighbor woman told the court how her child had gotten into a fight and shoved Dorothea's child into the mud. Dorothea came out and angrily threatened that the witness's child would never forget this offense. Within twelve hours the offending child began to grow ill, and he lay sick for three weeks. Who could doubt that Dorothea's curse had taken effect? Another neighbor told how he had been careful not to antagonize Dorothea because of her ill repute. Yet he told how other people had quarreled with her and had soon

[16] Margaret Archer, ed., *The Register of Bishop Philip Repingdon, 1405–1419*, 3 (Lincoln Record Society, 1982), 194–6 (reading *vnica . . . vice* for *vinca . . . vite*).
[17] Mariano da Alatri, "L'inquisizione a Firenze negli anni 1344/46 da un'istruttoria contro Pietro da l'Aquila", in Isidorus a Villapadierna, ed., *Miscellanea Mechior de Pobladura* (Rome: Institutum Historicum O.F.M. Cap., 1964), 233–5.
[18] Joseph Hansen, ed., *Quellen und Untersuchungen zur Geschichte des Hexenwahns und der Hexenverfolgung im Mittelalter* (Bonn: Georgi, 1901), 561–5.

suffered the consequences: illness of half a year's duration, death of a fine cow, or blood instead of milk from a cow. How had Dorothea done all this? The man could not explain – indeed, the witnesses were generally unconcerned about the precise mechanism of the supposed sorcery – but he feared that if she and her family were allowed to live they would inflict still more damage. Then he said no more, fearing that he might be ill repaid for his testimony.

In many ways Dorothea fits the stereotype of the "old hag". Many of the women prosecuted for sorcery seem to have been old women who had no family to support them, or who received no support from the family they did have. Doubtless they tended, like Dorothea, to be ill-natured sorts, who bore resentment toward those about them and inspired resentment in return.

There seems to have been a rise in the frequency of trials for magic in the later fourteenth century, with great numbers of trials especially in Switzerland and Italy. The increase may be in part a kind of optical illusion: in the fourteenth and fifteenth centuries parchment was gradually replaced by the cheaper medium of paper, which meant that more information got written down and preserved, which in turn means that from this era we have more documents of various kinds and more information about numerous aspects of European life and culture. Yet this is surely not the full story; in all likelihood there was a real and not merely apparent increase. The gradual shift from accusatory to inquisitorial procedure in the secular courts made this development possible. Once it became easier to secure conviction for sorcery, and once it became clear that an informant did not have to take on the responsibilities of a formal accuser, charges would eventually become more frequent.

The increase in frequency at this point, however, was not so pronounced as to suggest any single, momentous upheaval in European social relations as an underlying cause. One might think that the Black Death and other adversities of the late Middle Ages aroused frustration, suspicion, and hostility among the survivors and that these emotions found indirect outlet in trials for sorcery. There was no direct connection, however, with these calamities: sorcery trials did not typically involve accusations that people had caused the Black Death. They began, rather, with allegations that people had inflicted illness on children, caused cows to stop giving milk, seduced their neighbors, and worked other forms of mischief that could occur in any era.

These trials would be of interest in themselves, but they are of even greater concern because they paved the way for more dramatic prosecution to come.

194 Prohibition, condemnation, persecution

THE RISE OF THE WITCH TRIALS

There had already been an increase in sorcery trials in the fourteenth century, but a much more dramatic upswing in prosecution occurred in the second and third quarters of the fifteenth century, especially in France, Germany, and Switzerland. Not only were the trials more frequent: they were different in kind from most of the preceding cases. Far more often they now developed into catch-all prosecution. Rather than merely dealing with a single suspect, inquisitors and other judges would urge the people of a town or village to seek out as many suspects as possible. The ruling passion now was not simply to secure justice against the specific offender but to purge the community of transgressors. Furthermore, the nature of the charges shifted. No longer satisfied to show that the sorcerer had worked image magic or used potions, judges now sought evidence that they had participated in anti-Christian, diabolical rituals. No longer content with accusations of sorcery, or even with the suggestion that sorcery inherently entailed demonic magic, judges now wanted to portray the magicians as linked in a demonic conspiracy against the Christian faith and Christian society. The sorcerer, intent only on specific acts of malice against particular enemies, gave way before the company of witches committed to the destruction of Christendom. The term "witchcraft" is used in various ways, sometimes including sorcery or other forms of magic, but by the late Middle Ages the witch was someone who went beyond mere sorcery, someone who performed ritual acts of veneration to the Devil in league with other witches.

How cases of simple and apparently harmless magic might lead to fanatical prosecution for witchcraft is clear from a sermon preached in 1427 by Bernardino of Siena. The friar spoke against various sins of pride, one of which was the use of charms and divination. When people use such things, he said, they are renouncing God and worshiping the Devil. Even countermagic is evil: anyone who knows how to break the force of charms knows also how to work them. When such people say they only wish to cure the sick, one should cry out "To the flames! To the flames!"

Bernardino then held up as an example what happened in Rome when he preached there against the use of charms. At first people thought he was raving, but then he warned that if they failed to report the culprits they shared in their guilt. Soon a great many women were accused. One of them confessed even without torture that she had murdered some thirty children by sucking blood from them; another sixty she had let loose, though for doing so she had to propitiate the Devil with sacrifices. She had killed many other people, even her own son, with a magical powder. When she gave specific names and dates for these murders they corresponded to known deaths. Among other materials that she used were herbs gathered on the feast of St. John and on the Ascension. She also had foul-smelling unguents. She and her ilk would anoint themselves, and though they appeared unchanged to others they thought themselves transformed into cats. Bernardino reported with satisfaction that this woman had been burned as a witch. All others should be burned likewise, he maintained. Anyone who knew of such witches and failed to report them to an inquisitor would be responsible on the Day of Judgment for this omission.[19]

Witch trials inspired more witch trials, because the report of action in one place would stimulate passions elsewhere. Oral report alone might have sufficed for this effect, but it was supplemented by inflammatory written accounts. In the mid-fifteenth century, for example, an anonymous author in or near Savoy wrote a treatise on *The Errors of the Gazarii*.[20] ("Gazarii" was a local term for witches.) The author was probably an inquisitor, and in any case he had access to inquisitorial records. For him, witchcraft was a "sect" whose members assembled regularly at "synagogues" or assemblies to satisfy their anger, gluttony, and lust. Once a person has been seduced into the sect, his seducer brings him to the synagogue and presents him to the Devil. While presiding at this assembly the Devil assumes the form of a black cat, or sometimes a human being with some deformity. He interrogates the initiate and requires him to swear that he will be faithful to the sect and its master, that he will seduce others into it, that he will keep its secrets, that he will strangle as many children as he can and bring their bodies to the synagogue, that he will come at once whenever called to the synagogue, that he will disrupt as many marriages as possible by using witchcraft to cause impotence, and that he will avenge all harm done to the sect and its members. The initiate then kisses the Devil on the posterior as a sign of homage. Then all members of the sect hold a feast (in which the flesh of children is the *pièce de résistance*), followed by dancing, indiscriminate sexual intercourse, more feasting, and a parody of the eucharist.

Members of the sect have powders and unguents for working harm. To destroy crops they fill the skin of a cat with various kinds of vegetable matter, put it in a spring for three days, then dry and pulverize the concoction. On a windy day they go up a mountain and scatter the powder across the land as a sacrifice to the Devil, who in return for their

---

[19] Saint Bernardino of Siena, *Sermons*, ed. Nazareno Orlandi, trans. Helen Josephine Robins (Siena: Tipografia Sociale, 1920), 163–76. Cf. Richard Kieckhefer, *European Witch Trials: Their Foundations in Popular and Learned Culture, 1300–1500* (London: Routledge, 1976), 121–2, for cases in Rome that may be identical or related to this one.

[20] Hansen, *Quellen und Untersuchungen*, 118–22.

offering will destroy the crops. By touching people with an unguent (made from the fat of strangled children and the venom of toads and other animals) they can cause agonizing deaths. To procure the meat and fat of infants they strangle them at night, pretend to lament their demise, then exhume their bodies. Certain witches have confessed that they killed and ate their own children and grandchildren. Yet to conceal their conduct they pretend to be faithful Catholics, going to mass, confession, and communion often.

This treatise is one of the earliest to spell out the details of the pact with the Devil, which held a prominent place in the mythology of witchcraft:

when a person is initiated into the sect, after he has sworn his fidelity and given homage, the Devil takes a certain instrument and draws blood from the left hand of the one being led astray. The Devil then writes out a certain document with this blood, which he keeps for himself.[21]

Other trials inspired further literature. A sensational trial at Arras in 1459–60 led to the arrest of thirty-four people and the burning of twelve as witches. The inquisitor responsible for these proceedings extracted detailed confessions about the witches' sabbaths, and while there were many who feared that prosecution had gotten out of hand there were others who joined the inquisitor in this zealous effort to rid the town of such pestiferous company. An anonymous treatise lamented that this sect of witches was an unprecedented threat to Christendom, more loathsome than all paganism. The case inspired another treatise, by the theologian Johannes Tinctoris; a manuscript of this work contains an early depiction of the sabbath, with witches venerating the Devil in the form of a goat, and others flying through the air on extravagant woolly monsters.[22] The famed culmination of this literary tradition was the *Malleus maleficarum*, written in 1486 by the inquisitors Jacob Sprenger and Henry Krämer partly on the basis of trials that Krämer had conducted.[23] Nor was it only inquisitors and theologians who wrote sensational accounts of witch trials: as early as the 1430s, a secular judge in the Dauphiné added his own contribution to the genre.[24]

The stereotype of the witch was complex, and its sources were various. Certain elements came from the exercise of sorcery in the common

---

[21] Hansen, *Quellen*, 121.
[22] Ibid., 183–8. The depiction of the sabbath is reproduced in Norman Cohn, *Europe's Inner Demons: An Enquiry Inspired by the Great Witch-Hunt* (New York: Basic, 1975), plate 1.
[23] *The Malleus maleficarum*, trans. Montague Summers (London: Pushkin, 1928).
[24] Pierrette Paravy, "A propos de la genèse médiévale des chasses aux sorcières: le traité de Claude Tholosan, juge dauphinois (vers 1436)", *Mélanges de l'Ecole Française de Rome: Moyen Age–Temps modernes*, 912 (1979), 333–79.

tradition of magic: the idea that magical potions can be lethal, or can cause impotence or other afflictions. Other details seem to have come from the manuals of necromancy. The idea of scattering powder as a sacrifice to the Devil could well have come from this source. More specific notions were taken over as well. The Munich handbook, for example, instructs the necromancer not to make the sign of the cross when flying on a horse provided by necromancy, since the horse is in fact a demon and will flee the blessing. The same manual, in describing the illusory banquet that the necromancer can conjure forth, says that there may be a thousand kinds of food, all extraordinarily delicious, but the more one eats the hungrier one will become, because the food does not really exist. Both these notions are echoed in accounts of witchcraft.

Themes from much earlier tradition became woven into the witch stereotype. The notion of a pact with the Devil was grounded in the early medieval legend of Theophilus, and in the theological notion (held by Thomas Aquinas and others) that magic could work by an arrangement or "pact" between the magician and the demons, specifying the symbolic intent of various magical acts. The notion of a nocturnal orgy in the presence of a demon was a standard charge against heretics in the high Middle Ages – indeed, similar charges had been made much earlier against Christians in the Roman Empire – though calling this assembly a "synagogue" (and, from the late fifteenth century on, a "sabbath") was a sign of anti-Semitism. Witches were often thought of as flying through the air, a notion that could have come from various sources in folklore or from the necromancers' manuals. When theologians wanted to prove that such flight was possible they argued on biblical grounds: an angel carried the prophet Habakkuk through the air (Daniel 13–14), and demons, being merely fallen angels, retain this power. The concept of sexual intercourse with demons (called incubi if they took the form of men, succubi if they appeared as women) could also have come from many sources. Merlin's father was a demon, and when the Bible spoke of relations between the sons of God and daughters of men (Genesis 6:1) later medieval exegetes took this to refer to intercourse with incubi.

Theologians around the thirteenth century, including Thomas Aquinas, had refined and rationalized many of these notions. They had shown, for example, how it is possible for intercourse with an incubus to produce offspring: the demon appears first to a man as a succubus, obtains semen, then immediately takes the form of an incubus and transmits it to a woman. Other refinements occurred at roughly the same time: the pact with the Devil, for instance, was now seen as a formal act analogous to feudal homage.

A particularly important element in the stereotype of the witch was the centrality of women. The classic case of the misogynist witchcraft treatise is the *Malleus maleficarum*; earlier literature had seldom singled women out as specifically inclined toward witchcraft, but the *Malleus* and later texts routinely did so. In the courts, too, there was an increasing tendency to single out women for prosecution. In the fourteenth and fifteenth centuries women outnumbered men by about two to one as defendants in the witch trials; in the later fifteenth century the difference seems to have become more pronounced, and in following centuries it was greater still. This bias may owe something to the role of women as popular healers with herbs and charms, but there is no reason to think that women had a monopoly on these or other forms of magic. The association of women with witchcraft certainly cannot be explained as an outgrowth of the later medieval occult sciences and necromancy, since these were overwhelmingly the property of male clerics, both in fact and in legend.

Ultimately the vulnerability of women in this context must be seen as a corollary to the precarious position women held in late medieval society (and, for that matter, in almost every society through history). The general culture portrayed women as having weak intellect and will. When institutions were set against them women would have less power than men to resist. If the specific issue was witchcraft it would be hard for anyone, woman or man, to disprove the charges, since tangible evidence was not expected and confessions could easily be obtained through intimidation, false promises of mercy, or torture. But if women were in general less trusted and more feared, these means for coercion would be directed against them more than against men. General misogynist stereotypes would encourage prosecution, which would then encourage further development of stereotypes. The stereotypes, however, do not by themselves cause prosecution. They may give it direction and aid in arousing passion, but when this happens they are called into service to justify and encourage prosecution motivated by other factors.

The provocation to judicial action might be personal, even idiosyncratic. An old woman might quarrel with her neighbors. A man might attempt to excuse a love affair, claiming that he had been bewitched. A midwife might be lured into a cockeyed scheme for curing leprosy with the fat of a miscarried fetus. Any of these situations might speak accusations of witchcraft. If the accused implicated other suspects, perhaps in revenge, prosecution might escalate. Impassioned townspeople, having dispatched one alleged witch, might decide to purge their society of all her associates.

Thus massive trials occurred, especially in the second and third quarters of the fifteenth century. Secular judges in the Valais condemned large numbers of witches in 1428 and again in 1447. In the first case more than a hundred people are said to have been burned for killing people, destroying the crops, and working other harm through magic. This trial is especially important as the first for which we have firm evidence of the fully developed stereotype of the witch, complete with flight through the air and transformation of human beings into animals, along with more traditional notions such as eating of babies and veneration of the Devil.[25] In the Dauphiné fully 110 women and fifty-seven men were executed over a period from 1428 to 1447. Mass prosecution occurred elsewhere, usually under secular judges, though in 1485 it was the papal inquisitor Henry Krämer who apprehended forty-eight women and two men at Innsbruck.

While some cases may have started with apprehension of a single suspect and then proceeded to others, a trial might also *begin* with accusation of a large group. One wonders in such cases whether the judge came upon a group of heretics and applied to them the traditional stereotypes of devil-worship, or whether he perhaps stumbled upon some agrarian ritual that he little understood and misinterpreted as witchcraft. These are always possibilities, though there is little reason to think that such mechanisms underlay more than a small proportion of the witch trials. When we can see the background of a trial at all clearly, or even glimpse it faintly, what seems to lie behind the stereotypes is some form of magic.

Why, then, was there such an increase in the frequency and fervor of prosecution in the mid-fifteenth century, and why did trials begin to become sweeping witch hunts rather than focusing on individual suspects? Certain factors were important as necessary conditions for this development: widespread adoption of inquisitorial procedure, by secular as well as ecclesiastical courts; unrestricted use of torture; development of the witch stereotype, complete with the notion of a conspiratorial sect; and most important, suspicion (fed by stories of the necromancers) that apparently innocent magic might turn out to be demonic. But if these were the necessary conditions, what was the cause? The relationship between a condition and a cause is difficult to define. By way of analogy: when a long dry spell leaves a forest or a town vulnerable to fire, a spark may suffice to begin a conflagration, which will spread of its own accord. When all the conditions are set for the judicial hysteria of witch hunts, the precipitating incidents may be less important than this conjunction of prior conditions, and for a time the sensation may sustain itself.

If we need to locate a spark, however, at least one source is clear: the

[25] Carlo Ginzburg, "The witches' sabbat: popular cult or inquisitorial stereotype?", in Steven L. Kaplan, ed., *Understanding Popular Culture: Europe from the Middle Ages to the Nineteenth Century* (Berlin: Mouton, 1984), 39–51.

vigorous drive for reform of the Church in head and members, found throughout Western Christendom in the wake of the Council of Constance (1414–18). Reformist sentiment pointed toward useful reform of the Church, but, as we have already seen in the case of Bernardino, it was not free of fanaticism. A reforming theologian like John Gerson might direct his efforts mainly against genuine necromancers, and a reformer such as Nicholas of Cusa (1401–64) might find that women who confessed to the rites of witchcraft were merely mad, but even they were not immune to the fears of their age, and less discriminating minds would be less cautious.[26] The prosecutors were zealots, and like most zealots they were inspired by holy enthusiasm mixed with skewed perceptions. How their perceptions got skewed is a long story, and telling that story has been the point of this book.

CONCLUSION

If magic is a crossroads in medieval culture, it is one with numerous paths radiating from it. We have explored some of these paths at greater length than others. What should be particularly clear is the intersection of natural and demonic magic, and thus of the scientific and religious elements in the culture of medieval Europe. Distinguishing between natural and demonic forms of magic was not easy; agreement on the distinction was not to be expected. The history of medieval magic is essentially one of conflicting perceptions on just this issue. The tendency of the uneducated seems to have been to see magic as natural, while intellectuals were torn between three conceptions. Following early Christian writers, they might see all magic (even that of the common tradition) as relying at least implicitly on demons; with the transmission of Islamic scholarship in the twelfth century, intellectuals increasingly acknowledged (whether enthusiastically or grudgingly) that a great deal of magic was natural; yet the real and express invocation of demons by necromancers renewed old apprehensions and made educated people all the more suspicious that magic was really demonic, even if it appeared natural.

Special confusion emerged from special contexts. Early medieval missionaries in their conflict with Germanic and Celtic religion might preach against magic, yet in making accommodations to Germanic and Celtic culture they allowed practices which by late medieval definitions would count as magical and perhaps demonic. No doubt the confusion was heightened by the more or less simultaneous importation of different

---

[26] Françoise Bonney, "Autour de Jean Gerson: opinions de théologiens sur les superstitions et la sorcellerie au début du xvᵉ siècle", *Moyen Age*, 71 (1971), 85–98; Carl Binz, "Zur Charakteristik des Cusanus", *Archiv für Kulturgeschichte*, 7 (1909), 145–53.

kinds of magic from Arabic culture: the arrival of the occult sciences, grounded in metaphysics and cosmology, lent new respectability to nondemonic magic, but along the same route of cultural transmission came key elements in necromancy, and thus new disrepute for magic. The magical arts now stood both in higher respectability and in deeper notoriety than before, forcing intellectually respectable astrologers and magicians to distance themselves as clearly as possible from their disreputable cousins the necromancers.

The real victims of this tension were those who continued to employ the natural magic of the common tradition but were now thickly tarred with the brush of demonic magic. Those who prosecuted and condemned them were, after all, men with some education, who would naturally tend to see popular magic in terms of what other educated people were doing. Recognizing the threat of demonic magic in the clerical underworld, they would spontaneously project that model on to humbler magicians. To justify and promote their repression of popular magic they imagined not only a demonic element in this magic, but a conspiracy of demon-worshipers. Between the magicians and their opponents lay a wide perceptual chasm.

It has been proposed that "The greatest magician would be the one who would cast over himself a spell so complete that he would take up his own phantasmagorias as autonomous appearances."[27] By this definition, paradoxically, it was the theologians, preachers, lawyers, inquisitors, and other judges who themselves became the greatest of magicians.

[27] Novalis, *Schriften*, vol. 2 ed. Richard Samuel (Stuttgart: Kohlhammer, 1960), 612, Fragment 88, as translated in Jorge Luis Borges, *Labyrinths: Selected Stories and Other Writings*, ed. Donald A.Yates and James E. Irby (New York: New Directions, 1962), 208.

FURTHER READING

GENERAL

Cardini, Franco, *Magia, stregoneria, superstizioni nell'Occidente medievale* (Florence: La Nuova Italia, 1979).
Carroll, David, *The Magic Makers: Magic and Sorcery Through the Ages* (New York: Arbor House, 1974).
Cavendish, Richard, *A History of Magic* (New York: Taplinger, 1977).
King, Frances, *Magic: The Western Tradition* (London: Thames & Hudson, 1975).
Thorndike, Lynn, *The History of Magic and Experimental Science*, 8 vols. (New York: Macmillan and Columbia University Press, 1923–58).
Thorndike, Lynn, "Some medieval conceptions of magic", *The Monist*, 25 (1915), 107–39.
Wagner, Robert-Léon, *"Sorcier" et "magicien": Contribution à l'histoire de la magie* (Paris: Droz, 1939).

ANTIQUITY

Greek and Roman magic
Luck, Georg, trans., *Arcana mundi: Magic and the Occult in the Greek and Roman Worlds: A Collection of Ancient Texts* (Baltimore: Johns Hopkins University Press, 1985).
Pliny, *Natural History*, trans. H. Rackham *et al.* (Cambridge, Mass.; Harvard University Press; London: Heinemann, 1938–63); esp. vols. 8–10 (books 28–37).
Ptolemy [Claudius Ptolemaeus], *Tetrabiblos*, ed. and trans. F. E. Robbins (Cambridge, Mass.: Harvard University Press, 1940).
Scott, Walter, ed. and trans., *Hermetica: The Ancient Greek and Latin Writings which Contain Religious or Philosophic Teachings Ascribed to Hermes Trismegistus* (Oxford: Clarendon, 1924–).

Magic and Christianity

Augustine, Saint, *Concerning the City of God, against the Pagans*, trans. Henry Bettenson, new edn. (Harmondsworth: Penguin, 1984), especially sections from books 8–10.

"The divination of demons", in Roy J. Deferrari, ed., *Saint Augustine: Treastises on Marriage and Other Subjects* (New York: Fathers of the Church, 1955), 415–40.

Barb, A. A., "The survival of the magic arts", in Arnaldo Momigliano, ed., *The Conflict Between Paganism and Christianity in the Fourth Century* (Oxford: Clarendon, 1963), 110–25

Benko, Stephen, "Early Christian magical practices", *Society of Biblical Literature: Seminar Papers*, no. 21 (1982), 9–14.

Brown, Peter, "Sorcery, demons and the rise of Christianity: from late Antiquity into the Middle Ages", in Mary Douglas, ed., *Witchcraft Confessions and Accusations* (London: Tavistock, 1970), 17–45; reprinted in P. A. Brown, *Religion and Society in the Age of St. Augustine* (London: Faber & Faber, 1972), 119–46.

Jenkins, Claude, "Saint Augustine and magic", in E. Ashworthy Underwood, ed., *Science, Medicine and History: Essays on the Evolution of Scientific Thought and Medical Practice written in honour of Charles Singer*, vol. 1 (London: Oxford University Press, 1953), 131–40.

Kee, Howard Clark, *Medicine, Miracle and Magic in New Testament Times* (Cambridge: Cambridge University Press, 1986).

Remus, Harold E., "'Magic or miracle': Some second-century instances", *Second Century*, 2 (1982), 127–56.

Pagan–Christian Conflict Over Miracle in the Second Century (Cambridge, Mass.: Philadelphia Patristic Foundation, 1983).

Schoedel, William R., and Malina, Bruce J., "Miracle or magic?", *Religious Studies Review*, 12 (1986), 31–9.

Thee, Francis C. R., *Julius Africanus and the Early Christian View of Magic* (Tübingen: Mohr, 1984).

Ward, John O., "Women, witchcraft and social patterning in the later Roman lawcodes", *Prudentia*, 13 (1981), 99–118.

"Witchcraft and sorcery in the later Roman Empire and the early Middle Ages: an anthropological comment", *Prudentia*, 12 (1980), 93–108.

GERMANIC AND CELTIC MAGIC

Pagan survivals

Chaney, William A., "Paganism to Christianity in Anglo-Saxon England", *Harvard Theological Review*, 53 (1960), 197–217.

Crawford, Jane, "Evidences for witchcraft in Anglo-Saxon England", *Medium Aevum*, 32 (1963), 99–116.

McNeill, John T., and Gamer, Helena M., eds., *Medieval Handbooks of Penance* (New York: Columbia University Press, 1938).

Vogel, Cyrille, "Pratiques superstitieuses au début du XIᵉ siècle d'après le *Corrector sive medicus* de Burchard évêque de Worms (965–1025)", in *Etudes de civilisation médiévale (IXᵉ–XIIᵉ siècles): Mélanges offerts à Edmond-René Labande* (Poitiers: Centre d'Etudes Supérieures de Civilisation Médiévale, 1974), 751–61.

Norse magic

Bayerschmidt, Carl F., "The element of the supernatural in the sagas of Icelanders", in Carl F. Bayerschmidt and Erik J. Friis, eds., *Scandinavian Studies: Festschrift for Henry Goddard Leach* (Seattle: University of Washington Press, 1965), 39–53.

Davidson, H. R. Ellis, "Hostile magic in the Icelandic sagas", in Venetia Newall, ed., *The Witch Figure* (London: Routledge, 1973), 20–41.

Elliott, Ralph W. V., "Runes, yews, and magic", *Speculum*, 32 (1957), 250–61.

Runes: An Introduction (Manchester: Manchester University Press, 1959).

Jarausch, Konrad, "Der Zauber in den Isländersagas", *Zeitschrift für Volkskunde*, n.s., 1 (1929–30), 237–68.

Lid, Nils, "The paganism of the Norsemen", in W. Edson Richmond, ed., *Studies in Folklore* (Bloomington: Indiana University Press, 1957), 230–51.

Scott, F. S., "The woman who knows: female characters of *Eyrbyggja Saga*", *Parergon*, n.s., 3 (1985), 73–91.

Simpson, Jacqueline, "Olaf Tryggvason versus the powers of darkness", in Venetia Newall, ed., *The Witch Figure* (London: Routledge, 1973), 165–87.

Celtic magic

Ford, Patrick K., *Celtic Folklore and Christianity* (Santa Barbara: McNally & Loftin; Los Angeles: Center for the Study of Comparative Folklore & Mythology, 1983).

Gantz, Jeffrey, trans., *Early Irish Myths and Sagas* (Harmondsworth: Penguin, 1981).

Henderson, George, *Survivals in Belief among the Celts* (Glasgow: Maclehose, 1911).

Loomis, C. Grant, *White Magic: An Introduction to the Folklore of Christian Legend* (Cambridge, Mass.: Mediaeval Academy of America, 1948).

Loomis, Roger Sherman, *Celtic Myth and Arthurian Romance* (New York: Columbia University Press, 1926).

Mac Cana, Proinsias I., *Celtic Mythology* (London: Hamlyn, 1970).

Plummer, Charles, ed. and trans., *Bethada náem nErenn: Lives of Irish Saints* (Oxford: Clarendon, 1922).

THE COMMON TRADITION OF MAGIC

Medical and protective magic

Albert the Great, *Man and the Beasts: De animalibus (Books 22–26)*, trans. James J. Scanlan (Binghamton, NY: Medieval and Renaissance Texts and Studies, 1987).

Barb, A. A., "Birds and medical magic", *Journal of the Warburg and Courtauld Institutes*, 13 (1950), 316–22.

Bonser, Wilfred, *The Medical Background of Anglo-Saxon England: A Study in History, Psychology, and Folklore* (London: Wellcome Historical Medical Library, 1963).

Browe, Peter, "Die Eucharistie als Zaubermittel im Mittelalter", *Archiv für Kulturgeschichte*, 20 (1930), 134–54.

Bühler, Curt F., "Prayers and charms in certain Middle English scrolls", *Speculum*, 39 (1964), 270–8.

Cameron, M. L., "Bald's *Leechbook*: its sources and their use in its compilation", *Anglo-Saxon England*, 12 (1983), 153–82.

Dawson, Warren R., ed. and trans., *A Leechbook or Collection of Medical Recipes of the Fifteenth Century* (London: Macmillan, 1934).

Geier, Manfred, "Die magische Kraft der Poesie: Zur Geschichte, Struktur und Funktion des Zauberspruchs", *Deutsche Vierteljahrsschrift für Literaturwissenschaft und Geistesgeschichte*, 56 (1982), 359–85.

Grendon, Felix, "The Anglo-Saxon charms", *Journal of American Folk-Lore*, 22 (1909), 105–237.

Hälsig, Friedrich, *Der Zauberspruch bei den Germanen bis um die Mitte des XVI. Jahrhunderts* (Leipzig: Seele, 1910).

Hampp, Irmgard, *Beschwörung, Segen, Gebet: Untersuchungen zum Zauberspruch aus dem Bereich der Volksheilkunde* (Stuttgart: Silberburg, 1961).

Jolly, Karen Louise, "Anglo-Saxon charms in the context of a Christian world view", *Journal of Medieval History*, 11 (1985), 279–93.

Klapper, Joseph, "Das Gebet im Zauberglauben des Mittelalters", *Mitteilungen der schlesischen Gesellschaft für Volkskunde*, 18 (1907).

MacKinney, Loren C., "An unpublished treatise on medicine and magic from the age of Charlemagne", *Speculum*, 18 (1943), 494–6.

Pinto, Lucille B., "Medical science and superstition: a report on a unique medical scroll of the eleventh-twelfth century", *Manuscripta*, 17 (1973), 12–21.

Poulin, Jean-Claude, "Entre magie et religion: recherches sur les utilisations marginales de l'écrit dans la culture populaire du haut Moyen-Age", in Pierre Boglioni, ed., *La culture populaire au Moyen-Age* (Montreal: Editions Universitaires, 1979), 121–43.

Radimersky, George, "Magic in the works of Hildegard von Bingen", *Monatshefte für deutschen Unterricht*, 49 (1957), 353–60.

Remly, Lynn L., "Magic, myth, and medicine: the veterinary art in the Middle Ages (9th–15th centuries)", in Guy R. Mermier and Edelgard E. DuBrock, eds., *Fifteenth-Century Studies*, 2 (1979), 203–9.

Sheldon, Sue Eastman, "The eagle: bird of magic and medicine in a Middle English translation of the *Kyranides*", *Tulane Studies in English*, 22 (1977), 1–20.

Stannard, Jerry, "Marcellus of Bordeaux and the beginning of medieval materia medica", *Pharmacy in History*, 15 (1973), 47–53.

"Magiferous plants and magic in medieval medical botany", *Maryland Historian*, 8 (1977), no. 2, 33–46.

"Greco-Roman materia medica in medieval Germany", *Bulletin of the History of Medicine*, 46 (1972), 455–68.

Storms, G[odfrid], ed., *Anglo-Saxon Magic* (The Hague: Nijhoff, 1948).

206 Further reading

Stuart, H., "Utterance instructions in the Anglo-Saxon charms", *Parergon*, n.s., 3 (1985), 31–7.
Vaughan-Sterling, Judith A., "The Anglo-Saxon *Metrical Charms*: poetry as ritual", *Journal of English and Germanic Philology*, 82 (1983), 186–200.

Sorcery

Blöcker, Monica, "Wetterzauber: Zu einem Glaubenskomplex des frühen Mittelalters", *Francia*, 9 (1981), 117–31.
Crawford, Jane, "Evidences for witchcraft in Anglo-Saxon England", *Medium Aevum*, 32 (1963), 99–116.
Forbes, Thomas Rogers, *The Midwife and the Witch* (New Haven: Yale University Press, 1966).
Kieckhefer, Richard, *European Witch Trials: Their Foundations in Popular and Learned Culture, 1300–1500* (London: Routledge, 1976).
Siller, Max, "Zauberspruch und Hexenprozess: Die Rolle des Zauberspruchs in den Zauber- und Hexenprozessen Tirols", in Werner M. Bauer *et al.*, eds., *Tradition und Entwicklung: Festschrift Eugen Thurnher* (Innsbruck: Institut für Germanistik der Universität Innsbruck, 1982), 127–54.
Tucker, Elizabeth, "Antecedents of contemporary witchcraft in the Middle Ages", *Journal of Popular Culture*, 14 (1980), 70–8.

Divination

Braekman, W. L., "Fortune-telling by the casting of dice: a Middle English poem and its background", *Studia Neophilologica*, 52 (1980), 3–29.
Braswell, L., "Popular lunar astrology in the late Middle Ages", *University of Ottawa Quarterly*, 48 (1978), 187–94.
John of Salisbury, *Frivolities of Courtiers and Footprints of Philosophers*, trans. Joseph B. Pike (Minneapolis: University of Minnesota Press; London: Oxford University Press, 1938). (A substantial portion of this book, i.9 through ii.28, is essentially a catalogue and condemnation of divinatory practices.)
Metham, John, *The Works of John Metham*, ed. Hardin Craig (Early English Text Society, Original Ser., 132) (London: K. Paul, 1916). (Includes a collection of late medieval divinatory treatises in the English language.)
Owst, G. R., "*Sortilegium* in English homiletic literature of the fourteenth century", in J. Conway Davies, ed., *Studies Presented to Sir Hilary Jenkinson* (London: Oxford University Press, 1957).
Pack, Roger A., "A treatise on prognostications by Venancius of Moerbeke", *Archives d'Histoire Doctrinale et Littéraire du Moyen Age*, 43 (1976), 311–22.
Schmitt, Wolfram, "Das Traumbuch des Hans Lobenzweig", *Archiv für Kulturgeschichte*, 48 (1966), 181–218.
Thorndike, Lynn, "Chiromancy in medieval Latin manuscripts", *Speculum*, 40 (1965), 674–706.

Magical trickery

Roy, Bruno, "The household encyclopedia as magic kit: medieval popular interest in pranks and illusions", *Journal of Popular Culture*, 14 (1980), 60–9.

Volkmann, Kurt, *The Oldest Deception: Cups and Balls in the 15th and 16th Centuries*, trans. Barrows Mussey (Minneapolis: Jones, 1956).

MAGIC IN COURTLY CULTURE

Magicians at court

Hartung, Wolfgang, *Die Spielleute: Eine Randgruppe in der Gesellschaft des Mittelalters* (Wiesbaden: Steiner, 1982), especially 9–20.

Kyeser, Conrad, *Bellifortis*, ed. and trans. Götz Quarg (Düsseldorf: VDI, 1967).

Lindsay, Jack, *The Troubadours and Their World of the Twelfth and Thirteenth Centuries* (London: Muller, 1986).

Loomis, Laura H., "Secular dramatics in the royal palace, Paris, 1378, 1389, and Chaucer's 'tregetoures'", *Speculum*, 33 (1958), 242–55.

Ogilvy, J. D. A., "*Mimi, scurrae, histriones*: entertainers of the early Middle Ages", *Speculum*, 38 (1963), 603–19.

Magical gems and devices

Ball, Sydney H., "Luminous gems, mythical and real", *Scientific Monthly*, 47 (1938), 496–505.

Eamon, W., "Technology as magic in the late Middle Ages and Renaissance", *Janus*, 70 (1983), 171–212.

Evans, Joan, *Magic Jewels of the Middle Ages and Renaissance* (Oxford: Clarendon, 1922).

Kitson, Peter, "Lapidary traditions in Anglo-Saxon England", *Anglo-Saxon England*, 12 (1983), 73–123.

Marbode of Rennes, *De lapidibus*, ed. John M. Riddle, trans. C. W. King (Wiesbaden: Steiner, 1977).

Owings, Marvin Alpheus, *The Arts in the Middle English Romances* (New York: Bookman Associates, 1952), ch. 4, 138–64, "The supernatural."

Thorndike, Lynn, "De lapidibus", *Ambix*, 8 (1960), 6–23.

Magic in courtly literature

Bachman, W. Bryant, Jr., "'To maken illusion': the philosophy of magic and the magic of philosophy in the *Franklin's Tale*", *Chaucer Review*, 12 (1977), 55–67.

Comparetti, Domenico, *Virgil in the Middle Ages*, trans. E. F. M. Benecke (London: Sonnenschein, 1895).

Cooper, Helen, "Magic that does not work", *Medievalia et Humanistica*, n.s., 7 (1976), 131–46.

Green, R. B., "The fusion of magic and realism in two lays of Marie de France", *Neophilologus*, 59 (1975), 324–36.

Harf-Lancner, Laurence, *Les fées au Moyen Age: Morgane et Mélusine: la naissance des fées* (Geneva: Slatkine, 1984).

Kretzenbacher, Leopold, *Teufelsbündner und Faustgestalten im Abendlande* (Klagenfurt: Verlag des Geschichtsvereines für Kärnten, 1968).

Luengo, Anthony E., "Magic and illusion in the *Franklin's Tale*", *Journal of English and Germanic Philology*, 77 (1978), 1–16.

Mauritz, Hans-Dieter, "Der Ritter im magischen Reich: Märchenelemente in französischen Abenteuerromanen des 12. und 13. Jahrhunderts" (Dissertation, University of Zurich, 1970).

McAlindon, "Magic, fate and providence in medieval narrative and 'Sir Gawain and the Green Knight'", Review of English Studies, n.s., 16 (1965), 121–39.

Ménard, Philippe, "Chrétien de Troyes et le Merveilleux", Europe, 60 (1982), 53–60.

Sherwood, M., "Magic and mechanics in medieval fiction", Studies in Philology, 44 (1947), 567–92.

Spargo, John Webster, Virgil the Necromancer: Studies in Virgilian Legends (Cambridge, Mass.: Harvard University Press, 1934).

Whitaker, Muriel, Arthur's Kingdom of Adventure: The World of Malory's Morte Darthur (Woodbridge: Boydell, 1984).

Wood, Juliette, "Virgil and Taliesin: the concept of the magician in medieval folklore", Folklore, 94 (1983), 91–104.

ARABIC LEARNING AND THE OCCULT SCIENCES

General

Hansen, Bert, Nicole Oresme and the Marvels of Nature (Toronto: Pontifical Institute, 1985).

"The complementarity of science and magic before the Scientific Revolution", American Scientist, 74 (1986), 128–36.

"Science and magic", in David C. Lindberg, ed., Science in the Middle Ages (Chicago: University of Chicago Press, 1978), 483–503.

Kibre, Pearl, Studies in Medieval Science: Alchemy, Astrology, Mathematics and Medicine (London: Hambledon, 1984).

McAllister, Joseph Bernard, The Letter of Saint Thomas Aquinas De occultis operibus naturae ad quemdam militem ultramontanum (Washington, DC: Catholic University of America Press, 1939).

Molland, A. G., "Roger Bacon as magician", Traditio, 30 (1974), 445–60.

Shumaker, Wayne, The Occult Sciences in the Renaissance: A study in Intellectual Patterns (Berkeley: University of California Press, 1972).

Thorndike, Lynn, The Place of Magic in the Intellectual History of Europe (New York: Columbia University Press, 1905).

"The Latin Pseudo-Aristotle and medieval occult science", Journal of English and Germanic Philology, 21 (1922), 229–58.

Astrology and astral magic

Brown, J. Wood, An Enquiry into the Life and Legend of Michael Scot (Edinburgh: Douglas, 1897).

Clark, Charles, "The zodiac man in medieval medical astrology", Journal of the Rocky Mountain Medieval and Renaissance Association, 3 (1982), 13–38.

Coopland, G. W., Nicole Oresme and the Astrologers: A Study of His Livre de Divinacions (Cambridge, Mass.: Harvard University Press, 1952).

Curry, Patrick, ed., *Astrology, Science and Society: Historical Essays* (Woodbridge: Boydell, 1987).

d'Alverny, Marie-Thérèse, "Astrologues et théologiens au XIIe siècle", in *Mélanges offerts à M.-D. Chenu* (Paris, 1967), 31–50.

Garin, Eugenio, *Astrology in the Renaissance: The Zodiac of Life*, trans. Carolyn Jackson and June Allen (London: Routledge, 1983).

Gregory, Tullio, "La nouvelle idée de nature et de savoir scientifique au XIIe siècle", in John Emery Murdoch and Edith Dudley Sylla, eds., *The Cultural Context of Medieval Learning: Proceedings of the First International Colloquium on Philosophy, Science, and Theology in the Middle Ages – September 1973* (Dordrecht: Reidel, 1975), 193–218.

Grimm, Florence M., *Astrological Lore in Chaucer* (Lincoln, Nebr.: University of Nebraska, 1919).

Tester, S. J., *A History of Western Astrology* (Woodbridge: Boydell, 1987).

Thorndike, Lynn, "Traditional medieval tracts concerning engraved astrological images", in *Mélanges Auguste Pelzer: Etudes d'histoire littéraire et doctrinale de la Scolastique médiévale offertes à Monseigneur Auguste Pelzer* (Louvain: Bibliothèque de l'Université, 1947), 217–73.

Michael Scot (London: Nelson, 1965).

Wedel, Theodore Otto, *The Mediaeval Attitude Toward Astrology, Particularly in England* (New Haven: Yale University Press, 1920).

Wood, Chauncey, *Chaucer and the Country of the Stars: Poetic Uses of Astrological Imagery* (Princeton, NJ: Princeton University Press, 1970).

Zambelli, Paola, "Albert le Grand et l'astrologie", *Recherches de Théologie Ancienne et Médiévale*, 49 (1982), 141–58.

Alchemy

Albertus Magnus, *Book of Minerals*, trans. Dorothy Wyckoff (Oxford: Clarendon, 1967).

Libellus de alchimia, Ascribed to Albertus Magnus, trans. Virginia Heines (Berkeley: University of California Press, 1958).

Eis, Gerhard, "Von der Rede und dem Schweigen der Alchemisten", *Deutsche Vierteljahrsschrift für Literaturwissenschaft und Geistesgeschichte*, 25 (1951), 415–35.

Ganzenmüller, W., *Die Alchemie im Mittelalter* (Paderborn: Bonifacius, 1938).

Holmyard, E. J., *Alchemy* (Harmondsworth: Penguin, 1957).

Multhauf, Robert P., "John of Rupescissa and the origin of medical chemistry", *Isis*, 45 (1954), 359–67.

Newman, W., "An introduction to alchemical apparatus in the late Middle Ages", *Technologia*, 6 (1983), 82–92.

Norton, Thomas, *The Ordinall of Alchimy by Thomas Norton of Bristoll, Being a facsimile reproduction from Theatrum chemicum britannicum* (London: Arnold, 1928).

Obrist, Barbara, *Les débuts de l'imagerie alchimique (XIVe–XVe siècles)* (Paris: Le Sycamore, 1982).

210 *Further reading*

Partington, J. R., "Albertus Magnus on alchemy", *Ambix*, 1 (1937), 3–20.
"Trithemius and alchemy", *Ambix*, 2 (1938), 53–9.
Plessner, M., "The place of the *Turba philosophorum* in the development of alchemy", *Isis*, 45 (1954), 331–8.
Waite, A. E., trans., *The Turba philosophorum or Assembly of the Sages, Called also the Book of Truth in the Art and the Third Pythagorical Synod: An Ancient Alchemical Treatise* (London: Redway, 1896; repr. New York, 1976).

Books of secrets

[Pseudo-]Albertus Magnus, *The Book of Secrets of Albertus Magnus: Of the Virtues of Herbs, Stones and Certain Beasts*, ed. Michael R. Best and Frank H. Brightman (Oxford: Clarendon, 1973).
Eamonn, William, "Books of secrets in medieval and early modern science", *Sudhoffs Archiv*, 69 (1985), 26–49.
Manzalaoui, M., ed., *Secretum secretorum: Nine English Versions* (Early English Text Society, Original Ser., 276–) (Oxford: Oxford University Press, 1977–).
"The pseudo-Aristotelian Kitab Sirr al-Asrar: facts and problems", *Oriens*, 23–4 (1974), 147–257.
Ryan, William F., and Schmitt, Charles B., eds., *Pseudo-Aristotle, The Secret of Secrets: Sources and Influences* (London: Warburg Institute, 1982).
Schmitt, Wolfram, "Zur Literatur der Geheimwissenschaften im späten Mittelalter", in Gundulf Keil and Peter Assion, eds., *Fachprosaforschung: Acht Vorträge zur mittelalterlichen Artesliteratur* (Berlin: Schmidt, 1974), 167–82.

The Renaissance magus

Arnold, Klaus, *Johannes Trithemius (1462–1516)* (Würzburg: Schöningh, 1971).
Brann, Noel L., *The Abbot Trithemius (1462–1516): The Renaissance of Monastic Humanism* (Leiden: Brill, 1981).
Copenhaver, Brian P., "Scholastic philosophy and Renaissance magic in the *De vita* of Marsilio Ficino", *Renaissance Quarterly*, 37 (1984), 523–54.
"Astrology and magic", in Charles B. Schmitt *et al.*, eds., *The Cambridge History of Renaissance Philosophy* (Cambridge: Cambridge University Press, 1988), 264–300.
Couliano, Ioan P., *Eros and Magic in the Renaissance*, trans. Margaret Cook (Chicago: University of Chicago Press, 1987).
Ficino, Marsilio, *Three Books on Life: A Critical Edition and Translation with Introduction and Notes*, ed. and trans. Carol V. Kaske and John R. Clark (Binghamton, NY: Medieval and Renaissance Texts and Studies, 1988).
Shumaker, Wayne, "Johannes Trithemius and cryptography", in Wayne Shumaker, *Renaissance Curiosa* (Binghamton, NY: Center for Medieval and Early Renaissance Studies, 1982), 91–131.
Vickers, Brian, ed., *Occult and Scientific Mentalities in the Renaissance* (New York: Cambridge University Press, 1986).
Walker, D. P., *Spiritual and Demonic Magic, from Ficino to Campanella* (London:

Warburg Institute, 1958; repr. Notre Dame, Ind.: University of Notre Dame Press, 1975).

Yates, Frances A., *Giordano Bruno and the Hermetic Tradition* (London: Routledge; Chicago: University of Chicago Press, 1964). (Chs. 1–6 deal with fifteenth-century subjects.)

Zika, Charles, "Reuchlin's *De verbo mirifico* and the magic debate of the late fifteenth century", *Journal of the Warburg and Courtauld Institutes*, 39 (1976), 104–38.

NECROMANCY

d'Alverny, Marie-Thérèse, "Survivance de la magie antique", in Paul Wilpert, ed., *Antike und Orient im Mittelalter: Vorträge der Kölner Mediae-vistentagungen 1956–1959* (Berlin: de Gruyter, 1962), 154–78.

Kieckhefer, Richard, *A Necromancer's Manual from the Fifteenth Century* (forthcoming).

Manitius, Karl, "Magie und Rhetorik bei Anselm von Besate", *Deutsches Archiv für Erforschung des Mittelalters*, 12 (1956), 52–72.

Thorndike, Lynn, "Imagination and magic: force of imagination on the human body and of magic on the human mind", in *Mélanges Eugène Tisserant*, 7 (Vatican City: Biblioteca Vaticana, 1964), 353–8.

Waite, Arthur Edward, *The Book of Black Magic and of Pacts, Including the Rites and Mysteries of Goëtic Theurgy, Sorcery, and Infernal Necromancy* (London: Redway, 1898).

PROHIBITION, CONDEMNATION, AND PROSECUTION

General

Harmening, Dieter, *Superstitio: Überlieferungs- und theoriegeschichtliche Unter-suchungen zur kirchlich-theologischen Aberglaubensliteratur des Mittelalters* (Berlin: Schmidt, 1979).

Owst, G. R., "*Sortilegium* in English homiletic literature of the fourteenth century", in J. Conway Davies, ed., *Studies Presented to Sir Hilary Jenkinson* (London: Oxford University Press, 1957), 272–303.

Peters, Edward, *The Magician, the Witch, and the Law* (Philadelphia: University of Pennsylvania Press, 1978).

The witch trials

Barber, Malcolm, *The Trial of the Templars* (Cambridge: Cambridge University Press, 1978).

Ben-Yahuda, Nachman, "The European witch craze of the fourteenth to seven-teenth centuries", *American Journal of Sociology*, 86 (1980), 1–31.

"Problems inherent in socio-historical approaches to the European witch craze", *Journal for the Scientific Study of Religion*, 20 (1981), 326–38.

Blöcker, Monica, "Frauenzauber – Zauberfrauen", *Zeitschrift für schweizerische Kirchengeschichte*, 76 (1982), 1–39.

"Ein Zauberprozess im Jahre 1028", *Schweizerische Zeitschrift für Geschichte*, 29 (1979), 533–55.

Brucker, Gene A., "Sorcery in early Renaissance Florence", *Studies in the Renaissance*, 10 (1963), 7–24.

Camerlynck, Elaine, "Féminité et sorcellerie chez les théoriciens de la démonologie à la fin du Moyen Age: Etude du *Malleus maleficarum*", *Renaissance and Reformation*, n.s., 7 (1983), 13–25.

Cohn, Norman, *Europe's Inner Demons: An Enquiry Inspired by the Great Witch-Hunt* (London: Chatto, 1975).

Ginzburg, Carlo, "Présomptions sur le sabbat", *Annales*, 39 (1984), 341–54.

"The witches' sabbat: popular cult or inquisitorial stereotype?" in Steven L. Kaplan, ed., *Understanding Popular Culture: Europe from the Middle Ages to the Nineteenth Century* (Berlin: Mouton, 1984), 39–51.

Hansen, Joseph, ed., *Quellen und Untersuchungen zur Geschichte des Hexenwahns und der Hexenverfolgung im Mittelalter* (Bonn: Georgi, 1901; repr. Hildesheim: Olms, 1963).

Zauberwahn, Inquisition und Hexenprozess im Mittelalter, und die Entstehung der grossen Hexenverfolgung (Munich: Oldenbourg, 1900; repr. Aalen: Scientia, 1964).

Harvey, Margaret, "Papal witchcraft: the charges against Benedict XIII", in Derek Baker, ed., *Sanctity and Secularity: The Church and the World*, Studies in Church History, 10 (Oxford: Blackwell, 1973), 109–16.

Hopkins, Charles Edward, "The Share of Thomas Aquinas in the Growth of the Witchcraft Delusion", dissertation (Philadelphia: University of Pennsylvania, 1940).

Jones, William R., "Political uses of sorcery in medieval Europe", *The Historian*, 34 (1972), 670–87.

Kelly, H. A., "English kings and the fear of sorcery", *Mediaeval Studies*, 39 (1977), 206–38.

Kieckhefer, Richard, *European Witch Trials: Their Foundations in Popular and Learned Culture, 1300–1500* (London: Routledge, 1976).

Kors, Alan C., and Peters, Edward, eds., *Witchcraft in Europe, 1100–1700: A Documentary History* (Philadelphia: University of Pennsylvania Press, 1978).

Krämer, Heinrich, and Sprenger, Jakob, *The Malleus maleficarum*, trans. Montague Summers (London: Pushkin, 1928).

Lea, Henry Charles, *Materials Toward a History of Witchcraft*, ed. Arthur C. Howland (Philadelphia: University of Pennsylvania Press, 1939).

Levack, Brian P., *The Witch-Hunt in Early Modern Europe* (London: Longman, 1987).

Maier, Anneliese, "Eine Verfügung Johanns XXII. über die Zuständigkeit der Inquisition für Zaubereiprozesse", *Archivum Fratrum Praedicatorum*, 22 (1952), 226–46; reprinted in Anneliese Maier, *Ausgehendes Mittelalter:*

Gesammelte Aufsätze zur Geistesgeschichte des 14. Jahrhunderts (Rome: Edizioni di Storia e Letteratura, 1967), 59–80.

Murray, Alexander, "Medieval origins of the witch hunt", *The Cambridge Quarterly*, 7 (1976), 63–74.

Nicholson, R. H., "The trial of Christ the sorcerer in the York Cycle", *Journal of Medieval and Renaissance Studies*, 16 (1986), 125–69.

Quaife, G. R., *Godly Zeal and Furious Rage: The Witch in Early Modern Europe* (New York: St. Martin's Press, 1987).

Rose, Elliot, *A Razor for a Goat: A Discussion of Certain Problems in the History of Witchcraft and Diabolism* (Torronto: University of Toronto Press, 1962).

Russell, Jeffrey Burton, *A History of Witchcraft: Sorcerers, Heretics, and Pagans* (London: Thames & Hudson, 1980).

Witchcraft in the Middle Ages (Ithaca, NY: Cornell University Press, 1972).

Thomas, Keith, *Religion and the Decline of Magic* (London: Weidenfeld & Nicolson, 1971).

Wright, Thomas, ed., *A Contemporary Narrative of the Proceedings against Dame Alice Kyteler, prosecuted for sorcery in 1324 by Richard de Ledrede, Bishop of Ossory* (London: Nichols, 1843).

Ziegeler, Wolfgang, *Möglichkeiten der Kritik am Hexen- und Zauberwesen im ausgehenden Mittelalter: Zeitgenössische Stimmen und ihre soziale Zugehörigkeit* (Cologne: Böhlau, 1973).

INDEX

214